Daily
Reminders for
Living
a New
Paradigm

Daily
Reminders for
Living
a New
Paradigm

ANNE WILSON SCHAEF

HAY HOUSE, INC.
Carlsbad, California • New York City
London • Sydney • Johannesburg
Vancouver • New Delhi

Published and distributed in the United States by: Hay House, Inc.: www.hayhouse.com® • **Published and distributed in Australia by:** Hay House Australia Pty. Ltd.: www.hayhouse.com.au • **Published and distributed in the United Kingdom by:** Hay House UK, Ltd.: www.hayhouse.co.uk • **Published and distributed in the Republic of South Africa by:** Hay House SA (Pty), Ltd.: www.hayhouse.co.za • **Distributed in Canada by:** Raincoast Books: www.raincoast.com • **Published in India by:** Hay House Publishers India: www.hayhouse.co.in

Cover design: Karla Baker • *Interior design:* Riann Bender

Library of Congress Cataloging-in-Publication Data

Names: Schaef, Anne Wilson, author.
Title: Daily reminders for living a new paradigm / Anne Wilson Schaef.
Description: 1st Edition. | Carlsbad : Hay House, Inc., 2017.
Identifiers: LCCN 2016040442 | ISBN 9781401952402 (tradepaper : alk. paper)
Subjects: LCSH: Conduct of life--Meditations.
Classification: LCC BJ1589 .S43 2017 | DDC 158.1/28--dc23 LC record available at https://lccn.loc.gov/2016040442

Tradepaper ISBN: 978-1-4019-5240-2

10 9 8 7 6 5 4 3 2 1
1st edition, January 2017

Printed in the United States of America

*This book is dedicated to those who, in the desperate longings
of their inmost beings, know that we, as human beings, have within
all of us the marvelous capacity to know and live the magnificent
wholeness, peace, and serenity that is our birthright.*

*This book is dedicated to those who, as I did many years ago,
in a fleeting moment gazing at the stars in Boulder, Colorado,
have EXPERIENCED and KNOWN the oneness that is within and
around us. Whether this KNOWING was a moment in meditation,
a sense in nature, an intensity of awareness in a near-death
experience, we knew wholeness beyond a doubt. And to those who
have not yet had this knowing, yet still believe it is possible.*

*May this book support and help you along the journey
of remembering what is good and real.*

PREFACE

There are many good people who realize that we humans, as a species and as the societies/cultures we have created, are not only not functioning very well, we are actively destroying ourselves, all life on this planet, and the planet itself. Clearly we need a drastic change in what we are doing and how we are doing it throughout the planet. In our evolution as a species and as a planet, we have taken many detours. Hopefully, as we bumble along we will be able to learn from our successes and most especially from our failures and move into a new way of being with ourselves, one another, and the planet as a whole.

There are some who have very specific ideas about what this new paradigm should be and what it needs to look like. In the way we function now as humans, we want to know what the end point is while we are still on the journey. All too often this illusion that we *can* know it all motivates much of how we spend our time and energy.

Fortunately for us all, we cannot know where we are going or what the end of the journey looks like because the coming into being of this new way of living with ourselves, one another, and the planet is a process. It is a process that requires our participation and faith that as we participate as fully and as clearly as we can, we will help create new ways of being that are, quite frankly, at this point beyond our imagination. However, we do have some resources to bring to the table.

Deep within our cells, our DNA, the blood of our ancestors, our racial memories, and the core of our beings is the information of another way of living and being on this planet that can point us in a good direction. It is there deep inside all of us.

At this point in our human history, this information may be more easily accessed by those who have been disenfranchised by the dominant culture—women, minority groups, native people, and even alcoholics in recovery. All these groups are not so deeply embedded and enmeshed in the current dominant culture. They have less to lose by being "different" because they already are. They have fewer layers to dig through to reach this ancient wisdom.

Yet how lucky we *all* are that deep inside of us is our connection with the all that is and we can enter a process that "reminds" us of what we already "know."

In order to access this information, I have written this book to help us remember a process to get to what is buried deep in us all. I believe that reminding us of this truth is very important at this time in the process of evolution of the human race and the planet.

I have taken 30 themes and will provide a process of focusing on each of these themes every month. The 31st of those months that have them will be "wild cards" of issues I felt important to mention.

I hope these reminders will be helpful. We need to remember that there is still a great deal that we do not know as human beings and even more that we do not know *how* to know. And if we can just remind ourselves of the need to be open to these realities, we can trust the process of the unfolding.

In some ways this book can be seen as a process of "deculturizing" our minds so we can be open to broader perspectives, what Willis Harman called a "global mind change" . . . and more.

Thank you for joining with me.

All Is in Process

INTRODUCTION

Stop the world—I want to get off.

— TITLE OF AN ANTHONY NEWLEY MUSICAL

There is no way to live into a new paradigm without having a knowing about and an acceptance of the reality that *everything is process*. In our present world dominated by Western thinking, we tend to see and act as if what are actually *processes* are *things*—whether it be our cars, our houses, ourselves, our families, or even systems and cultures, and our world. We have come to a place where we want ourselves and our world to be tangible, "real," and most of all controllable.

Yet everything, at all times, *is* a process and is *in* process. Understanding the reality that everything is in process and living out of this reality is not easy for humans on the material plane. And in order to participate fully in our lives and every aspect of creation that surrounds us, we need to get this awareness of the reality that all is process deeply into the core of our being.

Knowing that all is a process and in process is similar to that old saying, "The only constant is change." Yet there is even one aspect of this old saying that reveals how much we humans long for "constants," stasis, and control in order (we think!) to feel secure.

As humans, we have so held on to the illusion of the possibility of stasis and control that even as "new paradigm" advocates hopefully can see, when we stand back a bit, that often imbedded in our ideas is a belief that 1) we can control what evolves; 2) we "know" what a new paradigm will look like; and 3) when we achieve it, it will stay that way. Only when we realize that everything is in process and that even the processes are in process will we realize that stasis and control are illusions. When we start with accepting and believing that all is process, our lives will change.

Participation

INTRODUCTION

Participation is an act of faith.

— CHEROKEE ELDER

Are you willing to believe that simply by participating as fully as you can in the process of life, that action will lead to more exciting and growth-producing service opportunities and present more and greater possibilities for being than anything you could ever have imagined for yourself?

Participation is just as key to living a new paradigm as knowing and believing that all is process. Indeed, participation is the way we *become* the process of our lives and of the all that is.

Our participation not only changes the situation in which we participate, it changes who we are and who we can become in ways that are almost always unknown to us. Participation exponentially expands the potential for new learnings, healing, and growth. It even opens doors we never knew existed. Though being able to stand back and observe ourselves is useful and necessary at times, we will never realize our potential by observing, watching, manipulating, and trying to control.

Participation is the essence of process and simultaneously is the vehicle of process. Participation generates previously unseen and unknown options. It helps us move from the abstract disembodied concept to the active practical and the experience of experiencing.

We will never *think* ourselves into a new/old paradigm that incorporates the wisdom of the ancients. The knowledge we have accumulated from our mistakes and our deep learnings requires our participation in order to show itself.

Thinking

INTRODUCTION

Sit down, shut up, and give your brain a rest.

— A.A. SPONSOR

In our culture, we have come to believe in and worship the power of our thinking. Our rational/logical minds have become the sanctuaries of worship for our way of life.

Now, don't get me wrong at the onset of this discussion. Our minds are wonderful gifts and logical/rational thinking has its place. And, when it is not balanced by the other aspects of our wisdom and awareness, this kind of thinking can easily become unbalanced and unbalancing as has happened in Western culture.

In order actually to *live* a new paradigm, we need to take a long, hard look at how and what we think. We need to explore the ways that the processes of our thinking are blocking our ability to live a new paradigm. We need to be open to balancing our thinking with other aspects of getting data and learn ways of integrating all the information that is available to us. We need not to rely so heavily on our logical-rational minds, concepts, and abstractions.

We need to remind ourselves that what and how we think are culturally influenced and need to be reminded that what and how we think can be modified, that this paradigm change is a process that cannot be done only through our thinking.

We know that our thinking is not real. And the detour the human race has taken in science, spirituality, education, and other areas has helped us forget what we know.

Beliefs and Assumptions

INTRODUCTION

The passing of any belief is never a happy event for those who hold it.

— DEANE JUHAN

When we know on all levels of our being the reality that everything is a process and is *in* process, and when we fully comprehend the necessity and magic of full participation, then perhaps we will be willing and ready to look at and examine *all* our beliefs and assumptions in order to achieve a new kind of balance and maturity.

Our beliefs and assumptions, conscious and unconscious, are the cheerleaders that demand our staying stuck.

In order to move on and embrace the change that living a new paradigm offers, we need to be able and willing to step back, look at, and seize the opportunity to reevaluate and change our beliefs and assumptions. We need to be open enough to 1) see where they come from; 2) be intellectually and emotionally honest to look at them and see if they make sense to us; 3) see if they are in any way impeding our physical, emotional, psychological, and spiritual growth; and 4) ultimately be willing to replace them with beliefs that are more open, open-ended, growth-producing, and healthy for all creation.

Unless we are *willing* courageously to examine and outgrow all our old beliefs and assumptions, we will never be able to *live into* a new paradigm.

Feelings and Emotions

INTRODUCTION

When Peter left me, the negative emotions that rose up
in me and exploded in me were just horrifying. But God kept telling
me that they were all part of me and I couldn't try to hide
them under the carpet because I didn't like them.

— EILEEN CADDY

Somewhere along the way—probably with the onset of the worship of linear/rational thinking—the human species seems to have forgotten that our feelings and emotions are a very necessary and important ingredient of who we are and what we have to offer.

Our brains have become so unbalanced with the overdevelopment of our logical/rational minds and the suppressing, ignoring, and denigrating of our feeling minds that we are, indeed, lopsided as a species at this point of our evolution.

We need to be reminded and remind ourselves that our feelings and emotions are not "out to get us," that they are, indeed, a very important part of who we are as human beings and what we have to offer as human beings.

Without our feelings and emotions working with our rational minds, we are, indeed, crippled.

We have participated in a centuries-old process of handicapping ourselves as human beings by ignoring and not developing a mutually respectful and working relationship between our rational/thinking minds and our feeling/emotional minds.

Honesty

INTRODUCTION

I always tell my grandson honest people is just like having money in the bank. Anybody can help you, anybody can trust you. That's it. There's no other way around. That's how the Indians were.

— ALTONA BROWN, ATHABASKAN ELDER

In order to live a new paradigm, we need to recognize, at all levels of our being, how much dishonesty has become integrated into our current world paradigm.

We *expect* people to lie to us, and all too often we are not even aware when we, ourselves, are lying. Dishonesty has moved beyond being epidemic. It is now endemic to our planet.

Businesses assume dishonesty in their corporate structures and practices. And we find it "normal" that we cannot make an assumption of honesty in their products, procedures, and practices. We make the same assumptions about our and other governments.

When I was a child everyone knew if a certain merchant put his thumb on the scale when he was weighing a steak or roast. Soon the word was out and he was out of business. There is no way we can live into a new paradigm if we, ourselves, accept dishonesty in ourselves and others.

We can begin the living of a new paradigm by a personal demand for honesty in ourselves and others.

Courage

INTRODUCTION

Decision is a risk rooted in the courage of being free.

— PAUL TILLICH

The task of *living* a new paradigm is one very tall order that requires every ounce of who we are and who we can be.

Ironically, this change will probably come from the disenfranchised because these are the ones who have a clearer vision that change must happen. Their senses are not so dulled by the "benefits" of the old paradigm. Thus, their vision can be clearer. For example, indigenous people and women have more "memory" of another way than those who have developed and run the current paradigm. For those who run the current paradigm, I have seen in their writings an unconscious assumption of "We will decide what the new paradigm will be and we will make it happen and run it." Wrong! Those assumptions and ways of doing things are what have created the current paradigm that is not working well.

We have the opportunity to have the immense courage to move toward something when we don't know what it looks like or how it will work and stake everything we have on it.

Courage is what makes an ordinary person extraordinary. And it is nondiscriminatory in who it chooses to grace with its presence.

Entitlement

INTRODUCTION

But I want it!

— ANONYMOUS

Entitlement is an attitude and a feeling of deserving without question whatever that person wants and thinks is important.

Entitlement has no true regard for others or awareness that one's actions, wants, or desires affect others. And if the "entitled" do have a wee awareness that others might be affected by their desires, wants, or actions, that awareness is discounted in the service of their self-centeredness.

When we learn about addictions, we learn that one of the cornerstones of addiction is self-centeredness and self-seeking. These joint characteristics are seen as central to the disease process of addiction. I have written in other places that we live in an addictive society and that the characteristics and process of the society directly parallel those of the active addict. So it should come as no surprise to any of us that self-centered entitlement has become so integrated into the society. "We deserve, we deserve, we deserve" is the mantra that we worship in our royalty, celebrities, and wealthy and have sought to emulate. Politicians, business leaders, and even ministers join in chanting the mantra—"We deserve, we deserve, we deserve."

The attitude of entitlement is key to the dysfunctional paradigm we have developed. We need to confront and change this attitude/belief to live a new paradigm. Our ancestors knew that everything, absolutely everything, they had was a gift.

Accepting Our Humanness

INTRODUCTION

*When you think about it, not accepting our
humanness seems a bit unrealistic, don't you think?*

Living a new paradigm can never be considered an easy task for us humans. There are so many detours we have taken as a human race in our quest to realize our potential.

For us to get off of and recover from our detours, it will be necessary for us to identify and then be willing to correct many of our spoken and unspoken assumptions about being human in order for us to live with ourselves and all creation.

For example, a very common illusion that many humans have is that we are, indeed, and can be gods. Most people would immediately deny that they harbor this illusion. And don't actions speak louder than words?

One of the current myths of the dominant system is that we know and understand everything or can through our science. This belief is so tightly held that anything that cannot be observed and understood by our current scientific paradigm quite simply does not, by definition, exist. This assumption, in actuality, ignores a large percentage of our experience and our lives.

Accepting our humanity and its possibilities and limitations is absolutely necessary to live another paradigm.

Respect

INTRODUCTION

The word respect does not exist
in many native languages. It is assumed.

Respect—the word *and* the concept—has almost vanished from modern culture. In indigenous cultures the active process of respect was inherent in every aspect of living, from the most mundane to the most elevated. For our ancestors, respect was not an abstract concept, it was a living, working process that permeated even the smallest act.

Respect implies an acceptance of the holiness of every facet and process of creation. When we show respect, we recognize that every aspect of creation is sacred and is to be honored in every way.

One of my grandmothers told me that the Cherokee only have to do four things in life. At all times and in every act, thought, and being, we have to:

1. Honor the Creator

2. Honor all creation

3. Be of service

4. Practice the ceremonies

Sharing respect in everything we do is the active component in all these guidelines.

Respect is the active honoring of everything and everyone.

The Abstractualization of Life

INTRODUCTION

Don't be afraid your life will end; be afraid that it will never begin.
— GRACE HANSEN

We live in a paradigm that more and more depends upon and lives out of the abstract and the conceptual.

We live on a material plane. Assuming that we are here to heal, learn, and grow, the material plane is our classroom, our lab, and our learning place. An old Cherokee medicine man once said to me, "When you are ready, come to me and I will take you into nature. There, you can learn everything you need to know."

Our current scientific, religious, political, and economic paradigm operates out of abstractions that have little or nothing to do with our "reality." There is nothing wrong with abstractions and conceptualization. And, when we forget that they are mere approximations of our reality, we get in trouble. In the process of forgetting that the abstractions and conceptualizations are just that, approximations, and as we build new conceptualizations and abstractions on top of them, we find ourselves living more and more in an unreal world, losing touch with what is real. If we are to move into a new paradigm that is more workable for this planet and its inhabitants, we have to become more realistic about the deceptive role of abstractions and conceptualizations.

We need to see abstractions and conceptualizations for what they are . . . substitutions and approximations of the "real."

Being of Good Spirit

INTRODUCTION

*Let us give thanks for this beautiful day. Let us give thanks
for the water, without which life would not be possible. Let us
give thanks for Grandmother Earth who protects and nourishes us.*

— LAKOTA DAILY PRAYER

If we are going to live in a new paradigm, we must first accept the role that negativity plays in the present paradigm and then realize that negativity is culturally learned and inherent in a closed system.

We must also be reminded that before our present paradigm and scientific approach, there were thousands of cultures that did not base their wisdom and scientific knowledge on null hypotheses and negativity. In the Western worldview, negativity is all too often seen as sophisticated and objective. Being positive about life is seen as being unrealistic and not scientific.

Once, when I was a keynote speaker at a conference, my topic was to speak on my first book, *Women's Reality*. Before I made the speech I met the woman who was to "respond" to what I said. She spoke eloquently about the book, how she loved it, and how much it "spoke" to her. Then, in her "response," she ripped it to shreds! I was shocked. "What happened?" I gasped.

"Oh," she said. "I teach at an Ivy League college. If I don't rip everything to shreds and tear it apart, I would not be respected and not have a job for long."

To learn to live in a new paradigm we need to question the negativity we have been taught and return to the good-spirited attitude that is imbedded in our souls somewhere.

Domination Over and the Illusion of Control

INTRODUCTION

Life is so constructed that we never get "caught up."

Domination over and the illusion of control are core concepts and actions in the current dysfunctional paradigm that the human race has developed at this point in our evolution. Whether it is dominating and controlling ourselves, others, nature, or the universe, our current system is built on these illusions.

In other writings, I have described the current dominant system as an addictive system. I have demonstrated how the system in which we live functions exactly the same as an active alcoholic. It has the same characteristics—self-centeredness, dishonesty, self-seeking behavior, secretiveness, distorted thinking, lack of reality, lack of acceptance of process, trying to dominate and control others, lying, deceiving, twisting words and concepts, manipulating, loss of self (when we are self-centered, we are out of touch with ourselves), and a disconnect from our spirituality. We need to remember that alcoholism is more than drinking. It is a way of life.

These behaviors and processes have become so integrated into our society that we have come to believe that they constitute "reality" and are "just human." Well, they don't and they aren't. It is only as we realize the nonreality of these beliefs and behaviors that we will find our way to a new/old paradigm.

Did I say that addicts have very poor memories? So, "remembering" another way of being in the world is very difficult.

Humor

INTRODUCTION

Humor is reason gone mad.

— GROUCHO MARX

As I read books, articles, and statements about the new paradigm, I notice how humorless they are.

In the current paradigm, being serious about something—anything—and being humorous about anything seem to be on some celestial dualism in which everything has to be one or the other. The belief is that if we are serious enough to want to live out of a new paradigm, we need to be *really* serious.

Some believe that changing our entire way of living and being in the world is a very serious matter and if we introduce humor, laughter, lightness, or teasing, they believe that we will somehow undermine the importance, the seriousness, the solemnness of truth. This belief seems to be akin to having to be quiet and whisper in church.

One of the aspects I always enjoyed in black churches is that their God seemed to be one who enjoyed a good laugh, a great shout, or a joyous feeling. Having fun and laughing can be very spiritual.

We will explore the role of humor in changing our paradigm.

Wonder and Awe

INTRODUCTION

Observation was certain to have its rewards. Interest, wonder, admiration grew, and the fact was appreciated that life was more than mere human manifestation; it was expressed in a multitude of forms.

— CHIEF LUTHER STANDING BEAR, OGLALA SIOUX

Wonder and awe are in very short supply in our current jaded, humorless perspective of the world. Yet without them, we will find that our wish to find a new paradigm for living may be difficult indeed.

If we truly believe that we are responsible for everything and should be able to dominate and control everything . . .

If we truly believe that we have the ability to know and understand everything and if we cannot, we define it out of existence . . .

If we think we should be perfect and never make mistakes . . .

Then there is not much room for the spontaneity of wonder and awe.

In most indigenous cultures, wonder and awe are rarely mentioned or discussed because they are *assumed* as essential elements of living—not existing, living.

Everything around us and everything inside of us can, if we let it, inspire a response of wonder and awe. There is absolutely nothing—a thought, an idea, a feeling, an awareness, a "knowing"—that cannot inspire awe.

For many cultures that have lived well on this earth, wonder and awe have been essential.

The Present Can Only Be Our Reality
if We Own Our Past and Our Future

INTRODUCTION

*Honoring our past and accepting it
creates our future.*

We are always being admonished to be in the present, which is not easy for most people. Of course the irony is how can we *not* be in the present, it is where we are!

Yet most people find it almost impossible to be in the present for two reasons: 1) We have not "cleaned up" our past, which is not only our personal past, it includes the past of our ancestors, our race, and our species and 2) We do not act in a way that recognizes that everything we do now has an effect on our and others' future.

Being aware of our past and future is not a dualism. It is a trilogism that includes our past, our present, and our future. We need to learn to be in all three while participating in the process of being as fully as we can in the wholeness of it all. David Bohm talked about the "enfolding and exfolding" of reality. Everything is happening at once. When Einstein was asked why we have time, his response was, "So that everything doesn't happen at once."

If you need a lesson in humility and the limitation of the human brain, try trying to "grok" time. Time challenges our human limitations and it also stretches us beyond our perceived knowings.

There is no way to live a new paradigm with a mechanistic view of time and the world in which we live.

Walking in Beauty

INTRODUCTION

Beauty is in the eye of the beholder.

— PROVERB

. . . and so is *ugly*.

There is a Navajo poem that is also a prayer, which says, "May you walk in beauty." That phrase has haunted me much of my life in a most pleasant, supportive way because it has nothing to do with material things or even material beauty, although both are wonderful.

Walking in beauty is a way of life, one that's very different from the current dominant paradigm. Yet I believe that this reality is essential to finding a new way to be for this human race of ours.

To walk in beauty is not a series of actions or prescribed behaviors.

It is not something we can think ourselves into.

It is not something others can teach us and our conscious minds.

Yet learning to live out of a feeling and an attitude of walking in beauty is certainly an important aspect of living a paradigm shift.

What do I know about walking in beauty? Nothing—and a lot. How does one communicate such a state of being?

By *living* it.

Taking Time

INTRODUCTION

God made time and he made plenty of it.

— MY ELDER NEXT-DOOR NEIGHBOR IN IRELAND
("IT'S AN OLD IRISH SAYING," SHE SAID)

In my experience, "old sayings" always mean more than what appears on the surface. And the acquired wisdom of a culture, no matter which one it is, is always a process of listening to and pondering—for a long time.

Growing up in Western culture, the opposite often seems to be true. Time was always in short supply—even more scarce than money.

I love it when I innately "know" that something has just come across my path that is very important and I should not only remember it, I should take it into my being and let something bigger and more vast than my conscious mind ponder the subtle wisdom hidden therein. This is why I love proverbs. Every time I revisit one, it pushes me to another level of truth.

This new level may seem just the opposite to the level of truth I lighted on before when I pondered it. And yet I cannot let myself get hung up on small details like that, because I have learned that levels of truth are just that and the next time, if I am lucky, have done my work and grown, I will be ready for a new learning.

Who am I to think I know it all yet?

A Belief in Healing

INTRODUCTION

Health is not merely the absence of sickness.

— HANNAH GREEN

In our modern-day culture, we have little belief in true healing.

Our medical complex (or should I say our industrial/medical complex?) is one of our largest industries, which consumes an inordinate percentage of our time and money in the current world. The question recycles: "Do we really have a belief in true healing?"

Years ago, I came to the conclusion that our forms of medicine and psychology were not that interested in actual healing at all levels. They are more interested in 1) Keeping people going so they can contribute to the economy; 2) Helping people to adjust to a sick system; 3) Making money; and 4) Being in control.

In order to help contribute to living a new paradigm, one must: 1) Stop to evaluate what goes under the guise of healing that is not healing; 2) See what goes under the guise of healing that is actually destructive; 3) Question the science on which our current dominant healing paradigm is based; 4) Look at other paradigms that have existed for healing; 5) Ponder the denial about illnesses; and 6) Explore other paradigms.

One might ask why a focus on healing is necessary to learn to live a new paradigm. The answer is easy.

The answer is because only people who are as whole as they can be will have the energy to build a more functional paradigm. This new paradigm requires a cooperative collective of wisdom.

Knowing and Living in Several Realities

INTRODUCTION

*When we limit ourselves to
one reality, we are impoverished.*

In order for us to live another paradigm different from the one in which we are now living, we have to come to know and live in several realities.

Most Westerners have grown up being told that our only reality is the material world, that our mechanistic science is *the* science and that this science wedded with the revealed religions is all that we need to understand, survive, and thrive in this world. Perception with our senses or extensions of our senses, reductionism, measurement, prediction, control: these, we are told, are all we need to function in this world.

We have been taught that wealth is measured in material possessions, and that domination and control of others, nature, and the planet is what's important. We have been taught that the unseen and the unknown are not only not important, they do not even exist. We have been taught that if it cannot be measured, perceived, and controlled by the methodology of our science, "it" does not exist.

Therefore much of our total reality does not, by definition, exist, and other realities are not considered.

If we are to live a fuller paradigm, we have to look beyond a static, partial reality.

Being of Service

INTRODUCTION

Being of service is a cure for self-centeredness.

Many indigenous people share a common belief that they are here on this planet to be of service. They do not look for situations to be of service like co-dependents do (so they feel better). Nor do they expect to be rewarded for being of service. Nor do they force their "being of service" on other people like do-gooders.

People who have being of service integrated into the core of their being do not think much about to whom, how, or when they are being of service. People who have the reality of being of service participate in the process of their lives and are open to the opportunities that are presented to them to be of service in whatever situation they find themselves.

Their "being of service" is not regulated, quantified, prepared for (as in degrees or training), or compensated for. When being of service is integrated into our worldview and beings, the process of our living our lives brings constant opportunities to our door. It is up to each of us to respond and participate.

Many times, "being of service" may not initially look like "being of service." It looks like participating. The benefits of being of service are many and varied.

Graciousness

INTRODUCTION

*When we know who we are in the scheme of things,
graciousness is a by-product.*

There are some words, like *graciousness*, *honor*, and *respect*, that one rarely hears in common usage in today's paradigm.

Not only have they seemed to have lost their usage in current Western culture, they come from the very core of existence of a worldview where they had valuable meaning in the culture. These three were not just words. They exemplified a way of being that was accepted, valued, and lived. These three words were not abstract, disembodied concepts. They were spiritual, emotional, and valued processes of being and interrelated. It is not without significance that these words have almost vanished from our lives and everyday usage. These ways of being are not static states. They are ways of living and being that are guideposts for becoming an active part of a paradigm that begs us to remember that deep in our beings we know another way—if we can but remember.

And let's be clear, we must be genuine from our very being to live out these ways. There is nothing more off-putting or more obvious than someone who is trying to disguise their inner core and pretend they are gracious (or have honor or respect).

Graciousness is a reflection of a state of being that comes from deep inside.

Moving Out of Our Comfort Zones

INTRODUCTION

Remember!
The unknown may be our best friend.

Take warning! If we really want to live a new paradigm, this means being open to the unknown in every way we can imagine and in ways we cannot imagine.

I have always had such admiration for alcoholics who risk recovery. Since most of them come from alcoholic or dysfunctional families, live in an addictive society, and are surrounded by addiction, they quite literally have no idea what sobriety looks or feels like. Yet when life gets hard enough, they are willing to risk the journey to the unknown.

Many, of course, just want to take the pressure off and then fall back into old behaviors. They give up drinking and hold tightly to their old behaviors. They do not confront the "ism" of alcoholism. They are referred to as "dry drunks." The comfort zones of their old behaviors are just too precious to them to let go of and they continue in behaviors that are destructive to themselves and others.

There are, however, those courageous souls who are willing to go for it and change every aspect of their lives, if necessary, for their sobriety/spirituality. These are the fearless ones. These are the ones who are willing to move outside their comfort zones and risk it all for the possibility of something better.

When we are willing to remember that we do not know what we do not know, we may be ready to live a new paradigm. Then, we are ready to move out of our comfort zones.

Letting Go of What We Think We Know

INTRODUCTION

If I can let you go as trees let go . . . Lose what I lose to keep what I can keep . . . The strong root still alive under the snow . . . Love will endure—if I can let you go.

— MAY SARTON

As we are nearing the ending of each month, it is important to pause to remember that this is a book of daily *reminders*.

Hopefully it is a guide to help and encourage us to know and respond to wisdom that is buried deep inside of us. And this wisdom has the knowledge and hope that we, as human beings, can live and have lived differently on this planet. Unfortunately, as humans we tend to be so absorbed in the "reality of the present" that we ignore the nascent knowledge and awarenesses that we carry within us.

So, this is a little book of "reminders" of what we know and can know, that we have forgotten or lost touch with. All of us have more wisdom in us than ever reaches our consciousness.

All of us have volumes of untapped and unused brainpower that has not been stimulated and nourished because of the assumptions of the cultures in which we find ourselves. In fact, it is quite possible that our ancestors used more of their brains than we do in order to survive. What we consider as progress may well be regression or at best lopsidedness.

Having said all this, and having reminded us that this book is about remembering what we have learned in the long history of the species, let us now participate in the exercise of letting go of what we *think* we know.

Accepting That Choices and Behaviors Have Consequences

INTRODUCTION

*Knowing we have choices generates a wealth of
wisdom as we process the consequences of our choices.*

The human race in general, and Western culture in particular, seems to have forgotten the reality that our behaviors have consequences—that when we choose to indulge in destructive behavior, there will be consequences to ourselves and others. There seems to be a cultural collusion to forget and ignore this reality.

Also, there appears to be an illusionary cultural agreement that no matter who we are and what it is that we have done or are doing, it does not really matter. We assume that our lives really will not be impacted by our choices. Not only have the adults forgotten this reality, their behavior and attitudes have resulted in future generations not having the experience of the opportunity to learn this reality. When young people do not observe that the adults experience consequences for their lying, acting out, or being dishonest, they are not being reminded of this reality by the adults. When adults do not have time or energy or concern to see that their children experience that their behaviors have consequences, how can they learn this important reality? This kind of reality is difficult to learn in abstract.

We seem to have developed a cultural amnesia for the reality that our behaviors individually and collectively have consequences.

We need daily reminders of the truism that choices and behaviors have consequences.

Humility

INTRODUCTION

Humility can never be taught or planned.
It is a human accidental discovery—when it emerges.

Humility is the basis of all moral/spiritual conduct. Without humility, living a new paradigm is not possible. Humility is a kind of realism and deep acknowledgment of who and what we are. It is a recognition that we do not and, indeed, should not run the world.

Humility is a relaxed, peaceful, even joyful awareness of our place in the scheme of things; it is a quiet acceptance of our strengths and, even more important, of our limitations. With this awareness and this acceptance, we are able to participate more fully in our world and be a part of it.

Humility is neither being less than nor more than any other part of creation. It is a deep knowledge and acceptance of *our* place and the place of all creation in the reality of that creation. Without humility, we cannot hope to live gracefully with ourselves, with one another, or with the beauty of creation.

Humility is the foundation of living out of our moral, ethical, spiritual being.

Knowing and Being Known

INTRODUCTION

*How empty we feel when we do not
"know" others and are not "known" by them.*

We have been so attached to, defined by, and dependent upon the material plane that it has become increasingly difficult to remember what it means to be human and what being human is all about and has to offer.

This confusion also means that because we are human and have come to believe that not only are we the highest form of creation and the most important, we have taken it upon ourselves to put ourselves first. This belief has supported the illusion that we can and should define, control, and dominate the rest of creation. This arrogance has resulted in destruction to ourselves, one another, and all creation.

Instead of being human and exploring our humanness in conjunction with and relation to the process of all creation, we have "removed" ourselves as being "superior." We have floundered around in the destructiveness of trying to be gods when our greatest wealth is that we have all the assets and limitations of being human on this planet at this time. Not only have we done a very bad job of trying to be god(s), we have not done a very good job of being humans. When one tries to believe that one is something one is not, that person does a terrible job of doing much of anything. Being human is difficult enough. Trying to be gods is not only ridiculous, it is impossible and very destructive to all creation.

To live a new paradigm, humans need to start by being realistic about what it means to be human.

Everything Is Spiritual/Sacred

INTRODUCTION

All our acts have sacramental possibilities.

— FREYA STARK

We need to be reminded that our ancestors were better at grasping the reality that everything is spiritual and that they lived out of that knowledge. If we are going to try to live a new paradigm, it will be important to approach everything we do as approaching the spiritual.

I have found in working with groups of people throughout the world that the current dominant paradigm has developed a void in our awareness that everything, absolutely everything, is spiritual. Even our religions, it seems, have forgotten this reality in the service of the material.

For many native people who have lived out of a different paradigm, the reality that everything is spiritual was so real that they had no word for "spiritual." It was a given so true that one did not need a word or concept for that basic reality. The reality that everything is spiritual is not a concept. It is not a thought. It is not a proper way to be. It is *the* reality.

If we are to begin living a new paradigm, we need to start living out of a practice that everything, absolutely *everything*, is spiritual.

Wholeness

INTRODUCTION

When I know that I am part of a whole,
I can never act alone again.

We live in a paradigm that abhors wholeness. All of us have been trained to reduce anything and everything to its smallest elements and then to analyze it. Few, if any, of us realize how thoroughly we have been indoctrinated by the methodology and thinking of this particular Western scientific paradigm.

The result of this permeating belief in and adherence to reductionism has resulted in a cultural blindness and inability to think, see, feel, and act out of wholeness. The reduction to elements has become so second nature to us that we have almost lost the ability to imagine or believe that, indeed, we are all part of an interconnected wholeness and that this interconnectedness, although rarely acknowledged, is our reality as humans and as an entire creation. Partials are so much easier to conceive of. Partials are so much easier to think in terms of. Partials are so much easier to control (we think!). And in a world where measurement, prediction, and control (or the illusion thereof) are worshipped, wholes present an uncomfortable problem we would rather ignore than deal with.

Unless we are willing to get out of our comfort zones and start moving toward a recognition that we live in a world of wholes and are all interconnected, we have no hope of building a new paradigm.

Joy

INTRODUCTION

So often, joy is so quiet we hardly notice it.

We need to be reminded that living out of a new paradigm could be quite joyful.

As Richard Wagamese says of the Anishinaabe, "When you quit lookin' around at nature, you quit learnin' the natural way. The world gets to be somethin' you gotta control so you're always fightin' it. Us, we never fight the world. We look around lots, find its rhythm, its heartbeat, and learn to walk that way."

How much grief and exhaustion our control paradigm has cost us over the centuries! How much time and energy has been uselessly wasted in trying to control our world instead of living with it.

How easily we have embraced a paradigm built on the illusion of control when we could have been living peacefully with our world and participating with it instead of believing that we had the answers and needed to control every aspect of creation.

We have lost the joy of participation because of the illusion of control.

Emotional Brilliance

INTRODUCTION

In the province of Munster it is a common thing
for the women to follow a funeral, to join in the universal cry
with all their might and main for some time,
and then to turn and ask—"Arrah! Who is it that's dead?
Who is it we're crying for?"

— MARIA EDGEWORTH

One of the consequences of living in the current paradigm in which we are living is that our emotional brilliance is assaulted constantly.

Emotional intelligence is as or probably more important than logical intelligence when it comes to living well with ourselves, others, and the planet. Yet we get little or no encouragement to develop our emotional intelligence.

In fact, quite the opposite is true.

Our current culture denies the existence of emotional intelligence and has tried to erase it from our cultural memory and functioning.

What do you know about your emotional intelligence (brilliance) and what are you doing to support it?

All Is in Process

WE ARE A PROCESS

I just can't seem to get it together.

Of course you can't, because we are a process.

Everything about us is a process. From the time we are conceived until we breathe our last breath (and probably beyond!) we, ourselves, are a process. How much easier our lives become when we accept the reality that we are a growing (hopefully), healing (hopefully) process of learning.

The temptation to believe that we can make ourselves a static entity is seductive and, if we stop to think about it, completely unrealistic and unrelated to our experience of ourselves. Yet how often do we fall back on our old tried-and-true beliefs that we will work through all of our issues (or refuse to work through them!) and then we will "have it all together" and be just fine forever?

The truth is this being we call ourselves is a constant work in progress and the sooner we see ourselves that way the sooner our lives will become easier.

We have threads of who we are that run through our lives and, if we are lucky, we will always be becoming and growing into who we can be.

Participation

THE BEAUTY OF PARTICIPATION

*Full participation can be
the expression of our freedom.*

Nonparticipation is one of the vehicles we have developed to make our world static, closed, and be uninvolved. Full participation requires that we act even when we have no certainty or control over the possible outcomes.

The very act of participation changes the current situation and opens the door for new possibilities that are beyond our imagination and experience. For example, I have often seen in myself and others that by merely *saying* something about how we are feeling, most often the feelings change and we change.

When we say, "I am just furious about that!" the feeling of fury changes.

When we say, "I am so tired," we often feel less tired.

Participating verbally can often bring great change to a situation. Sitting back and stewing rarely has the same effect. So our participation even on a verbal level can shift our experience and the situation.

For those who want to make a paradigm shift, learning to participate on many levels is a must.

Thinking

Cultural Thinking

*Insanity can result from trusting
your disembodied thinking.*

Our minds are active and fickle. They are also creative, amazing, and wonderful. They are heavily influenced by the culture in which we live. Most of our minds have been influenced by Western science, math, and education at this time in the history of our human race. And there still remain other cultures that remind us that there are other ways to think and perceive the world.

An American thinks with different content and processes than a German. There may be many similarities because we are both part of Western culture, science, and philosophy. And there are differences—significant differences because of the way we have been acculturated. Add a Chinese, Tibetan, Japanese, or Korean into the mix and the differences increase exponentially. And, these cultural differences can give us a clue that what and how we think is not reality.

We need daily reminders to help us remember that our thinking is just that, *our* thinking, as a person and as a culture, and not reality. I have found that this lesson can be forgotten on a daily basis.

So, we need reminders.

Beliefs and Assumptions

BEGINNING TO EXPLORE

Learning to see when I am acting out of unchecked beliefs and assumptions may be one of the greatest skills I ever acquire.

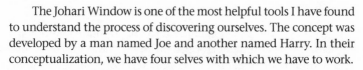

The Johari Window is one of the most helpful tools I have found to understand the process of discovering ourselves. The concept was developed by a man named Joe and another named Harry. In their conceptualization, we have four selves with which we have to work.

1. We have the Public Self, which is the self that we present to the public. In general, we know who this self is and feel in control of ourselves and our world with this self. It is who we want the world to see us to be.

2. There is the Hidden or Private Self. This is the self that we are aware of, that we only show to those with whom we are intimate and at times would rather others don't see at all. And, also at times, the self we want the option to deny.

3. There is the Unaware Self, which is the self that others see though we have no awareness of its existence whatsoever. This self is often a threat to our self-image.

4. There is the Unknown Self, which is unknown to ourselves and unknown to others. This self holds repressed memories and feelings, cultural and ancestral memories, and a mixture of unknown information. Deep healing happens when this self comes into the private and public self.

Our beliefs and assumptions operate in all our selves and are dangerous when they reside mostly in 2, 3, and 4.

Hopefully, the normal process of growth and healing for each of us results in the shrinkage of 2, 3, and 4. This shrinkage then results in our not needing to spend much energy concealing them.

Feelings and Emotions

OUR FEELINGS AND EMOTIONS ARE INTEGRAL TO OUR BRILLIANCE

There is no part of us that is not our teacher.
When we pick and choose, we lose.

Years ago my former agent said to me, "You are emotionally brilliant." That comment stopped me in my tracks and resonated throughout my being. I felt then and I feel now that it was and is the best compliment ever given to me.

As I have grown and matured, I feel that I have plumbed deeper and deeper levels of its meaning for me. One awareness that has come to me is that there is a great deal of difference between information and wisdom. We are constantly bombarded by information and our brains and computers are filled with facts—which are fun and interesting. Yet in and of themselves, "facts" have little ability to heal, teach, or help us grow if they are not also run through our feeling, emotional minds to help us connect with their *meaning* for us. When we remember to take the time to weigh what information means for us, how it will affect our lives, others, and the planet, information takes on a very different perspective.

Our feelings and emotions add perspective to information.

Honesty

PERSONAL HONESTY

This gives us great joy, for we now consider that we stand upright before you and can speak what we think.

— SA-GO-YE-WAT-HA, SENECA CHIEF

Beginning to practice personal honesty is like filling our lungs with fresh, pure air after having lived in a polluted city for much of our lives.

Many of us may have deluded ourselves that we are honest people. Yet it takes a great deal of personal dedication and practice to see the subtlety of our dishonesty when we live in a culture that not only condones dishonesty, it demands it. Recovery from the habit of dishonesty is definitely not supported by the culture.

We live in an addictive culture and one of the cornerstones of addiction is lying or self-deception. A great deal of our personal and creative energy goes into deceiving ourselves about 1) who we are; 2) what we are feeling; 3) what we want for ourselves; 4) who we can be; and 5) who we don't need to be. Very few people know what they are feeling or whose thoughts and perceptions they are thinking or perceiving.

For us to participate fully in a new paradigm, we have to embark on a new paradigm about ourselves. We have to be willing to face our blind spots and our unknowns. And, we will need help.

Courage

PERSONAL COURAGE

Here I stand. I can do no other.

— MARTIN LUTHER

Personal courage is usually an afterthought in reaction to the circumstances of life. Few, if any, people decide that they are going to be courageous people and then practice the principle in all their affairs.

Most of us are like Martin Luther (one of my heroes), who definitely did not set himself up to take on the entire Catholic church and then do so. He was a quiet monk who slowly and cautiously came up against practices and principles that from his perspective kept the Catholic church from being "the church." Step by step, he found himself taking small stands because, from his perspective, the church was selling its soul and the purity of its message for financial and political reasons. He loved the church and continued to do so even when it rejected him. Yet he persevered—not because he wanted to be a hero; not because he wanted to destroy that which he loved the most; not because he had a clear vision in mind to replace the church he knew. He persevered because he loved the church and he wanted the best for it, and in his heart of hearts he took his stand to save the church from itself. That took courage.

Luther's statement, "Here I stand. I can do no other," is, I believe, a lesson for us all, regardless of what spirituality we embrace.

Entitlement

THE SPIRITUAL INHIBITOR

Who actually believes they deserve anything?

Entitlement is a serious spiritual inhibitor.

Who knows when entitlement seeped in as a characteristic of the present dominant system that humanity has evolved? I am very clear that it is certainly not part of the beliefs of any indigenous system that I have ever encountered. Yet the assumption of entitlement seems to be growing exponentially in our materialistically oriented world.

In order to participate fully in the emergence of living a new paradigm, it seems that coming to terms with our being wedded to the notion of entitlement needs to be addressed. There is no question but what this assumption is closely tied to the materialism, the wasting of our human resources, and the destruction of whole groups of plants and species in our environment. This feeling of and belief in entitlement must be confronted in ourselves personally and in its institutional form if we are to move into a new way of living with ourselves, others, and the planet.

Entitlement is so inherent in the dominant system on this planet that it is assumed and not seen as unusual.

Accepting Our Humanness

THE BIG PICTURE

*Accepting the limitations of being human
is the beginning of maturity.*

Because we are human, we will probably never be able to see fully and understand the big picture. Because we are human, we have human brains, human perceptions, and process all the information that comes to us from a limited perspective. This reality means that try as we might, and wish as we might, we will never, never "get it all" . . . ever. This truth is our reality, and the sooner we accept this reality the better options we have to learn more.

The wisdom of this perception of our limitations is something every indigenous person knows. Processing this reality in this way is not because indigenous people are not educated or know less—far from it. It is because they, in general, are wiser and know a great deal more, and their culture teaches them the reality of their humanness.

Native people have learned from their ancestors that the actual reality of the human organism is that our minds and beings are incapable of getting the whole picture. That's just the way it is.

Isn't it a relief to know that we are so constructed that we are only able to get *some* pieces of the puzzle? And, if we accept that reality, we have more and more to learn.

Respect

RESPECTING THE SMALL THINGS IN OUR LIVES

Respect is an attitude of gratitude.

As a child, I was taught to approach everything with which I came into contact with respect. I believe this attitude of respect was taught to me in the womb. The word *respect* was rarely used and every action was laden with respect.

When I was young, one of our prized possessions was an old cast-iron skillet. It had, I believe, been in our family for generations and we used it every day. After each use, it was carefully wiped out. If necessary, clear, clean water was used to loosen anything that might have stuck in or dirtied it. Actually, almost nothing ever stuck in it because it was so well "seasoned." Soap was never used. Soap was much too harsh for something so precious! After it was wiped out and cleaned, it was rubbed with oil and set aside for its next call to duty.

At a very young age, I was given the responsibility to monitor the old skillet and to determine when it needed to be "seasoned." This monitoring was a grave responsibility with such a valuable object and I took it very seriously.

All objects were treated with the respect they deserved. Remembering the old skillet helps me be respectful of everything I approach today.

The Abstractualization of Life

BACK TO REALITY

Every eye forms its own fancy.

— MRS. O'MALLEY (IRISH PROVERB)

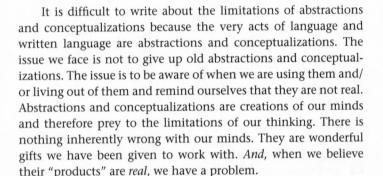

It is difficult to write about the limitations of abstractions and conceptualizations because the very acts of language and written language are abstractions and conceptualizations. The issue we face is not to give up old abstractions and conceptualizations. The issue is to be aware of when we are using them and/or living out of them and remind ourselves that they are not real. Abstractions and conceptualizations are creations of our minds and therefore prey to the limitations of our thinking. There is nothing inherently wrong with our minds. They are wonderful gifts we have been given to work with. *And*, when we believe their "products" are *real*, we have a problem.

I know a woman, educated at an Ivy League college, who was asked if she would write a book on divorce. She knew nothing about divorce. She had never been married or divorced. Without any research, she wrote the book. As I watched her process, I was appalled. As she thought about divorce, she would develop an idea. She would not test out that idea. She simply believed it. Then she would think out the implications of that idea and build on her thoughts. The whole book was logical and rational. It just made no "sense" and was not grounded in reality.

We have built an entire world on abstractions. And building an abstraction on an abstraction does not work too well.

Being of Good Spirit

MODELS FOR LIVING THE GOOD SPIRIT

Every race was put on this earth for a reason. The Hawaiians were for sharing the true essence of Aloha—love for everyone and everything.

— REVEREND AKAIKO AKANA, HAWAIIAN KUPUNA

One of the reasons so many of us enjoy being around indigenous elders is that most of the "old ones" approach life out of a place of openness and goodness.

This spirit of goodness is probably one of the reasons that the indigenous people let the colonizers stay. No matter how bad a situation may be at the time, there is always the possibility that something good can come out of it depending on what we do with it.

Optimism need not be unrealistic. If we live our lives out of an attitude of "Woe is me," we will probably find the woe hiding around every corner. Just as beauty is in the eye of the beholder, so is ugly in the eye of the beholder.

Often we fail to realize that a welcoming smile, a twinkle in the eye, and a spirit of openness can bring sunshine into a cloudy room. Of course the feeling of good spiritedness has to be genuine and we cannot generate this feeling in our minds. It has to come from our beings.

Remember, good spiritedness, like many other forms of goodness, is contagious.

Domination Over and the Illusion of Control

THE BIG PICTURE

Why do we try to control everything? Aren't we occupied enough with living our life in a good way?

— CHEROKEE ELDER

The belief in the validity of the urge to dominate the earth and others probably goes far back before the Old Testament and, for some, it has been used to excuse some rather dysfunctional behavior. In our current paradigm, not only are domination and control sanctioned, they are seen as a necessary virtue. In any hope for a new paradigm, we must not only face our illusion that either is good, we must face our illusion that either is possible, let alone desirable.

At this point in the development of the human species almost all of our foreign policies, our national identities, our national borders, our materialistic focus, and our military industrial complexes, let alone our governments, are built on the illusions of the necessity and acceptability of the alcoholic-like thinking processes of domination and control. If we are willing to see reality and trust what we have learned from addicts, we can see that these cherished illusions are very deadly and dysfunctional. Most of our leaders cannot see this reality because the very system in which they have chosen to function is based upon these illusions. The recovering alcoholic has had to learn that these illusions are destroying their lives. Are all of us ready to challenge these illusions as the alcoholic needs to do to recover?

This illusion of control needs to be a daily question we ask ourselves and a daily reminder to seek an alternative.

Humor

HAVING FUN ON VALENTINE'S DAY

Having fun can never be planned;
it is always lurking just out of sight.

Not only has Valentine's Day become—like most other holidays—a very commercial holiday, it has become a serious commercial holiday.

There is probably nothing more intimate than laughing together. Recently I was at a film with some friends. It was not a very good film; in fact, it was a pretty bad film. Yet at one point in the film my friends and I and a few people in the audience shared a spontaneous belly laugh. I was aware of the feeling of intimacy I had with my friends and these few others. How rare spontaneous belly laughs are these days!

Often, people who know each other very well find that one form of intimacy they have is telling stories about themselves—which they both know, in which they are the butt of the joke. And they laugh together in happy, tender memories.

Humor is a way of bonding.

Wonder and Awe

EARLY WONDER AND AWE

*The great thing about getting older is that you
don't lose all the other ages you have been.*

— MADELEINE L'ENGLE

Approaching all of life with wonder and awe is a natural aspect of an indigenous paradigm, and is essential to live a new paradigm.

As I wrote that sentence, I remembered having the privilege to be present when my daughter first discovered her hand. Since birth, she had been waving her hands around in what seemed like random movements, with her eyes taking no notice of what "they" were doing. Then, one day, she "saw" her hand for what seemed like the first time (I had not been there all the time and I was as in awe of the expression on her face as she seemed to be with her experience of her hands).

In that moment, her eyes fixated on her hand. It was as if the earth suddenly stood still. Her mouth opened in what was a toothless expression, much bigger and more wondrous than a smile. At first she was quiet and speechless as her gaze fixed on the wondrous object before her eyes. Then as she discovered that she could turn it slowly, getting various perspectives and maybe even having some preverbal awareness that she was somehow related to this amazing piece of work, she began to emit soft gurgles, soft squeals, and happy sounds. My eyes filled with tears for having the opportunity to experience these shared moments of awe and wonder.

Often tears are the only appropriate response for awe and wonder.

The Present Can Only Be Our Reality
if We Own Our Past and Our Future

OWNING OUR PAST

*If what the kahunas (teachers) taught is true—that it is possible
for an aumatua (an ancestral spirit for two generations like one's
deceased parent or grandparent) to guard and inspire a beloved relative
on earth—I shall watch over you from above and guide you righteously.
I do not know at the present time how this is done but I shall find out
from the Hui O Aumatua (guild of ancestral spirits) when I join them
after I awaken from nature's trance-sleep of death.*

— MARY JULIA GLENNIE BUSH, HAWAIIAN KUPUNA

When we think what a short time it has been in the human
existence on this planet that we actually have recognized that
psychologically and experientially our past not only informs our
present, for many, our past all too often *controls* our present.

Quite truthfully, even though there has been some impressive progress in the last 100 years of dealing with the influence
our past has on our psyches, feelings, behavior, and beings, we
are barely at ground zero with a general recognizing that we are,
indeed, personally affected by our past. We have really not even
scratched the surface of knowing how to heal from our past as
individuals and little has been done to heal our ancestors, our
families, our communities, our nations, and our species.

There are some who are working at all these levels and they
are few and far between. Yet healing our ancestors and healing
our nations is possible.

In this book we will focus on healing our individual pasts so
we, as individuals, have the possibility to choose to participate
in a new paradigm of living. Perhaps if more individuals take
responsibility for healing their pasts, we will evolve to the hun-
dredth monkey.

Walking in Beauty

MEMORY

*Remembering the words of our teachers
is a walk in beauty.*

Just writing the words *walking in beauty* brings a flood of memories and tears to my eyes.

One of the dearest people in my life was a Navajo elder who is now working his magic, I'm sure, on the other side. He was a gentle man, an unassuming man, and a brilliant man. Words of wisdom came out of his mouth unheralded with pomposity.

Over the years with him, I learned that he was a Christian. I was surprised with his commitment to Christianity at first because I knew that he devoutly practiced his Navajo spirituality. After I got to know him better, I discovered that he was a devout Baha'i and one of the international leaders in that spirituality.

He once said to me, "I don't care *how* a person prays. The important thing to me is that he *does* pray. Then he can always stand beside me."

As usual for someone who walks in beauty, his words live on within me and perhaps will with you now.

Taking Time

GRANDPARENTS

*Grandparents are a form of wealth
above and beyond the material plane.*

How lucky a person is to have grandparents in her/his life, and how even luckier one is to have great-grandparents! This is because grandparents and even more so great-grandparents have time to take time.

How wise are native cultures in which much or most of the parenting is done by the grandparents and great-grandparents. Now don't get me wrong, parents are just fine in their place. And in our current culture, they are so busy trying to cope with the stresses and strains of the material plane that they rarely have time for the important things—the foundations of what really matters.

Also, parents have not had the longevity of the years to teach them that what we think is important when one is younger, probably isn't that important when all is said and done.

Another piece of this phenomenon is that the really important lessons are learned through experience and example—often struggle, failure, and disappointment, and then reflection—and parents have not had much time for that.

Those who have "the old ones" around are the lucky ones. And, no matter what age we are, we can still seek out "the old ones."

A Belief in Healing

BROADENING OUR VIEW

Healing is not just physical or personal.

— CHEROKEE ELDER

All the native healers I have known have a strong belief in healing as an integral part of life. In fact, when one asks the question of why we are here, in the current dominant paradigm, the answers vary significantly from group to group. Some would say that there is no reason. We are just here and we need to make the most of it. (There are probably more people in this category than most of us would like to admit.) Others would say that we are here to carry out some particular religious mandate and healing is not an issue because ultimately we humans do not really matter. Others would say that we as humans are not really significant and in the larger scheme of things do not really matter, while still others would say that we human beings are the most important part of this planet and any healing should be focused on what humans need. Clearly we have a lot of confusion when it comes to who, what, when, and where should healing occur.

From what I have seen of a new paradigm, all of us are here to heal, learn, and grow, and this occurs when all aspects of creation work together.

Knowing and Living in Several Realities

THE UNSEEN—THE UNKNOWN

*Remember, Elizabeth Anne, it is the unseen
and the unknown that are most important.*

— MANILLA WILLEY

These words were spoken to me by my mother when I was very young. I believe that much of my life has been spent trusting what she said and coming into knowing what she meant. I have made progress and I am very sure that I have a long way to go to grow into truly knowing, living, and incorporating what she was telling me.

For many years, in my highly scientific, mathematical world of high school, studying premed, and doing graduate work in psychology, with a heavy emphasis on experimental psychology (my advisor, a wonderful man, hated to see me "waste" my talent on clinical psychology; it was "so unscientific"), those words of my mother simmered on the back burner of my being. Yet, I kept adding small amounts to the pot so it would not simmer dry as I learned proficiency to survive in my material-plane world. Luckily, I had been raised in a traditional Cherokee way so the unseen and unknown, even when I was unaware of it, was not far away.

If we are to expand ourselves and live new paradigms, we will *have* to expand our realities—always.

Being of Service

A PERSONAL LIFE

When I feel I deserve a personal life,
I find that being of service snaps me out of it.

One of the main obstacles to truly being of service that people raised in the current dominant culture have is the belief that we should have and have the right to have a personal life. Having a personal life in this sense means doing what *I* want, when *I* want, how *I* want, with no one and nothing interfering. This belief of the inalienable right to have every aspect of our lives exactly when, where, and how we want it springs directly from an addictive paradigm. It is based on the form and reasoning of the addict. It is not necessarily related to human nature and it is, indeed, related to the nature of the addictive process.

In the work I have done with addicts and addicts in recovery, I have found that one *has* to be of service and let go of the illusion of a personal life in order to experience the peace and joy of recovery (of course, combined with many other significant life changes).

Being of service is essential to the process of recovery and living in a sober way.

Recovery from the focus on a self-centered, self-defined life is essential for recovery from the addictive process and necessary to live a new paradigm.

Graciousness

ALWAYS ERR IN THE DIRECTION OF GRACIOUSNESS

Always err in the direction of graciousness, Elizabeth Anne.

— MARY ELIZABETH REED

I remember my great-grandmother saying this to me as a child. And I always knew that when she said something and repeated it, what she was saying was important and needed attention.

Now Grandma Reed, as I called her, was a very gracious, gentle person. During the Great Depression, she never turned a hungry person, stranger or friend, from her door and she always found a way to be gracious even with the most obnoxious. To her, every being reflected the Creator and deserved our courtesy and graciousness. She even practiced this graciousness toward the plants, roots, bark, and leaves she used for healing. Grandma Reed believed that we always had choices as human beings and it was necessary and up to each of us how we exercised these choices. And exercise them we must.

She taught me many things and was an encyclopedia of information about healing, and, even more important for me, she was an encyclopedia of wisdom about how to *be*. I came to know that the way we *are*, as we move through the process of life, always reflects the relationship we have with the Creator and all creation. And these relationships are reflective of who we are and who we can be as part of the whole of creation. So I always tried to err in the direction of graciousness whenever possible . . . living the Creator in me.

Erring in the direction of graciousness actually is a pretty good way to live and essential for the process of moving into a new paradigm.

Moving Out of Our Comfort Zones

MAKING GOD LAUGH

Why wouldn't God like to be entertained too!

Some time ago, I became convinced that God created human beings for entertainment and that our role as a species is to make God laugh. Indeed, we may bumble around with everything else and the one thing that we seem to have perfected to a fine art is being laughable.

How firmly we believe, even if we do not articulate it to ourselves or others, that we can get our lives, our relationships, our houses, our cars, our selves, just the way we want them and they will stay that way forever. How silly we look trying to make this illusion real.

We flail around trying to create a world according to *ourselves* and wonder why it does not work very well. We not only try to control and manipulate ourselves, we try to control and manipulate others, and we feel frustrated and angry when none of our attempts to control and manipulate work that well. And when they do work for a while, we are not happy with that either. If you were God, wouldn't you keep laughing as you watch generation after generation of mere mortals try to create a world according to themselves?

We probably are actually doing a very good job of entertaining God.

Letting Go of What We Think We Know

EMPTYING

To be empty is to be available for filling.

— ZEN KOAN

One of my favorite Zen stories, which I find many opportunities to repeat, is the story of the college professor.

It seems that the college professor became aware that his field of information did not bring him wisdom. Being distressed about this new awareness and his current state of affairs, he decided to consult a Zen master (how wise he was to try to get out of his familiar paradigm and explore other ways to live!). So he went to the Zen monastery and requested a session with the head monk and teacher. When the professor entered, the old monk was seated on the floor before a plain table. He gestured for the college professor to sit on the mat on the floor across the table facing him. When the professor was seated, the monk nodded to him and the professor said, "I have come to learn from you. I have several degrees and often I feel I know nothing. Please teach me." The old monk turned and asked a student to fetch him a pot of tea and two cups. Neither the monk nor the professor spoke as they sat. The old monk put a cup in front of himself and one in front of the college professor. Then he started to pour tea into the professor's cup. He poured until the teacup was full and continued to pour until the tea was running all over the table and onto the floor. "Stop, stop," shouted the professor. "The cup is too full. Can't you see it is overflowing?"

The old monk quietly smiled and said, "And so it is with you. Your mind is too full. You need to empty it before more can get in."

And so it is with us.

Accepting That Choices and Behaviors Have Consequences

REMINDERS

*If we consider what we are doing that we might be tempted
to lie about before we do it, we may not lie so often.*

— CHEROKEE ELDER

We need daily reminders that our choices have consequences. Unless we experience the consequences of what we do
and the result of the choices we make, we tend to forget that
there actually are consequences for what we do.

How tricky are the minds of human beings! We get away
with one little experience of no known consequences and quickly
our minds deceive us into believing that no consequences have
become a rule, not the exception. We speed and do not get a
ticket and then are angry and "unfaired against" if we get a ticket
the next time. We cheat on our taxes and no one catches it so
we generalize that experience, cheat in our business and then
develop a style of ignoring, cheating, covering up, and lying. We
can actually convince ourselves that 1) we have done nothing
wrong, 2) if others do it, so can we, and 3) those who catch us,
point it out, and demand better from us are mean and unfair.

We often move into the belief that we are being victimized
for being invited to face the consequences of our behavior.

Unless someone reminds us of reality, our minds can take us
from victimized to victim in seconds.

Humility

BEYOND THINKING

Humility is very, very quiet.

— CHEROKEE ELDER

Humility is beyond our thinking. We cannot define what we *think* humility is and then try to do it. In fact, not only is "thought-into" humility the worst kind of humility, it is no humility at all. Many people believe that humility is a good thing and try to emulate it—and never succeed because humility is not a *product*. It is not a product of our thinking mind. It is not a product of our trying to control our own perceptions of ourselves or the perceptions of others. It is not achieved by deciding that we want to be humble and then trying to achieve it.

We may be pleased with our performance and yet no one else is fooled.

Humility is a by-product.

Humility is an outgrowth of a process of participatory living.

We cannot make humility. We cannot buy humility. We cannot manufacture humility. We cannot think ourselves into humility. Indeed, we have no control over humility whatsoever. We *can* be open to unconsciously grow into it. Thank goodness!

Knowing and Being Known

FACING THE TRUTH

Sometimes you have to get to know someone
really well to realize you're really strangers.

— MARY TYLER MOORE

When one says that we are human, it seems so obvious on the face of it. Yet if we take a close look at the history of the human race over the centuries, it becomes quite obvious that a paradigm has evolved that tries to affirm that humans are gods created to rule over and dominate the rest of creation. This trend has certainly come to the most absurd level of this illusion in the current dominant paradigm.

Native people the world over do not seem to have needed this illusion to try to live with and in process with the whole of creation. Their elders have passed down a wisdom that is more integrated with all of creation. Unfortunately for all of us, their acceptance of their humanness and willingness to live interactively with all creation has not survived in a technological, materialistic, mechanistic society. Indeed, instead of human beings putting their creativity into living with all creation and being a part of creation, the human race has focused on being gods or like their idea of what gods would be like, manipulating and controlling everything, including themselves, and destroying everything, especially everything unlike themselves.

Humans have put little energy into exploring what it means to be human, living out of that reality, and cooperating with all creation. We need to remember who we are and what we can be when we are realistic about ourselves.

Everything Is Spiritual/Sacred

OUR BEINGS

Not to see everyone and everything as spiritual is not to see them.

— CHEROKEE ELDER

I once heard someone say, "We are not human beings trying to be spiritual, we are spiritual beings trying to be human." For me, someone had just turned over the hourglass and the sand started flowing in a different direction. What a difference it makes if we see ourselves as inherently spiritual trying to find out how to be human and live on a material plane!

What happens to our psyches if we give up the struggle to be religious or spiritual and accept the fact that we already are? What a way to eliminate posturing and conning from our repertoire and change our focus to become more of who we are and living out of that reality. How would our lives be different if we accepted the fact that we *are* spiritual, and focus the struggle we feel on the reality that we have to learn how to be functional human beings on this planet from our spiritual base? Religions have attempted to help us remember that reality, and, unfortunately, religions have been set up by human beings who share our limitations and possibilities. The truth is that deep inside all of us is a spiritual being who is connected to knowledge and wisdom that goes far beyond our human limitations.

What would happen if we shifted our focus, starting with being spiritual beings trying to be human? Some who lived a different paradigm remembered this reality. What do we need to remember to live a fuller paradigm?

Wholeness

THE REALITY OF WHOLENESS

*A person who believes . . . that there is a whole of which
one is a part, and that in being a part one is whole; such a person
has no desire whatever, at any time, to play God. Only those
who have denied their being yearn to play at it.*

— URSULA K. LE GUIN

Wholeness is not an abstract concept. It is our reality. Whenever we try to dismiss or deny our reality, it forces itself on us, demands our attention and makes us deal with it.

We can get away with manipulating abstract concepts. We can think about them. We can play around with them. And we can put them aside and ignore them whenever we wish. Our concepts are playthings. They amuse us and afford us hours of entertainment. They are like trying to have a baby by masturbating. They can be fun and occupy heaps of our time and attention and, in the end, they are not real. With all our play with concepts, we do not get the baby.

Even the concept of wholeness has become one of our new playthings. Yet when we face into the reality of wholeness, it demands our full attention. At this time in history, the reality of wholeness demands that we accept it as reality. We no longer have the luxury to abstract wholeness into nonexistence. The earth is demanding that we give up our childish ways, our mental toys, and deal with our reality.

The truth is, reality—when we face it—can be so much more fun than abstract concepts.

All Is in Process

EVERYTHING AROUND US IS IN PROCESS

Life doesn't happen in stacked events.
It unfolds and unfolds and unfolds.

— CHEROKEE ELDER

When I was a young housewife, mother, and professional woman, I suffered under the illusion that I would get my house just the way I wanted it and then I could turn my attention to other things, like my profession. I also believed (I realized much later) that my car, the appliances, the couches, and the walls could be taken to the place of perfection and then they would stay that way forever. How frustrated I became when the slip-covers wore out, the walls needed to be painted (again!), or the carpets needed to be replaced! Before I learned better, I saw these realities as a personal attack on me.

How much easier my life became when I recognized that everything in this material world is a process. The car rusts; that's a process. Replacing it with a new car may support the illusion. *And* the reality is that everything on this material plane is in a process of decay and transformation. Our science may feed our illusion and wish to deny the decay, and we may try to deny the aging of our bodies and our houses. Yet the process of transitioning into something else is our reality.

How exhausting it is to try to deny that everything around us is in process and to believe that, ultimately, we can stave off that process.

Participation

THE POSSIBILITY OF PARTICIPATION

Take care and go gently and contentedly on with doing good work.

— JOHN CASTEEL

Remember that the purpose of this book is to *remind* us of truths that we know deep in our being. These truths often, in our current societies, are ignored, discarded, lost, and forgotten. Our society has increasingly put more and more emphasis on non-participation so that, to a great extent, many of us have almost lost the ability and the incentive to participate.

I knew a man who once said that his father's goal in life was "to make enough money so that he never had to do anything for himself." I felt so sad for his father. And my experience of him is that he is completely ungrounded and lost. He did not want to cook his own food, wash his own clothes, mow his own lawn. He wanted to live in his head with his abstractions and concepts. In so doing, he had become groundless and spiritless.

It is amazing what an effect washing our own dishes, the intimacy of knowing and preparing our own foods, or straightening up our workspace can have on us! Moreover, moving from being an observer of our own lives to being a participant can change our perspective on ourselves and our lives completely. We never see the possibilities for participation when we don't participate.

When we start seeing the opportunities for participation, our options are endless, and . . . so are we!

Thinking

UNRULY THINKING

We can think ourselves into anything.

— LEE PIPER, CHEROKEE ELDER

Have you ever had the experience of having a crazy thought . . .
That person hates me.
My beliefs are the only true beliefs.
Everything is a conspiracy.
There are no conspiracies. It's all bunk.

. . . and then thought yourself into believing the flavor of
the month?

Most of us have had a similar experience. And, hopefully,
we have been able to get some perspective and regain some
balance. As we begin to step out of our everyday thinking, our
group/national thinking, and our fantasies, we begin a process
for growth that could lead us to wisdom. We can, indeed, talk
ourselves into anything. And we often do.

We need to be able to get perspective on our thinking, from
ourselves and others, to begin to live another paradigm. And we
need daily reminders *not* to believe our thinking.

Beliefs and Assumptions

ABOUT OURSELVES

Almost all of us have unknowingly acquired limiting, self-sabotaging misperceptions that undermine our strength, health, and desires.

— BRUCE LIPTON AND STEVE BHAERMAN

Few of us, when we are young, have any awareness about the beliefs and assumptions we are being taught about ourselves and our world from those around us, or that they are just that—beliefs and assumptions. We also have little awareness that what we are being taught is not necessarily real or true.

One of the truths about our realities of being born as human beings on this planet is that we are born into a swirl of beliefs and assumptions that are thought to be true and real by those who think them. We can never underestimate the power of the beliefs and assumptions we are taught about ourselves at an early age. Part of our responsibility as people is to outgrow our belief that what we have been taught about ourselves is "real" in order to grow into who we can be. For some, who have been taught negative things about themselves based on the beliefs and assumptions of the family, it is like physically tearing off a layer of "reality" that feels like our skin . . . and . . . it isn't.

Many of our tightly held beliefs and assumptions about ourselves are often not true and not useful. In fact, they are harmful. And it may *feel* like dying to let them go. I have never seen anyone actually die in doing so.

Feelings and Emotions

WE ARE AFRAID OF OUR FEELINGS AND EMOTIONS

Our feelings and emotions are the doors to our oneness.

— CHEROKEE ELDER

Most people tend to be afraid of their feelings and emotions. We must remember to ask ourselves, "Why?" when they are so clearly a part of our inherent makeup and intelligence.

In our current development as a human race, many of us have come to believe that feelings and emotions are dangerous and destructive and the best way to handle them is to suppress and repress them at all costs. We conjure up an image of the three witches around this boiling pot and we are terrified that this pot may boil over at any point and who knows what might happen.

Instead of remembering that they are a part of us and are here to help us through this life, for many they represent the unknown and the uncontrollable and must be controlled.

What a mistake this cultural belief is for us all.

Fear of the unknown within myself is fear of myself and my reality.

Honesty

FAMILIAL HONESTY

We start our learning of dishonesty in our families.

— CHEROKEE ELDER

Dysfunctional families have many secrets and most families are dishonest on one or more levels. In fact, most of us in this culture, indeed, do begin our education in dishonesty in our families. "Put on your happy face." "Company's coming, watch yourself." "You don't really feel that way, now, do you?"

And it is the unspoken dishonesties that prove to be the most difficult to unearth because they are never really *said*. They are insinuated or inferred. If and when we ever would deign to question them as children, we were almost always dismissed as dumb or crazy. "Where on earth did you get that idea?"

For example, I have a friend who thoroughly believes the lie that he is dumb. He's not! He is brilliant—very brilliant. He is also dyslexic and learns in a way different from most. By the time he was six or eight, his family had convinced him that he was retarded and would never be able to take care of himself, nor should he have to. In his 50s, he is finally challenging this family lie that was perpetuated on him. And he is furious! Yet, for him to live his life fully, he has to challenge a lie he learned at his parents' knees.

Family lies are deep and difficult to confront. Yet we must confront them if we want to live a new paradigm. What lies did your family teach you . . . about yourself and others?

Courage

COURAGE AS AN AFTERTHOUGHT

Courage is every day.

Does action come out of courage or does courage come out of action . . . or both or neither? Here is a good example where setting up a dualism is dysfunctional (as it usually is). In truth, both are true—and there is more. We often cannot or will not take action if we cannot call upon our courage *and* taking the action increases our courage *and* courage is cumulative, and we do not know how courageous we are until we take the action. Indeed, thinking about courage often makes us less courageous.

How do we know if we are courageous or not?

We don't. And even when we have been, if we were truly courageous and acting in the moment, there probably wasn't time for self-reflection. Thinking too much about courage may be the worst thing we can do to be courageous.

The truth is, we can always do more than we think we can— especially when what we do comes out of the rightness of our being. Participating breeds courage.

Entitlement

ENTITLEMENT AND HIERARCHY

Feeling entitled is always a trap.

Entitlement is based on a belief in hierarchy and a one-up/one-down operating philosophy that has permeated our society. Indeed, the concept of hierarchy permeates every aspect of the current dominant belief system.

Few realize the influence of hierarchy in our everyday lives and how it affects the way we operate. For example, almost all our institutional structures are built on the concept of hierarchy. In this concept there is someone at the "top" who has more power than others, who is "in control," and who is more "entitled." The illusion of control stems from a hierarchical system. In this system, power goes from the top down and by the time it "trickles down" there is little left. Of course, everyone wants to be on top and will stand on another's shoulders (or head!) to be there. The revealed religions also are all based on the concept of hierarchy and perpetuate the illusion that this is the way things have to be. Politicians love this concept and feed on it. They now are even saying that everyone should be in the top one percent, which is a statistical non-possibility.

If we believe in, practice, and perpetuate hierarchy, there is no way we can move into living a new paradigm.

Accepting Our Humanness

THE RELIEF OF OUR LIMITATIONS

To err is human; to forgive, divine.

— ALEXANDER POPE

To know and accept the fact that as humans our ability to understand the big picture is, by definition, limited, can be a big relief. This knowledge opens the possibility that we can eagerly learn as much as we can and do not have the impossible pressure to know it all. It just seems that our brains and beings are not constructed to know it all. So when we forgive ourselves for being human, well, that is divinely special.

Being human means that we are here on a journey—a journey to take in as much as we can, process as much as we can, and make progress as individuals and as a species. Knowing this reality means that we have endless opportunities to learn as much as we can with no pressure to know it all or no illusion that we can know it all.

We have a mandate to heal, learn, and grow as people and as a species. And, in spite of ourselves, even when we don't realize that mandate or try, something is happening. We have so believed that we are in charge, and yet we can clearly see that all too often we have not done so well. Knowing that already knowing and understanding everything is not our mandate for this life can be quite a relief and liberating.

We have put ourselves in so many impossible situations by refusing to accept our humanness.

Respect

OUR BODIES

To respect our bodies is to honor the Creator.

— CHEROKEE ELDER

There were two early activities that I did regularly with my great-grandmother when I was young: one was she bathed me every night and the other was we brushed one another's hair. Our house was cold and the best heat was in the living room. So Grandma would prepare my bath in an old galvanized tub near the stove in the living room and she would bathe me there. She would never use terry washcloths because she said they were too harsh for my tender skin, and she would use a very old, very soft square torn from an old sheet. Her touch was so gentle. She approached my body with such respect. Bathing was never rushed and she showed me how to respect my body. I need only to recall this experience to be reminded that my body is to be respected.

Another memorable experience with my great-grandmother was brushing one another's hair. Tears come to my eyes as I remember the respect and gentleness of such a simple activity. "Not too rough, Elizabeth Anne," she would say. "We must be gentle with our hair. We are lucky to have such beautiful, fine hair."

The way she said it, I knew that we would be lucky to have nice coarse hair—or no hair at all so we could have a good head rub. The clear message was that whatever it was, we were lucky to have it; we were lucky to have these wonderful bodies and we should treat them with respect, though those words were never spoken.

Like many things, we learn respect through actions.

The Abstractualization of Life

WORK

Our minds tend to blur the real and the unreal.

— CHEROKEE ELDER

In our culture, the more abstract and concept-driven our work is, the more it is valued. We are paid much more for "thinking" jobs than we are for "manual labor." We ignore this inequality by using the excuse that the thinking jobs require more education (often training in abstractions). Yet few of us would want the plumbers, carpenters, and electricians who are building our house not to know what they are doing.

Like my friend whose father told him that his goal in life was to make enough money so that he would never have to do anything for himself, this goal does not seem to be an unusual one in our culture. What he and many in our culture do not understand is that with their abstractualization and conceptualization of their lives, they are making themselves emotional and spiritual cripples. And, at the same time, they are being outdistanced by those who keep their feet on the ground and their hands in the dirt. If we choose to work in abstract professions, it is absolutely essential that we ground ourselves with the earth and our surroundings.

If our work and our wealth keep us in abstraction, we need to wash our own clothes, cook our own food, dig in our gardens, and find ways to keep grounded.

Being of Good Spirit

SQUISHING GOOD-SPIRITEDNESS

*Happiness, like matter, can neither be
created nor destroyed. It occurs.*

— CHEROKEE ELDER

Can you remember as a child how squeals of glee and peals of laughter just bubbled up from our inner beings and joy flowed up out of every cell? There were times that the joy was so intense that we just *had* to squeal—there was no alternative.

You may also remember being shushed. "Be quiet!" "You'll disturb people." How much goodness of spirit have we had shushed out of us? Yet somewhere deep inside of us, our bodies remember the feeling of exploding joy, aliveness, and good spirits.

One of my favorite elders, who was a teacher and mentor, once said to me: "We were not 'plugged in' all the time listening to recorded music. Our 'music' was the happy laughter of children and the sounds of nature. That's what lifted our spirits."

Are we willing to ignore the noise and let the laughter of children and the sounds of nature revive our good-spiritedness?

Domination Over and the Illusion of Control

OF THE SELF

*It seems strange that our learning that we
have no control may be our salvation.*

For addicts to recover, they have to face the unreality of their illusions and the painful destructiveness of them if they are to return to their spirit to have any life at all. Alcoholics are told that in order to recover they have to let go of their illusion of control. Painfully, they have to learn that they cannot control people, places, or things. They have to learn that they cannot control anything, and when they slip into the illusion that they can, not only do they get sicker, they are destructive to themselves and others.

In alcoholics or addicts, the illusion starts when they believe they can control their addiction. Of course the very definition of our addiction is something over which we are powerless. Being powerless does not mean that we have no personal power per se. It means that we have to recognize that we have no power over people (ourselves), places, and things—or our addictive behavior.

Trying to control our feelings, our memories, our thinking, or our behavior is like trying to control a tornado.

Humor

ABOUT OURSELVES

If you are willing to make yourself the butt of a joke,
you become one of the guys, a human being . . .

— LARRY WILDE

Self-humor is a way of bonding with ourselves and also putting ourselves in proper perspective. It is also a way of being very truthful and tender with ourselves. For example, many years ago before my father died, one of the top items on his bucket list was to rent a houseboat and spend a week on Lake Mead. I very much wanted to give him that, so I made a reservation for a two-bedroom houseboat. When the time of the reservation rolled around and it was too late to cancel and get my money back, he was too ill to go. What to do? I didn't really want to go without him. I *really* did not want to lose all that money. The trip *might* be fun. So I enlisted a friend and off we went on the adventure.

Almost everything that could go wrong did. We arrived around noon and by the time we were "checked in" (they were fools to let me have it!) it was late. We went to the nearest anchoring place and stopped. The next day we realized we needed a smaller boat to get around—more money. Getting the smaller boat took all day. Then the storm hit. Our radio said that it was unusual to have two hurricane-like storms come together over Lake Mead. That storm lasted three days. A rat ate a hole in my favorite cashmere sweater. My friend was so fearful of the rat that we had to keep the light on all night. The battery died. The water level of the lake dropped and after two days of trying to get out, we had to get a tow to unstick us. In "docking," I ran right up over the dock. Great learnings about greed, stubbornness, et cetera. I laugh until I cry every time I tell the story.

Learnings like that are pure gold.

Wonder and Awe

THE WEATHER

Nature is one of our best "awe-inspirers." Respect her.

— LAKOTA ELDER

Nothing can inspire wonder and awe like the weather.

I have written about the Arkansas thunderstorms and the wonder they held for me as a child. As an adult, I love sitting at a window looking out across Peace Valley in Montana. From my perch on the second floor of the old Boulder Hot Springs, I can see the storm building in the mountains to the west. It is awesome as what initially seemed insignificant slowly builds and twists, belches and roars, flashes and rumbles, and makes itself into one of those afternoon thunderstorms the West gives us. It challenges the mountains to stop it as it deftly slides over them into the valley. It can take as much as an hour or two before it slouches and crashes across the valley, sometimes stumbling on the mountains in the east before it moves on and visits another valley. Time spent with a thunderstorm is always time well spent. The Montana thunderstorm never disappoints and it provides an almost daily opportunity for wonder and awe.

Then there is the experience of driving up the long Peace Valley to Boulder Hot Springs. It is 36 miles from the south tip of the valley to the hot springs. One time when I rolled in at three in the morning, I had turned off the interstate and was not sure that I would make those last 36 miles when the Northern Lights began to play. Quite unexpectedly, I was immediately wide awake and filled with a peaceful wonder and awe with the opportunity of such a gift.

The weather is always there to inspire and put us in our place.

The Present Can Only Be Our Reality
if We Own Our Past and Our Future

ACCEPTING THE INFLUENCE
OF OUR PAST

*No matter what has happened to us, however
bad it was, we can and need to learn from it.*

— CHEROKEE ELDER

For some, it seems like a self-evident fact that our past experiences affect who we are today. We carry them with us every day of our lives and they affect our perceptions, our feelings, our emotions, our thinking, our "intelligence," our awarenesses, our choices of friends, our choices of work, even our choices of a way of life. Our past experiences influence those with whom we choose to relate, and how we relate to them. Our past experiences influence whether we are brave, timid, fearful, confident, shy, angry, happy, or able to utilize the talents we have been given. In fact, our experiences in life even influence *how* we view our innate talents.

Now do not get the idea that I am dredging up the old nature/nurture dualism from old psychology books. I'm not.

First of all, dualisms are limiting in and of themselves, and secondly, there is simply nothing to be gained from that false issue.

I am more concerned with a general acceptance of the reality that we are profoundly affected by our life experiences (as Freud knew) in our early years and they have to be dealt with for us to move on with our lives, make the contributions we can make, and begin to live out of a fuller paradigm than we are now doing.

Walking in Beauty

REMEMBERING

For some, it is easier to remember the bad, yet, if we are open to them, good memories always balance everything out. We even have choices about what we remember.

— CHEROKEE ELDER

When I think of walking in beauty, I immediately think of my great-grandmother.

In my memory of her, she was always very poor, and lived very simply. When I was very young, she lived with us. It was during the Depression, and my early memories were of people coming to my great-grandmother for healing. Everyone was always welcomed, and, with no words spoken, knew that it was just fine that they had come.

We always had one room or one area of a room that I would now call the pharmacy and Grandma would invite them to sit there among the herbs and "medicines." She was always so welcoming and focused on the person that I am sure that almost immediately they felt that they were the center of the universe and no issue was too small or too large to discuss with Grandma.

She always gently, matter-of-factly explained my presence very straightforwardly—"This is my great-granddaughter. She is a healer too and is here helping me." Who could possibly question the good luck of having two healers, even if I was under five years old?

My great-grandmother walked in beauty with every word and every motion.

Taking Time

SIMPLE THINGS

Remember, everything you do is a sacred act.

— LEE PIPER, CHEROKEE ELDER

One of my Cherokee elders casually shared with me the importance of brushing my teeth carefully at night. She pointed out that during the day, all sorts of "bad stuff" comes at us and tries "to get into us." She said that at night it is very important to take all the time I need to brush my teeth and rinse several times, spitting out my bad thoughts or energies I have taken in. It is also good for my teeth and gums.

I am so aware that in our busy modern life we rarely give ourselves the luxury simply of taking time—with anything. Few around us remind us of the absolute importance in our lives of taking time. Taking time is simply not part of our modern culture, and when we "have time," we fill it up with entertainment, television, talking, or keeping our minds busy. God forbid that we should have idle minds.

"Idle minds are the devil's workshop." What kind of culture is this proverb pushing us into?

People who walk in beauty are experts at taking time often during the day.

A Belief in Healing

WHOLENESS

*When you need healing, go lie down and press your
face against your mother; the earth, she will heal you.*

— PHIL LANE, SR., YANKTON SIOUX ELDER

When we believe in the integrity of wholeness, we can only
understand illness and healing in context. The current paradigm
of trying to heal individuals as individuals out of their context
makes no sense at all.

In Samoa, I understand that when a person comes to a traditional healer and is "sick," the healer asks what is going on in
the family, what is going on in the village, and what is going on
in the larger area, then they zero in on what the individual needs
to get well.

In Western culture, we have gone so far in the other direction that not only do we focus on the isolated symptoms in the
individual, we prefer to look at those symptoms in isolation and
"treat" them in isolation.

It is very recent that we started to look at trends and clusters
of symptoms.

People exist only in context. We need never to forget the
importance of context.

Knowing and Living in Several Realities

SLEEPING REALITIES

I love to sleep. It is one of my better skills.
I reach other realms when I sleep.

If we are to remember how much we know about living in other paradigms, we must first remember that we know that other paradigms have existed in the memory of the blood of our ancestors. This memory is sleeping within us. We have only to awaken and remember.

Those of us who were raised in native/tribal tradition may be closer to those roots. Essentially, even though the memories may be dim, we all remember wisdoms of other times and other ways. These memories are sleeping in all of us humans and, if we are only open, they will respond. This "responding" will be easier if we can let ourselves be open to having access to the intelligence beyond and behind our thinking minds.

Our thinking minds have been so "trained" that in order for us to go beyond our thinking minds, all of us will have to learn to question our training. Underneath that "training" is our knowing. Both are valid. They are just useful in different ways.

Opening to our known unknowns can be a bit frightening. Yet not doing so at this point in the history of humankind can be even more frightening, if you think about it.

Being of Service

DAILY OPPORTUNITIES

Each day is a new beginning.

— A.A. SLOGAN

Even in our carefully ordered and controlled lives which have been built out of our best dysfunctional building blocks, life is so constructed to present us with many opportunities to be of service. Being of service can be as simple as holding a door for a stranger, fixing a meal when everyone else is too tired, or stopping along the highway to help someone who is clearly in trouble.

Being of service requires us to be aware of and participate in and with our context. It requires us not to fall into the illusion that we *are* the context and what defines our context. To the contrary, it requires us to be aware of our context so that we can participate in it as fully as possible. There is a saying in the 12-step program of Alcoholics Anonymous, "What goes around, comes around." Often what is meant by this saying is that we reap what we sow, or what we do to others will come back to haunt us. And this saying can also mean that the useful service we provide will return to us tenfold.

We cannot truly perform a service when we have an agenda. And when we are being of service out of our core, the return is always different from and better than we expected.

Graciousness

THE EQUINOX

*Wisdom is the reward you get for a lifetime of
listening when you'd have preferred to talk.*

— DOUG LARSON

How easy it is to forget that the universe always errs in the direction of graciousness with us humans and all creation!

How gracious it is to have seasons, equinoxes, and solstices to remind us of the vast processes that affect our lives! How wonderful it is that in spite of our tendencies toward self-centeredness and believing ourselves to be the center of the universe, there are seasons and cycles that remind us that we are a part (a very small part) of processes and, indeed, processes that are much larger than ourselves. These processes remind us of the wholeness and our oneness within the larger process.

How gracious is that reminder?!

If we look around us, we are constantly reminded of the graciousness of the generosity of air to breath, food to eat, and water to quench our thirst. How gracious the earth is to us! How gracious all creation is to us!

We are surrounded by models that invite us into our experience that "err in the direction of graciousness." We have only to learn to reply in kind.

Moving Out of Our Comfort Zones

CREATURES OF HABIT

*A habit is something we have learned
that needs to be questioned.*

I once heard someone say, "I am a creature of habit. When I fall into a rut, I feel happy and comfortable. I start hanging pictures on the wall of the rut. I like static."

How much we like and strive for static. We absolutely demand that we and our world become static. We are going to get our bodies just the way we want and they are supposed to stay that way. Everything is supposed to stay the way we want it. We absolutely refuse to acknowledge that everything is in process. We even demand that our god(s) be static. We are comfortable in our ruts with pictures on the wall.

Well, if we want to live a new paradigm, one that is not destructive to ourselves and the planet, we will have to be willing to move way, way out of our comfort zones and beyond. If we want to live a new paradigm, we have to remember that trying to fit it into our well-decorated ruts of any kind probably will never fit the bill.

If we want to live a new paradigm, we need to be willing to admit that there are comfort zones of which we have no awareness, which we may be challenged to let go of.

When we move away from a universe we have tried to make static to one of participating in an unknown process, who knows what might happen or what it might look like?

Letting Go of What We Think We Know

LEARNING WITH OUR WHOLE BEING

*Coming unglued may mean that I
am moving to a new phase of equilibrium.*

We may not know as much as we think we know. And what we *do* know may not ultimately be that useful.

Our current culture is burdened with information. Indeed, this period in history is known as the Information Age. There is no doubt that we have more information available to us world-wide than ever before.

We have a German exchange student living with us and her iPhone is constantly in her hand. She always takes it to bed with her. She has told us that she and her friends Google everything. The minute they hear of something they do not know or understand, they Google it. "I Google everything. And so do all my friends," she said to me. Indeed, they have instant access to facts and information—some of it accurate and some if it not. Yet when she asks me about something, she gets the information embellished with stories and memories attached to the information, experiences and self-owned opinions, illustrations and active demonstrations, joking about myself and others, and laughter about our mistakes and learnings. She and I enjoy the information, and sometimes, painful learnings. The "facts and information" are balanced with other kinds of learnings.

When we learn with our whole being, we have more than information and facts.

Accepting That Choices and Behaviors Have Consequences

THE ROLE OF CO-DEPENDENTS

In an addictive society, addicts have no problem
to forget that there are consequences to their behaviors.
Addicts easily twist their worlds into
fantasies of their own creations.

Before any of you quickly rush to deny that you are actually an addict and therefore move to abstain from this discussion, I would like to remind each of us that when we live in a society that functions like an active addict and has been designed and built by persons trained and educated in the addictive society, none of us is exempt. Each of us is culturally trained to behave, think, and believe like an addict and develop behaviors that are integrated into the society. The very act of recovery is taking the responsibility to remember that the addictive behavior is not reality *and* that it *is reality in an addictive society*.

The problem is—we do not remember anything different. The problem is—addicts have bad memories. The problem is that we all need help to remember something our species, at this point in our history, is focused on forgetting. The problem is—we all need experiences that help us remember what is real—that choices and actions have consequences.

We as humans—especially humans who have bought into the addictive society—will choose to get away with whatever we can unless we make an active choice to participate in a different paradigm.

Humility

DEFINING HUMILITY OUT OF EXISTENCE

*Humility is not a commodity, a skill, or a learned behavior.
Humility is like the gentle rain that happens.*

— CHEROKEE ELDER

Perhaps true humility is so rare in today's world because it cannot be generated, made, controlled, or bought. We have built our civilization on what has been consciously generated, made/manufactured, and controlled. And humility simply does not fit into any of these processes or approaches to life. In fact, we have not only come to have disdain for processes and things that we cannot control, we have tried to define such realities out of our awareness and existence.

"If we cannot make and control it, 'it,' by *our* definition, does not exist."

This is the mantra of our age. If we did not or cannot produce it, if we cannot control it, if we do not understand it, and if our tools cannot understand it and/or prove its existence, then, by definition, "it" does not exist.

Unfortunately, humility seems to have fallen into the arena of nonexistence. We can talk about it as if it were real and does exist, and we do not believe in it and its value.

Would you behave differently if you actually *believed* in humility?

Knowing and Being Known

BEING HUMAN AGAINST ALL ODDS

We need to accept the gifts we have been given as humans.

— FREDERICK FRANCK

My good friend, philosopher, teacher, and artist Frederick Franck, wrote a wonderful book he titled *To Be Human against All Odds*. I believe that it was retitled by some publisher to be more in keeping with the dominant system at some point. What Frederick tried to do in that book was to help explore what it means to be human. He was not interested in buying into the illusion of our being gods. He was interested in our gifts of empathy, clear thinking, being aware of our connectedness, and what we could do as we participated as part of the whole. His point was not that we are better than or above the rest of creation; his point was that we have not taken advantage of our uniqueness as humans to be of service to all creation.

In our present paradigm, we have so overdeveloped our rational/logical minds and we have so underdeveloped our emotional, intuitive, feeling minds that we are lopsided as beings and have not made the balanced contribution that we are capable of making for the betterment of all creation.

When great parts of us are unknown and unused by ourselves, there is no way we can make our full contribution to ourselves or others.

Everything Is Spiritual/Sacred

Our Bodies

Our bodies are sacred temples.

— Mary Elizabeth Reed

How would we live differently if we remembered that our bodies are spiritual? Our bodies are not our enemies. They are not here to be used and abused. Nor are they out to get us in spite of the way we have treated them. What might we do differently if we truly believed they were spiritual? What might happen if we recognized them as one manifestation of the spiritual? I remember, years ago, I was talking with two young men about sex (no topic is off-limits for me!). I noted the shock on their faces when I said that I had been brought up knowing that making love was a sacred act that had the potential of putting us more in touch with the Creator. I was surprised to find out that they had never heard this reality before.

They had grown up believing that 1) sex was forbidden, 2) sex was bad, 3) sex "should only take place under certain culturally approved rules," 4) sex was the most important thing about a relationship, 5) sex was for procreation, 6) sex needed to be controlled, 7) sex was about orgasm and "getting your rocks off," and on and on . . . They had heard nothing about sex being sacred and a way of experiencing a connection with a reality greater than ourselves.

If we do not remember that our bodies are sacred gifts, no wonder sexuality has become so violent and distorted in the current paradigm.

What would you do differently if you remembered daily that your body is sacred?

Wholeness

THERE IS A MAGIC IN WHOLENESS

Wholeness is not an idea, it is our reality.

Richard Wagamese quotes an Anishinaabe woman as saying, "The Anishinaabe are pretty big on magic. Not so much the pullin' rabbits outta hats kinda magic but more the pullin' learning outta everything around 'em. A common magic that teaches you how to live with each other."

Our current worldview, with its reductionistic, scientific approach to acquiring knowledge, has a side effect of separating and dividing us from ourselves, one another, nature, and all creation. This has resulted in a splintering of our wholeness and a losing of awareness that we are all, indeed, connected and are one with all creation.

How can religions that say they believe in one God also deny that we come from the same creation? Try as we might, we just cannot make those two approaches come together. If we are all created by the same Creator, then we are "related." If we are all related, then why can we not respect one another and see differences as an opportunity for growth?

Perhaps the magic of beginning to see all creation as a whole will then help facilitate us to work together for the good of all.

If we can remember that all of creation is connected in wholeness, then just maybe we will begin to see "the other" as one with us. We can work "magic."

Joy

EXQUISITE/PAINFUL JOY

Intense joy can be very quiet.

We have become so dependent on alcohol, drugs, and partying to "have fun" that we have lost touch with the fact that down deep in our beings we have a great capacity for pure joy and happiness.

The other day I was visiting a friend who is in great pain from cancer. He has been completely disfigured by a surgeon who wanted to prove how skilled he was, and my friend is in total misery. I love him and spent a long time with him just holding hands and being with one another. It was good for both of us and painful too.

On the way home, right about sunset, I was driving into the most magnificent wisps of coral clouds hanging in an azure sky, and my heart soared in pure joy with such beauty. I marveled at the juxtaposition of the pain and sadness I felt with and for my friend and the exquisite joy and peacefulness I felt as the sunset performed its miracle on me. Tears of joy ran down my face for the joy of having such a friend, the exquisite pain of his passing process, and the gift and reminder of the passion of all life in the magnificent sunset.

Life has a way of giving us peaks of joy even in the most difficult of times. We need to remember to be open to them.

Emotional Intelligence

FEELINGS

The senses are contradictory and deceiving. We never
look at anything with our senses. We look with
our feelings. Only our feelings can be trusted.

— ALEX PUA, HAWAIIAN KUPUNA

When we are emotionally intelligent, we *know* what we are
feeling and we can *feel* what we are feeling.

We trust that our feelings have important information for us
and that they provide a breadth and a depth of information that
is not readily available to our thinking minds.

This information helps us have a deeper understanding of
what is going on inside ourselves and within others.

Our emotional intelligence warns us of impending danger
or trouble long before our rational-logical mind discovers that
anything is going on at all.

With a high emotional intelligence we are less easily conned
and/or fooled.

There is a reason we have an emotional intelligence.

All Is in Process

OUR CHILDREN ARE A PROCESS—NOT A THING

God has no grandchildren.

— A.A. SLOGAN

Every person has her/his own process of life. I have seen so many parents who steadfastly hang on to the illusion that they will mold their children into what they want them to be and then they will stay that way for life. This is one of the most damaging parental illusions that we can commit. It shows no regard for our children's reality as people and beings in the process of becoming. All too often people want to ignore their children's process and force them into being little clones of themselves, seemingly in an effort to prove their own validity.

Our responsibility as parents is to be clear enough in our own process of becoming that we can facilitate our children in their own process of becoming—even when it differs significantly from our own life process. To love and nurture our children is to be able to step in when needed to help them discern what their life process needs to be for them at that time, and to support that process as best we can, even when we do not completely understand it. Good parenting is never an easy process and it can be so much easier and productive if we can step back and recognize that our children have an inner process grounding them that knows much more than we do. As we participate in life with them, we may also be privileged to participate in their process of life. God has no grandchildren! Why would our God be better, wiser, more knowledgeable than our children's?

Perhaps good parenting is a process of helping our children get acquainted with their inner process—their higher power.

Participation

PARTICIPATION WITH— NOT CONTROL OF

There is a quiet, serene confidence in knowing that all things do not stand or fall according to one's own achievements or the correctness of every decision one makes.

— JOSEPH A. SITTLER

In our current paradigm, many of us have forgotten how to participate without trying to control ourselves and others. In this context, participation does not mean coming into a situation and trying to control the situation. Nor does it mean predetermining a specific outcome and trying to get ourselves and others to get there.

It is more like starting a day with a few things in mind of what needs to be done and then being completely open to what the day brings without being wedded to our agendas.

Most of us will immediately say, "Then nothing will get done!" This simply has not been my experience. In fact, more often than not, *more will get done* when we are trusting the process and participating. It may not get done in the preconceived timeline. It may not look the way we thought it would. It may not get done in the manner we thought. And creativity (the spirit?) may have a chance to step in. The illusion of control has ruined many a project and caused an inferior product to be produced.

If we give ourselves time to remember, we will realize that participation and innovation are partners.

Thinking

EARLY LEARNINGS ABOUT THINKING

If we can't trust our thinking, what can we trust?
This is an important question to ask.

When I was a young woman completing my doctoral training in psychology, I decided to do my internship at Bellevue Hospital in New York City. I certainly learned a lot, and a great deal about schizophrenia. I even began to call Bellevue the schizophrenic capital of the universe. Although the general public thought of schizophrenia as a "split personality," we were taught that it was a *thinking disorder*. In schizophrenia, people thought thoughts that were not based in reality, they believed them, and often acted on them—sometimes in violent ways.

As I worked with people in recovery, I began to see that what A.A. called "alcoholic thinking" looked very much like schizophrenia. Addictive/alcoholic thinking seemed to be on the same continuum. I mentioned this in a speech and a participant told me that when the concept of schizophrenia was developed, alcoholism was included under the diagnosis. I did some research and found that she was right.

So what does this mean? If we live in an addictive society and the thinking of the addict and the schizophrenic are on the same continuum, what does this say about the process of the way we are taught to think and how we do it? We need to be reminded that there are times when our thinking is very logical and rational, *and* it just doesn't make any sense.

We see this kind of thinking in politics and business all the time. "Schizophrenic/addictive thinking" cannot be trusted.

Beliefs and Assumptions

ABOUT OUR FAMILIES

*The great gift of family life is to be intimately acquainted
with people you might never even introduce yourself to,
had life not done it for you.*

— KENDALL HAILEY

Just as many of the beliefs and assumptions we have held about ourselves have doubtful value, the beliefs and assumptions we have held about our families need to be checked out and tested with our emerging reality. Some families make this more difficult than it need be.

Most child-development experts think of the role of adolescence as a time when we necessarily push back from the beliefs and assumptions of our families and try to "think for ourselves." This process is certainly harder in some families than others. For example, I know one young woman who when I said to her "What are your options?" she blankly looked at me and said, "There are no options . . . my family's way and . . . there is no other way." Coming of age is a difficult process in that kind of concrete, constructed world.

Many families also have some very fixed, clear notions about who they are as a family based on their beliefs and assumptions. "We are a perfect family." "Our way is not only the right way, it is the only way." "We are better than other people." And on and on. Whether the beliefs are positive or negative in nature, both can be disastrous for personal growth and awareness. There is always an unspoken belief that to be a good person (and to survive) one must agree with the beliefs and assumptions of the family.

Even when the beliefs and assumptions about our families are "good" ones, they can be destructive if rigidly held and are not open to change.

Feelings and Emotions

OUR FEELINGS AND EMOTIONS ARE OUR DOORS TO GROWTH AND HEALING

Our feelings are our most genuine paths to knowledge.

— AUDRE LORDE

We need to remind ourselves how important it is to make friends with our feelings and emotions. Our feelings and emotions are almost always the doors into our repressed memories and awarenesses. Our thinking/conscious minds will never get us there. And unless we get to those repressed memories and awarenesses, we will never have the possibility to heal and grow from our experiences—all our experiences. No matter what our experiences have been, they are *our* experiences and they are the grist for our mill to learn as much as we can from this human experience and become the fullest and most whole person we can become.

Our feelings and emotions may not be easy doors for us to walk through and when we do, we need to remind ourselves that the outcome is always powerfully growth-producing.

Honesty

COMMUNITY LIES

*Communities also can absorb
the disease of the culture.*

All of us need to confront the dishonesties that we grew up with in our communities if we are to live a new paradigm.

"We are better people because we live in this community and go to this school."

"We are not as good as those people because we do not have as much money as they do."

"We have to watch very carefully how successful people act and dress to be successful."

"Having one color of skin is better than having another."

"You can't date someone from that community because they are not as good as we are."

Community lies are very powerful and can constrict our lives in ways we can hardly imagine. And we take them in not realizing that not only are we getting harmful information, we are also learning the process of taking in and living lies that are destructive to ourselves and others.

Whether we want to believe it or not, our communities have a great influence on us and the lies that are perpetuated in these communities distort us from within. To live a new paradigm, we have to face and change these distortions of perception.

Courage

DAILY COURAGE

Courage is fear that has said its prayers.

— DOROTHY BERNARD

We have a million opportunities a day to practice and build our courage.

We see a child being abused by its mother. Do we do or say something?

We see animals being tortured. Do we say something?

We see the earth being destroyed. Do we even have the courage to feel, truly *feel* the pain we feel or have we taught ourselves not to feel such things?

If we have shut off the intimacy that we need to have with ourselves to be people of honor and integrity, do we have the courage to feel those feelings that were buried so long ago when we did not have the wisdom or skills to deal with them?

I see so many people who have shut off so many memories, feelings, and emotions because they have believed that shutting them off was the way to survive. Do we have the courage to peek behind these doors one at a time?

Remember, our inner beings will only hand us what we are ready to handle.

Entitlement

THE CONCEPT OF ONE UP/ONE DOWN

How arrogant (and foolish and unrealistic)
to feel superior.

An offshoot of the belief of and adherence to the concept of hierarchy is the practice of one up/one down.

Some people who feel entitled firmly believe that they don't necessarily want to be "one up." They just don't want to be "one down." So they always go one up just in case. Being a woman, I have tested this belief many times. Although there has been some progress, many men automatically *assume* that when they meet a woman she will go one down and "things will be as they should be." When she (or any other person of "less status" in a hierarchical system) doesn't go one down, a moment of unease and shuffling ensues and then the person who believes in hierarchy goes one down, resenting every moment of it.

Clearly the belief in hierarchy and a one-up/one-down system is more powerful than the possibility and opportunity to be "equal."

These beliefs and habits are very strong and deeply seated in all our institutional structures. Yet if we truly want to move into a new path for the human race, it is time to let them go.

Accepting Our Humanness

EVERYTHING IN OUR PATH IS AN OPPORTUNITY FOR LEARNING

Yet, self-surrender and letting go in loving trust draw out what is most human in each and every one of us, and, therefore most divine.

— BERT WHITE

As humans, everything that happens to us and everything we encounter is an opportunity for growing and learning.

This exciting possibility demonstrates the conservation of the universe . . . nothing that comes into our lives is useless or wasted unless we waste it. Every experience—good, bad, painful, and happy—is there as a learning possibility. Whether that learning happens or not is up to us. At some ultimate level, nothing is either good or bad. It's what we do with it. It's what we learn from it. It's how we use it to grow and become a fuller person; that, in the end, is what counts.

We don't have good or bad. We have opportunities.

From my own life, I have learned that if I don't get the lesson the first time around, it will come around again . . . and again . . . and again. And each time I refuse to get the learning, it will be harder the next time.

The intensity of the whack we get alongside our heads to get a learning is directly proportionate to our denial, stubbornness, and illusion of control.

Respect

RESPECT IS AN APPROACH TO LIFE

We need to have respect and love for all things and all people.
— DON COYHIS, MOHICAN

Washing dishes offers us an opportunity to practice respect. From my perspective, there are more opportunities to practice respect when we do our dishes by hand, and even in the way we load and unload our dishwashers we can practice the presence of respect.

I have many visitors who come to my house and stay various lengths of time. Before this many-visitor period, I had one set of dishes for more than 35 years. Suddenly, it seemed to me, the chipping/breaking descended upon my dearly loved and used dishes. The first phase was that I would go to the kitchen or cupboard and there would be a chipped or broken dish, or I would find one in the trash or a favorite mixing bowl had disappeared.

"Do you know where [blank] is?" "What happened to this plate?" "Didn't we have twelve of these bowls?" became oft-expressed questions.

Then began the training, which they seemed to have missed as children. "We need to respect everything, absolutely everything."

"We can get another one?"

"That's not the issue," became an oft-expressed response.

Every single little thing deserves our respect. Remembering this will help our personal paradigm shifting.

The Abstractualization of Life

PARENTING

The thing about having a baby . . . is that thereafter you have it.

— JEAN KERR

The abstractualization of parenting is resulting in generations of "lost" beings.

If we want to live into a new paradigm, we cannot do so without becoming realistic about what we as a culture are doing with the role of parenting. We need to see how parenting and raising children have become abstract concepts that have little or nothing to do with the job itself.

When we have children "because we have a right to have children," "because we deserve to have children," "because the church tells us we must," "because everyone else is," "because we want to maintain our genealogical line," "because it is the next thing to do to fill the void," "because no one can keep us from 'doing what we want,'" or for any other abstract reasons, our children probably will not have very good parenting. Probably 75 percent of the people who have children do not want to *raise*, *teach*, and *nurture* children. What a different world we would have if we did not treat parenting and having children as an abstraction.

We need to see how abstractions and conceptualizations have come to dominate the way we live our lives.

Being of Good Spirit

APPROACHING NATURE

Nature is who we are and more than we are.

— CHEROKEE ELDER

Do we remember that we are part of nature and not above it?

Do we remember that we need nature as much or more than it needs us?

Do we approach nature as our teacher?

Do we have the patience to sit with her and wait with her until she deems us ready to learn from her? How can we learn to live a new paradigm unless we are willing to humble ourselves to the rocks who have been here much longer than we have and have seen more than we ever have? There is an old Zen Buddhist saying that the rocks have sat Zazen longer than any of us and have much to teach us.

Every year I write a page-a-day calendar for Women Who Do Too Much. I enjoy the process, especially the one of gathering quotes from women. And women seem to appreciate the calendar. One year I had the idea to suggest that one day a month, women should get a rock and see what they could learn from the rock. My publisher actually got a couple of negative calls and I even received one piece of hate mail about the "stupidity" of those entries.

Magical things happen when we approach the rocks from an attitude of good-spiritedness and see what they can teach us. Find a rock, put it on your desk. Touch it every day. See what it can teach you.

Domination Over and the Illusion of Control

OURSELVES

*It is only our fear and lack of faith that cause
us to need to be in what we think is control.*

— BERT WHITE

The way we approach ourselves is key to our learning to live another paradigm.

Most of us do not realize that part of our "job" of being human is to establish a healthy relationship with ourselves. Yet the relationship we have with ourself includes many facets of ourself and also the process of the way these selves relate to one another. We have the public self, the private self, the self that others see, of which we are unaware, and the unknown self. In addition, we have our conscious self, which is the self that minds the day-to-day business; our unconscious self, which has taken on all kinds of scary images because it is the unconscious or unknown self; and then there is the self that is connected and one with the all that is. Most of us want to deny and ignore this myriad of selves and invest in the illusion that "What you see is what you get." Yet we want to live in illusion and believe in simplicity of "I am who I am." A big part of this journey is getting friendly with all these parts of ourselves and learning to work with them so we can become more whole and more in touch with ourselves and our connection beyond ourselves. Trying to control the selves we do not recognize or want to recognize is impossible and not very smart.

To live a new paradigm is to recognize and explore not giving into denying, controlling, and disbelieving.

Humor

RELIEF

*I'm always afraid I'll wake up one day
and find myself turned serious.*

Humor is often necessary to bring a welcome relief to a very tense situation.

For example, right now I am on a seven-week boat trip from Florida around South America to Australia. Sometimes people who are not accustomed to being at sea for long days at a time get a bit tense and testy. This testiness is not directed at anybody. It is just that landlubbers are accustomed to being on land. Interesting, the powers that be on the boat have scheduled a staff tug-of-war on the pool deck today. Now this is a British ship and it tends to be a little stiff and proper. Formal dress for dinner and such things. So today, very wisely, the entertainment staff has scheduled a staff tug-of-war. The chefs just walked by in full dress with white clothes, chefs hats, and face makeup. The waiters in the exclusive Queens Grill are dressed in grass skirts with coconut "bras" and full face makeup.

Even the British in their own way recognize that a bit of frivolity on occasion (carefully controlled, of course) is good for relieving tension and to be used sparingly . . . when appropriate and agreed upon, of course.

Wonder and Awe

NATURE

Every now and again take a good look at something not made with hands—a mountain, a star, the turn of a stream. There will come to you wisdom and patience and solace and, above all, the assurance that you are not alone in the world.

— SIDNEY LOVETT

Have you ever seen the ocean turn pink like the inside of a ripe guava? The pink is so intense and so beautiful that it never ceases to stop me in my tracks. And I am not a great admirer of pink in and of itself. Yet when my entire world—the sky, the ocean, and the land—turns pink at the end of the day as I am simply driving along on the highway, tears fill my eyes and I whisper a "thank you" for the privilege that I am experiencing.

What a feeling of awe I have when the mating eagles return "home" in the winter and take up their watch of the lake on their old snag. I am so glad they have safely returned and are keeping a watch over our house.

Or, speaking of wonder and awe, have you ever awakened to the calling of the whooping cranes? Or fallen asleep to the call of the bobwhite or the whip-poor-will? No lullaby was ever more soothing or comforting. Who would not experience wonder and awe to have the exquisite privilege to be a part of all this? Who would not want to protect and preserve it so that the generations to come can have the same experiences? Nothing can inspire like nature. When we surround ourselves with steel and concrete, we limit our opportunities to live with wonder and awe.

One of our easiest ways to return to sanity is for nature to put us in our place.

The Present Can Only Be Our Reality
if We Own Our Past and Our Future

WE ARE THE SUM TOTAL
OF OUR EXPERIENCES

No man is rich enough to buy back his own past.

— OSCAR WILDE

We are the sum total of our experiences and we are more than the sum total of our experiences. Part of our challenge in life is to live this paradox.

In the many years that I have worked with people from all over the world from different races and cultures, I realize that I have always assumed that *they* know and assume that they are carrying their individual history with them, even if they have no awareness of this reality. There seems to be an inverse relationship between their awareness of this reality and how much they are affected by it. That is to say, the less they are aware of this reality and the specifics of this reality, the more they are affected by it.

I have worked with many people who have few, if any, memories before, say, puberty. For these people, in some very real way, they had no childhood and they, therefore, do not have the learnings, the happiness, the foundations of their life.

When I meet someone like this, I see their lack of any memories, any childhood, as a red flag that not only is there something missing, something very important is missing and robbing them of their wholeness.

On some ultimate level for our wholeness, it is not important *what* happened to us that we can't remember. It is the *process* of working through it and getting the learnings that will best serve us in the future.

Walking in Beauty

GATHERING HERBS

*We were contented to let things remain
as the Great Spirit Chief made them.*

— CHIEF JOSEPH

"Let's go gathering, Elizabeth Anne," were some of the most favorite and exciting words of my early childhood. This meant that Grandma and I would go out to spend several hours in the woods and fields gathering "medicines." These forays into nature were gently exquisite for me as a child. I had Grandma all to myself. There were no chores that had to be done. We always talked in hushed and reverent voices like we did in church. And gratitude, stated and unstated and felt, permeated everything we did.

When I think of walking in beauty, I think immediately of these gentle forays into nature to gather medicines to help heal others.

It was very clear to me that Grandma had no illusion that she or the herbs did the actual healing. They were just tools to assist the Creator, who wanted us to be whole and healthy.

The whole day with Grandma in the meadows and forests was spent walking in beauty.

Taking Time

DOING NOTHING

How wonderful it is to do nothing . . . and rest afterward.

— MEXICAN SAYING

I love it.

Doing nothing is almost a lost skill in modern culture. And resting afterwards—well, that's just indulgent!

As a writer, I have learned that much of my most productive time is when I am doing nothing. Years ago, I used to believe that I had a writer's block and was "procrastinating" and avoiding my writing when I was getting ready to write. I would clean the stove, reorganize my desk and my studio, and in general fritz and frither. Later I came to see that during this "procrastination" time, I was actually writing or more accurately keeping my hands busy to fool my mind so that the information I needed to write (which was not yet in my conscious mind) could get through.

We need to be reminded that we desperately need time to frither, putter, fiddle, and moodle to let our memory of another way to be in this world come through.

Living a new paradigm is not possible if we don't take time.

A Belief in Healing

MECHANISTIC SCIENCE

Healing is a process, not an event.
— MARY ELIZABETH REED

The model we now have for healing is based upon the machine. Humans are assumed to function like machines and our bodies are expected to function like machines. In some cases, "healing" is assumed to be as simple as taking out a worn part or replacing that worn part. In this healing paradigm, there is a reductionistic, limited approach to healing.

I recently heard that a young doctor who was having problems with kidney stones had his parathyroid gland removed because it relates to the use and elimination of calcium in the body and kidney stones are made of calcium. I was horrified!

There was no consideration of the other—known and unknown—functions of that gland and the myriad of problems that removing that gland would cause.

"If your eye offends you, pluck it out."

We have been so simplistic in our mechanistic approach to our universe that we have lost awareness of the complexity of illness.

Knowing and Living in Several Realities

EARLY TRAINING

Remember, Elizabeth Anne, it is the unseen that is the most important.

— MANILLA WILLEY

I grew up in a very interesting and balanced household with respect to realities. My father, who was part Cherokee, had, on the surface, "bought the package." He was a bit ashamed of his Cherokee heritage and wanted to be a "modern man in a modern world." He was brilliant in science and math. He made sure that I excelled in both and loved both. Math games and scientific experiments were part of my everyday feeding. I was using trigonometry to solve math problems in eighth grade in a three-room country school. (My teacher just shook his head and shrugged when I came up with the "right" answers and he had no idea why.)

My mother and grandmother were free to bring in the other levels of knowledge. Occasionally my father tried to pooh-pooh my mother's "premonitions," and it was impossible to see that he did not respect (and fear!) them because (scientifically/statistically) she was always right. He had to respect accuracy! Mother and grandmother would just pat my head with a patient smile.

So I grew up knowing about ghosts, spirits, and the unknown, how they can help and inform us. I grew up knowing in my very soul that I had a lot of help—from somewhere—and that I should be grateful. And I was. I trusted my mother's intuition and premonitions. It took me years of testing out the validity of my own to trust them.

Living a new paradigm means having a leap of faith with what can't be scientifically "proved" and yet is known.

Being of Service

RICHNESS OF OURSELVES

To serve others we need first to honor ourselves and our Creator.

— CHEROKEE ELDER

In order to be of service to others, we will more easily be of service if we recognize and value who we are and the gifts we have been given. We do not need to be arrogant and/or feel that everyone could benefit from our gifts. And it certainly helps if we are willing to take action with what the situation demands and do what we can. When we just "pitch in," the door to wonderment opens. Being of service can be one of those doors to wonderment that was snoozing in our unconscious.

How very wonderful it is to discover that we have talents secret even from ourselves, and that we can do things we never imagined we could do because we would have never risked on our own. We actually needed that opportunity for being of service to learn about ourselves!

If we had not risked being of service to someone or something else, we may never have had this opportunity to learn about ourselves.

Of course, we can also learn something about ourselves if we refuse to be of service. It may not be a pretty picture; still, it is a learning.

Graciousness

THE GRACIOUSNESS OF SPRING

*Never forget that nature is always
our most gracious benefactor.*

Spring, again and again, and again, and again, brings us the promise of renewed life, rebirth, and the cycle of process that sustains us. For me, there is no season that is more gracious than spring.

When I was a child, I lived in the Cherokee adopted country of the Ozarks. The Ozarks are very gracious in the spring.

At the end of each winter, I always anxiously awaited the advent of the redbuds and the dogwoods. The redbuds and dogwoods for me heralded the graciousness and promise of spring. Until they arrived, the woods, except for the evergreens, of course, were hardwood forests and the winter woods were basically death-like with the bare dark trees and branches hanging forlornly everywhere. Then the redbuds appeared as if by magic. Tiny, little, bright, magenta blossoms along the dark branches, like pure delight suspended in cheering patches of color. Soon after, the canopy of dogwoods appeared seemingly suspended unsupported in the air. I always cried and still do with the surprise and beauty of it all. Only as an adult did I learn that people in other parts of this world did not have this kind of spring graciousness in their lives. I grieved for them.

When someone or something is gracious to us, we mellow and change. A new paradigm simply must be filled with graciousness within and without.

Moving Out of Our Comfort Zones

THINKING WE KNOW

*Get a "cherished illusions" box and
deposit written-down illusions in it daily.*

One of the cherished comfort zones I find creeping into the writings of those of us who truly have come to know that the present paradigm the human race has developed is definitely not working is the reliance on old patterns of *how* we think and *what* we think.

In Western culture, we have developed stylized patterns not only of *what* we think, we have developed stylized patterns of *how* we think. And we have come to believe that they are real. We have tried to "static" our universe. We refuse to believe in the basic reality that all is in process. This truth is one we have to face if we are to move ahead as a species. So many "new paradigm" people want to move from this old paradigm to this new paradigm and they believe (thinking) that they know what it will look like.

Well, we just can't know what will happen if we participate in the process and do not try to predetermine the outcome.

Challenging our cherished illusions is a lifetime process.

Letting Go of What We Think We Know

PARENTAL TEACHINGS

The events of our lives happen in a sequence of time, but in their significance to ourselves they find their own order . . . the continuous thread of revelation.

— EUDORA WELTY

At some point in the process of growing up, we have to stand back and reevaluate what we have learned from our families and parents.

When I was a psychotherapist, I used to tell my clients, "There are two ways to be controlled by your parents. One is to believe what they believe, do what they tell you to do, live how they live, and adhere to their beliefs and values." Then I would say, "The other way to be controlled by them is to rebel against everything they are and everything they have taught you." "Either way," I would say, "you are being controlled by them, their beliefs, and their values."

As with any dualism, we need to seek a third option. The third option is to do the long and difficult process of working through both ends of the dualism and finding out what is true for you and fits for you, your experiences, and what you have learned for yourself. Maturity is found in taking what fits for you from the teachings of your family and your culture and letting go of the rest. For us as human beings, a major part of our work to become adults is sifting, choosing, letting go of what does not fit for us, and redefining what does fit.

Just knowing what our parents want us to know does not lead us to wisdom. Rejecting everything our parents taught us is not wisdom either.

Our wisdom is a lifetime process.

Accepting That Choices and Behaviors Have Consequences

THE SEDUCTION OF BEING A VICTIM

When you find yourself in the middle of a mess,
sit down and examine your role in it.
You'll feel better.

Modern psychology in its theories, assumptions, and beliefs has helped develop and perpetuate the cult of the victim. Part of the focus of psychology has been to identify *why* we are the way we are and zero in on, essentially, who wronged us. Mothers get an undue share of the responsibility for why we turned out the way we have. Fathers get some, families get a lot, teachers get their share, school bullying gets a big share, the church gets its share, the schools, the society—you name it. All can be the reason we turned out the way we did.

Psychology in its theories and interpretations gives us many people to blame, and therefore gets us off the hook from taking responsibility for how we turned out and who we are. The ultimate result of this psychological belief system is that all of us become victims of something and are no longer "responsible." We end up feeling angry, resentful, and justified in our bad behavior. We need to remember that victims don't get better, they just get bitter. The outcome of this ideology is victims who came to believe that their bad behavior is justified because they have been victimized. And victims always become perpetrators.

Remember, living as a victim does not leave much room for growing, learning, and healing.

Humility

HUMILITY HIDES ITSELF

To be humble is not to make comparisons.

— DAG HAMMARSKJÖLD

Humility only appears when we are not looking for it.

It is like one of those sly things in nature, like morel mushrooms or jacks-in-the-pulpit that recede into the background when one is actively searching for them.

Basically, humility cannot be caught or captured. It cannot be pressured or apprehended. It cannot be sought after and found.

It frustrates the modern mind and psyche because it does not fit into a technological, materialistic, mechanistic paradigm.

By-products never do.

Some of the most important aspects of human possibilities are by-products.

Our frantic lookings, are, indeed, amusing to our Creator.

Knowing and Being Known

TRANSPARENCY

Differences challenge assumptions.

Each of us as persons has unique gifts, skills, limitations, and possibilities. In order to utilize our full potential and become the persons we can be, a major part of our journey is to come to know ourselves as fully as we can.

When we think of the process of knowing and being known, some of us may feel a bit frightened. Indeed, in this cultural paradigm much of our emotional and spiritual energy is spent in hiding who we *really* are from ourselves and others. What would people think if they knew what I really think? What would people think if they knew the things I have done? If people knew my secrets, they would never have anything to do with me.

Few realize how much energy it takes to hide our truth and reality from ourselves and others. Whole professions have evolved that are financially supported by encouraging "patients" to share their "secrets" and have the "catharsis" of exposing themselves to someone who is supposed to remain a "stranger" and keep their secrets "confidential."

How little we really know in the current paradigm about "knowing and being known," which can be the greatest of human experiences.

Everything Is Spiritual/Sacred

THE THINGS AROUND US

Spirituality is not static. It is an every-second event.

I recently had a guest staying at my house who used one of my beautiful stainless steel pots to steam some fresh corn. After she finished using the pot she washed it and turned it upside down on a towel on the kitchen counter to dry. Later that day, I walked by the kitchen and saw the big beautiful pot upside down. I was horrified to see that the bottom of the pot was covered with burnt-on stains where it had boiled over and, unattended, had been blemished.

I stopped what I was doing and spent the next hour apologizing to the beautiful old stainless steel pot while I cleaned it. I felt sad and embarrassed that something that had served me so well had been neglected and abused. I felt bad that I had not protected it in my own house. Somehow my guest had forgotten to remember that the beautiful pot was sacred. It had come from the earth, which is sacred, and served me well for many years. It deserved to be treated well and appreciated for its service.

It is not that I have to keep everything perfect. Certainly my house is not perfect and everything in it and the house itself is treated as sacred and spiritual.

When everything is recognized as spiritual, we need to remember to treat it with respect and value it.

Wholeness

SHORT-SIGHTEDNESS

The only thing that will redeem mankind is cooperation.

— BERTRAND RUSSELL

Virginia Satir, when she was introducing the concept of family therapy to a group or to a family, used to tie everyone together with one long rope. Then she would ask the "family" to perform a simple task like walking across a room. It was always a time of great hilarity watching a group of self-centered people try to perform that simple task. The "leaders" would be sure that they knew exactly how to do it and if everyone would just be willing to take directions from them, they could accomplish their goal. Unfortunately, usually each "leader type" was devoted to her/his solution.

Perhaps, after some false starts and mishaps, the family group would be able to maneuver across the room. And, getting across the room was not the most important learning. The most important learning was kinesthetic, practical, experiential learning that when one person lifted an arm, another person was choked. Or when one person insisted on doing it her or his way, someone else was injured.

Only when they learned to cooperate, negotiate, and function out of their wholeness did they realize that they could accomplish a task without harm to others.

Joy

CAPACITY FOR JOY

Never underestimate your capacity for joy.

How joyful it is to know that all is process and all is in process.

Seeking and being open to participate in the process of our lives is so different from feeling that we have to control our lives. Controlling ourselves, people, places, and things is a thankless and impossible task. We never have the pure joy of accomplishment because we never really succeed. Never succeeding can be very discouraging and destructive to our self-esteem.

Unfortunately, when we are trying to control our and others' lives, we have little or no time to participate in the flow of the process of life and we are always exhausted. There is little joy in exhaustion unless it comes from participating in the process of life with others in the completion of a job well done. When we learn to let go and participate in the process of our lives and others' lives, joy is a natural result.

Participating in the processes that life presents to us is much more rewarding than anything we could have created.

All Is in Process

OUR RELATIONSHIPS ARE A PROCESS

Relationships cannot be controlled. We have the opportunity to participate in their happening.

So much pain is generated from the illusion that we will get our relationships nailed down in one form or another and then they will stay that way forever. Where in the world did we get the notion that our relationships are like our couches?!

I can remember back when I was a psychotherapist, hearing so many women complain about their relationships with their spouses. Their stories went something like this:

"He was very attentive and solicitous until we made a commitment and then something changed. It was like he put a lot of energy into the courtship and as soon as the 'deal was sealed,' he moved on to bigger and better conquests." So much of our approaches to relationships have been to establish them and then think the job is done.

We often hear that we have to "work" on relationships, as if they are a static thing like we think of our cars that need regular maintenance—a scheduled night out together; occasional flowers—mechanical "fixes." Yet our relationships are not a thing. Relationships are a living process that require us to participate in one another's processes of life. When we see our relationship as a process, we don't need to dissect it as if it were a cat to be studied.

We need to participate in our relationships as fully as we can with respect and honesty. We need to trust that we cannot control them or know where they should go or what they should be like.

Participation

UNPREDICTABLE CHANGES

Those who build a house are built by it.

— MAORI ELDER

I once worked with a manager of a small hotel. The owners and management team had decided that they did not "run the place" in the old paradigm. Being new in the profession, the manager elected to go to several conferences, seminars, and workshops on hotel management. Almost all the ideas she came back with—with the exclusion of some technical and legal advice—were not only not helpful, they were destructive to their "managing in a new paradigm." She began to develop into the belief that she was the "head person." She thought she knew or was supposed to know more than the other staff. She set up some competitive "games" where staff got "points" for good work, accumulated the "points" and then were awarded prizes, which aroused competitiveness and anger. And she seemed to develop a steel rod up her back, becoming very defensive whenever anyone differed with her perception. Clearly, they were not heading into the new paradigm we had hoped for.

Then, something amazing happened.

Staff began not showing up. Often, they were not able to find good staff. Staff were not doing a good job. When she came to me, my response was, "You're the manager. If no one is there to do the job, you have to do it!" Grudgingly, she cleaned the baths, attacked the stack of dirty dishes, made the beds, and cleaned the rooms when housekeeping was running behind. She *participated*. In no time, she began to have some major personality and management-style changes! She, the hotel, the staff, and the customers were happy!

Participation changes us in ways we could never imagine!

Thinking

OBJECTIVELY LOOKING
AT OUR THINKING

When I start mistrusting what I think,
I am moving from information to wisdom.

I have learned a great deal about our thinking process from the 12-step program of Alcoholics Anonymous, which is, itself, a step in the direction of the process of making a paradigm shift.

I once heard a man in recovery say, "I have been in A.A. long enough to know not to trust anything that I think." At the time and even now, I thought that was brilliant!

I had seen that alcoholics (like others in the culture) have some very crazy thoughts, like "That person is angry with me." They don't check them out and yet they believe them. This process is and should be a concern for us all because there are many nonrecovering addicts in high places running things, and if they believe their thinking and *act on it*, we are all in trouble.

So when I heard this one man say that his recovery had helped him have some relief from the *way* he thinks and *what* he thinks, I had hope for us all.

We need to be reminded every day that we cannot always trust what or how we think or what we do with our thinking.

It takes time to spot "crazy thoughts."

Beliefs and Assumptions

OUR COMMUNITIES INFLUENCE OUR BELIEFS AND ASSUMPTIONS

Assumptions are dangerous things.

— AGATHA CHRISTIE

When we are thinking about our beliefs and assumptions and the ways that they can interfere with our willingness and ability to live a new paradigm, we cannot overlook the role that our communities play in how we see ourselves, how we see ourselves in relation to others, and how we see the world and the assumptions we make about the world.

There are communities that see themselves as inferior as a group. Different people handle feelings of inferiority in different ways. Some, as a group, become meek and passive and others vocally belligerent and aggressive. One of the worst attitudes that our families and our communities can imbue us with is that of arrogance and entitlement. For those laboring under the illusion of being better than others and deserving of special treatment because of the belief they have in "who they are," it is extremely difficult to learn anything; they can't have the necessary humility even to be open to see that their beliefs and assumptions are just that, beliefs and assumptions. Unfortunately, people who believe that they are "better than" have removed themselves from the wholeness and have great difficulty being part of a wholeness and oneness that is bigger than any one of us can be by ourselves.

When we believe we are "better than" we have removed ourselves from the process of all life.

Feelings and Emotions

FEELINGS AND EMOTIONS ARE ESSENTIAL FOR OUR HEALING AND GROWTH

That's the truest sign of insanity—insane people are always sure they're just fine. It's only the sane people who are willing to admit they're crazy.

— NORA EPHRON IN *HEARTBURN*

In my experience, all of us have experiences as we grow that are hurtful and often harmful.

None of us had perfect families. None of us lives in a perfect society. This is simply true for all of us. Our families may not want to admit it and our societies may not want to admit this truth. And, at this point in our evolution as a species, we need to remember that this reality *is* simply our truth. There is nothing more crippling than trying to live the myth that we are perfect, our families were perfect, or our societies are perfect.

Some of the most damaged individuals I have worked with are those who are desperately trying to live out one of these myths. They, of course, cannot deal with and work through their reality when they attempt to live out their illusions.

Thankfully, our emotions and feelings are here to teach us that these illusions are just that—illusions.

Our feelings and emotions are our doors to illusion busting.

Honesty

INSTITUTIONAL DISHONESTY

Why have we come to accept dishonesty—anywhere?

Institutional dishonesty has become accepted and acceptable in our current world paradigm. Corporations are continually searching for ways to legally extort money from the working classes and society in general. Schools are set up to educate us to fit into a dysfunctional society that is destroying the planet and all life on it. And all of us are so busy trying to survive the insanity that we are creating that we lie to ourselves and tell ourselves that there is nothing we can do and we do not even try.

Each religion tells its followers that it is the one true religion while ignoring that we all are on this planet and have different pieces of the truth. And each focuses on building and maintaining the institution while ignoring the unique importance that honesty plays in spiritual growth. Religions, at this point in history, seem to have accepted the agreed-upon "truth" that dishonesty is an essential and necessary part of all human institutions and it needs to be ignored and supported. Our institutions have become training grounds for dishonesty. Even teachers and administrators are changing test results so that their schools look better.

Dishonesty has become institutionalized. The first step is naming. The second is nonacceptance.

Courage

BEING AFRAID

I have not ceased being fearful, but I have ceased to let fear control me. I have accepted fear as a part of life, specifically the fear of change, the fear of the unknown. I have gone ahead despite the pounding in my heart that says: Turn back, turn back; you'll die if you venture too far.

— ERICA JONG

So many people say to me, ". . . but I'm afraid." And they say this as if that is the end of the conversation. They are afraid, so they must stop; I must stop; everything must stop.

My usual response to this "stopper" is, "Great! So? It's great that you are feeling something. Being afraid is great. Go into the fear. See what's there." Where did we ever get the idea that we should stop whenever we feel fear? If I did that, I would have never written a word when I faced a blank page—nor would most of the other writers I know.

Our fear is great. It's our friend. It keeps us on our toes. It makes us see clearer. It increases our alertness. It opens old creaky doors for new light and new wisdom to stream in.

Feeling fear is one of the building blocks for courage and alertness.

Hooray for feeling fear.

Feeling fear helps us practice courage in small steps so we are ready when the big ones confront us.

Entitlement

ON THE ROAD TO CHANGE

Everyone needs to develop an attitude of gratitude.

— BLOOD ELDER

We have, on this planet, living models for a new way of being here that do not include the illusions of entitlement, hierarchy, or one up/one down. Our indigenous cultures seemed to have been able to avoid this pitfall when they were developing their cultures. These cultures firmly believed that everything they were and had was a gift. Life itself was seen as a gift. It was not something earned, fought for, or that one was entitled to.

It is, quite simply, a gift and we had no control over receiving it. Just as life is a gift, everything else we have is a gift—not earned, gifted.

We did not get it from "being good." We did not get it from being better than others. We did not get it because of accumulated wealth, education, or possessions. Indeed, there is absolutely no way that we could have made all we have been given happen.

How sensible and reality-oriented is that knowing if you really think about it? Our life is something that was given to us.

How could we possibly feel "entitled" knowing that fact?

Accepting Our Humanness

MISTAKES

*The spiritual warrior is the person who makes 30 to 50
mistakes a day, goes to the Creator after each one,
and learns from them.*

— DON COYHIS, MOHICAN

When we accept the fallibility we have as humans and the limitations we have, we tend to shift our perception on the meaning and importance of mistakes.

Most people hate making a mistake, they hate being caught in a mistake, and they will do anything not to make a mistake. Many do a lot of work to deal with "mistakes." However, when we shift our perception of what it means to be human, the reality of mistakes shifts.

When we know that we are human and we know that we are here to learn and grow, especially spiritually, we welcome mistakes. Mistakes begin to be seen as an opportunity for learning.

A Native American friend of mine once said to me, "We welcome mistakes. The spiritual warrior makes thirty to fifty mistakes a day, turns to the Creator after each one, learns the lesson to be learned, and moves on."

Only if we suffer under the illusion of perfection or believe we can be and *are* gods do we see mistakes as a problem.

Striving for perfection or believing that it is possible is doomed to be an exercise in pain, futility, and frustration.

Respect

RESPECTING OUR FOOD

Notice what you are eating and be grateful.

— CHEROKEE ELDER

I could warn how lethal it is to ourselves and our planet not to respect our food and from my experience of watching preachers trying to frighten people into "believing," I have come not to think that this approach is very effective.

What I *do* know is that when we approach our food with an attitude of respect, it tastes better, it is more supportive of and healthy for our body, we need less of it to feel satisfied, it is more fun, more fun to work with, and it elicits more creativity from us.

One of my favorite places in the world is Tassajara. It is a Zen monastery that is located deep in the California coastal hills, down a hair-raising road past Carmel Valley. Once you get there, you are glad that you do not have to face that road again too soon.

One of the greatest things about Tassajara is the food. It changes depending on the cook and it is always, always delicious. After spending some time in the kitchen, I realized why. It's not *what* they cook; it's the *way* they cook, regardless of what the food is or the kind of food each chef prefers. At Tassajara, they approach the food with *respect*. They let the food tell them what it wants done to it.

No food assumptions at Tassajara—just respect.

The Abstractualization of Life

THE ABSTRACTUALIZATION OF LOVE

I wish I'd a knowed more people. I would of loved
'em all. If I'd a knowed more, I woulda loved more.

— TONI MORRISON IN *SONG OF SOLOMON*

Recently someone said to me, "I love you . . . I think."

Whoa! What's wrong here?

Years ago, when I was a psychotherapist, the local gay and lesbian community decided that I was "safe" and open-minded and came to see me in droves. I was shocked to see that this community was approaching love relationships in the same way the heterosexual community approached them. I was a bit disappointed because I had hoped that because they "did not fit into the old paradigm," at that time, they might get busy and develop a new paradigm . . . No such hope. What I saw was that both communities believed that intimacy could be achieved through sex and romance.

What I came to see over time was that both sex and romance were abstract concepts of love, and neither worked as a path to true intimacy. Sexual attraction is fun, exciting, and interesting, *and* it does not necessarily or often lead to intimacy. Real lovemaking is a by-product of intimacy. Red roses, candlelight dinners, and romantic settings are not intimacy. They are abstractions which often disappoint.

Love and intimacy cannot be manufactured in our minds or by a commercial culture.

Being of Good Spirit

ENEMIES

*I want to thank the Creator for all His gifts. I don't always
understand the gifts of those who say negative things about me
and who attack me, and I do trust that the Creator has given me
these gifts so that I can learn and grow spiritually.*

— LENORE STIFFARM, BLOOD

Jesus talked about "loving our enemies." Do we even need to
have enemies? Others may be "enemies" to us and in truth, there
is no law that says that we *have* to reciprocate in kind. Is there?
What if we accept that there are going to be people who don't
like us and that is just the way it is. Do we have to act like them
and hate them back? If we truly believe that we are all part of one
creation, how can we not assume a connection with everyone
and everything? How can we not want the best for them? Isn't
a starving Iraqi child or a starving Native American child, or a
starving African child the same as if our child were starving?

When we actually stop to think about it, it just does not
make any sense to be mean-spirited against anyone or anything
if we are part of a greater whole. Others will do things we don't
like; that is just normal and it is taking an extra step to be mean-
spirited toward them.

Our ancestors knew this truth and our cells need to "remember" this reality if we are to live into and out of a new paradigm.

Domination Over and the Illusion of Control

OUR RELATIONSHIPS

*It has been wisely said that we cannot really
love anybody at whom we never laugh.*

— AGNES REPPLIER

Most people in our culture approach relationships from a position of domination and control. Although most would never admit it, there is a prevalent cultural belief that we can make others love us. If we just wear the right clothes, use the right underarm deodorant, behave in the correct way we can *make* someone love us. Men and women both use the illusion of domination and control to establish their "security." Again, many would deny this reality and all too often it exists. In this kind of dynamic, we need to recognize that we not only distort ourselves, the other, and the relationship, we distort our relationship with that beyond ourselves.

I remember watching as a friend of mine "decided" what kind of relationship she would have with a man who clearly stated that he did not want to marry and have children. She ignored who he told her he was, got pregnant—twice, insisted they marry, planned his career for him, and "waited" until he made enough money so she could be a stay-at-home mother. Twenty years later, they are (bitterly) divorced and it is pretty clear that neither of them wanted her "plan" implemented. She is dealing with the implications of her domination and control. He married a woman with children of her own and has added two more. All are sad, angry, and bitter.

We need to remember: dominating is destructive to the dominator and the one being controlled. To live a new paradigm, we have to change our belief in and practice of these behaviors.

Humor

WE HUMANS ARE VERY DEAR

Time wounds all heels.

— JANE ACE

Recently I was very privileged to be able to listen to a series of lectures by a renowned authority on wildlife, birds, and flora and fauna of the South Pacific. In many of the lectures, he talked of the mating behavior of various birds. For example, the boobies have very large feet. Some have blue feet, some have brown feet, and some have red feet. These beautiful feet are necessary for the survival of the species as they display them to one another in their mating behavior—the bigger and the brighter the better, or so it seems.

He showed slides of another seabird that has a wonderful blue pouch at the front of his throat, which the male blows up to impress the female. *I* was impressed!

The very next day, I was privileged to observe a long-past-middle-aged couple getting acquainted. They stared at one another intently when either said anything. They laughed much too loudly at the slightest possible amusement, touched the other's hand whenever possible, and, in general, would have made a teenager shrink with embarrassment. At first I was annoyed with the "disruption." Then, I began to see him as puffing up his blue throat. In my mind, this was followed by an imaginary display of the most beautifully striped and painted feet. Although I doubted that this mating behavior would propagate the species at this point in their lives, with their puffed-up throats and their colorful feet they did seem quite dear actually.

A little humor goes a long way to soften our reactions. It is difficult to judge when one sees others as "dear."

Wonder and Awe

OUR BODIES

*At the moment you are most in awe of all there
is about life that you don't understand, you are closer
to understanding it all than at any other time.*

— JANE WAGNER

I was raised to honor and respect my body and the bodies of others.

Since I grew up in a family of healers, seeing the body as a beautiful sacred gift was inherent in everything we did. Very early on my great-grandmother with her gentle hands and voice inspired me to see the human body as a miraculous process, awe-inspiring and wonderful in its design and creation. For example, look at the design and function of the body. It is quite creative and very functional. We are surrounded by poisons and pollutants (increasing more and more, I might add), and we have so many mechanisms to deal with them—very efficiently.

The kidneys, the liver, the skin, the lungs, and the elementary canal all quietly go about their work, with the help of the endocrine system. The blood, arteries, veins, heart, cells, and lymphatic system wondrously do their best to rid our bodies of all the toxins we mindlessly take in and carelessly surround ourselves with. Anyone who has studied anatomy can only sit in awe and wonder at the miracles that our bodies perform every day.

When we recognize the processes our bodies are performing for us every day, every minute, every second, every nanosecond, it is good to remember awe and wonder are appropriate responses.

The Present Can Only Be Our Reality
if We Own Our Past and Our Future

THE PROCESS OF OWNING OUR PAST

You never know when you are making a memory.

— RICKIE LEE JONES

I have come to believe that one of the most effective conservation mechanisms that exist in our world is our storage of
memories. Somewhere in our bodies and minds everything we
need to work through our experiences and heal is stored.

I was horrified at one point when I read of a medication being
developed to erase all our bad memories so we would not have to
deal with the pain. What a tremendous loss this would be!

I approach the whole issue quite differently. In my experience, we have our inner "governor," who will only let these memories come up when we have reached a level of maturity, strength,
and awareness to deal with them and learn from them. So the
fact that we are beginning to have flashes of old memories is an
indicator of our having done our work. These flashes are an indi-
cation of how strong we are. Then, in the process of letting these
memories/experiences come into our consciousness, we have the
amazing experience of working them through, getting our learnings from them, and healing. Almost always, what we need to get
and learn could never have been "figured out" by the conscious
mind. It is something beyond and beneath our conscious mind
that takes charge when we have old, unknown experiences that
need to be remembered and healed.

Relearning another way than our paralysis with these
repressed memories will give us the options to have the strength
to live a new paradigm.

Walking in Beauty

THE BEAUTY AROUND US

Tell them how we loved all that was beautiful.

— ANONYMOUS AMERICAN INDIAN

I will never forget the way my great-grandmother approached the medicinal roots, stems, and leaves of the plants she gathered. For example, when we were digging a sassafras root to be used for tea (one had to drink good, strong sassafras tea in the spring to thin and purify the blood before the hot weather) she would always stop to inspect the plant from which she would take some of the root. She wanted to make sure that the plant was ready and willing to "give" us the medicine. This process involved a lot of listening, *hmm* sounds, head nodding, and waiting. I learned never to ask what was happening. She said I would learn and know if I waited, watched, and "listened" carefully. I knew that listening did not mean just with my ears. To listen the way Grandma meant it was to listen with my entire being.

How do you explain this kind of listening to a four-year-old so they too can walk in beauty? You don't! You show them and wait with them to "get" it.

When everything was right and we had made sure what we took would not kill the plant and that there were plenty of other healthy plants, we took what we needed—only what we needed, because the plant needed us to come again and we needed to come again. Then we left a gift and a prayer of gratitude and concern.

The whole process of gathering medicine is walking in beauty.

Taking Time

MEDITATION

*Half an hour's meditation is essential except
when you are very busy. Then a full hour is needed.*

— FRANCIS DE SALES

I know some people swear by a particular form of meditation and spend hours doing it in order to reach a quiet mind and new levels of awareness. I am a bit nervous about the structure becoming the answer (form as a "fix"). And, if it works for you, go for it! In my experience, Westerners are not that good at Eastern meditation, and for some it is just another vehicle to try to control themselves for a desired outcome.

From my travels around the world and living and working in various cultures, I am very clear that no one thing works for everyone and each of us needs to find what works for us to somehow get out of our own way and reach the other levels of knowing that give us broader and deeper levels of reality to help us move along our journey.

In the process of trying out various approaches and seeing others do the same, my observation is that 1) Westerners do not handle gurus very well—they "worship" them, do their hierarchy thing, and in general leave themselves, and 2) sitting meditation does not work for some. For these people, they do their meditation while washing the car, doing the dishes, folding the laundry, or vacuuming the rug. I know one woman who has the cleanest carpets around because she vacuums them to within an inch of their life. "That's my alone time," she says.

We all need alone time. It is up to us to find out what works for us.

A Belief in Healing

THE ROLE OF ADDICTION

Nothing is ever all bad . . .

From my perspective, it is not possible to look at the larger picture of illness and healing in this culture without looking at the role that addictions play in the "disease," dis-ease, of the current culture.

I have come to believe that addictions are completely integrated into the dominant culture. The society we have created not only encourages addictions, it demands them so that we can tolerate what we have created. If we were "fully conscious" and did not distract ourselves and "medicate" our awareness, we would be able to see very clearly what we have created. Our addictions blur our awareness, distract us, and demand more and more of our attention. So our addictions serve the purpose of our not seeing what we see and knowing what we know. They are also very lucrative to the corporate world in many ways. Addictions are not only integrated into our society, they are essential to its continuance of the way it is and making change—true change—less likely.

Addictions support a denial of our reality and a building of illusions.

Knowing and Living in Several Realities

THERE ARE NOT ONLY TWO REALITIES

*Reality this week is nothing like
what I was freaked out about last week.*

— PETER SIDLEY

In our current dualistic paradigm, we will go so far as to tell ourselves that there are two realities: the real one and the unreal one.

It is truly amazing how much greater effect the *processes* (which we rarely name) of a particular paradigm have on us than the content! This is more true when we actually deny that the processes exist. (Maybe that is because we deny them!) So we stick with our guns with the process of setting up a dualistic world even when one of the aspects "doesn't exist!" Because of the denial of many realities existing simultaneously and our dualistic thinking, if we need to come to the acceptance of the existence of many realities in order to live a new/different paradigm, then our work is cut out for us. For myself, I have solved this dilemma in coming to believe in different levels of truth. We start out as children with a certain level of truth—usually our family's level. As we grow and mature, with rebellion or whatever, we challenge this level of reality and move on to another level, usually the opposite of the one we previously held. Then, as we mature (assuming some do—others stay stuck and quit growing at a somewhat unsophisticated/primitive level of reality). Then, as we evolve the third level looks a bit like the first and it is more complex and inclusive and so it goes.

At each level, we have the learnings from the ones before and a compassion and understanding of those at less complex levels. As we grow, we learn about different realities, if we are open and do not get stuck in our illusions.

Being of Service

WHAT ABOUT ME?

I am not the center of the universe.
I am not the center of the universe. I am . . .

I have found that in our current me-me-me and my-my-my culture, one of the main obstacles to being of service is related to the "me psychology" that has been so instrumental in forming Western culture.

- *You have to take care of number one!*

- *Who will take care of me?*

- *Who will see that my needs will be met?*

- *I can't waste time being of service to them. I have such great needs myself.*

- And so on!

From my experience, when people are indulging in these types of thoughts and beliefs, this is exactly the time they need unselfishly to be of service to someone else. The minute we take the focus off of ourselves is the minute we start to feel better with ourselves. It just works that way.

You say you want to live out of a different paradigm? When was the last time you completely, unselfishly focused on being available and helpful when your service was needed?

Graciousness

A SOFTENING

We are all "getting there." What a relief it is to know that we will never arrive!

Graciousness requires a softening within ourselves and with others. Hard facts and Western, scientific information are not very gracious. In order to tap into our ability to be genuinely gracious, a softening process must occur in the way we think, what we feel, what we do, and how we interact with others. Any new paradigm demands and requires this kind of softening in order to *be* a real shift. And this softening needs to occur in the core of our being, because it is a softness that is predicated on the vulnerability of our being to all that surrounds and interacts with it. In order to be gracious we need to be what might be seen in the currently dominant culture as very vulnerable.

Old Mr. Danforth, the founder of Ralston Purina and the Danforth Foundation, used to say that we needed to have tough minds and tender hearts. We may have erred a bit too far in the tough part and lost the balance of graciousness. Without graciousness, we become too tough to welcome a paradigm that we do not yet know or understand.

We learn graciousness by being gracious in all that we think and do.

Moving Out of Our Comfort Zones

CHALLENGING OUR THINKING

*When I have an investment in the outcome,
I am insulting God.*

Western culture has adopted the thinking patterns, processes, and content of the alcoholic. If you do not believe this, tune in to Congress in action. The thinking patterns of the culture are those of the schizophrenic and the alcoholic. Years ago, when I started getting interested in addiction and studied the thinking patterns of the addict, I noticed the similarity in the thinking patterns of the addict and the schizophrenics that I worked with when I interned at Bellevue Hospital in New York City. The schizophrenics were just farther down on the continuum. We all knew that schizophrenia is a thinking disorder. And the thinking of the addict mirrors that kind of thinking, as does the current Western paradigm. Most native peoples, until they have to learn these schizoid-like patterns, think very differently. These schizoid patterns can be learned and they can be unlearned and they function like a mental virus, disembodied and dangerous. I have watched people in recovery who, when they come to a point of knowing that they cannot continue in recovery with their usual thinking, realize that they not only have to change *what* they think, they have to change the *way* they think. This awareness is followed by a period of desperate lost-ness. It is at this point the unmotivated give up. To continue on the path to recovery and a paradigm shift, those who persevere wander through a period of lost-ness. What can they trust if they cannot trust what and how they think?

Back to basics.

Letting Go of What We Think We Know

THE ROLE OF PEERS

*The more I traveled, the more I realized that
fear makes strangers of people who could be friends.*

— SHIRLEY MACLAINE

When we are at the point of testing out what our parents have taught us, sometimes our peers become our point of reference. In essence, we are asking a group of people who are in the same state as we are to be our point of reference. Indeed, peer references may be an essential part of the process of growing up. And many people stay stuck in that stage of their development for their entire lives, even if their information for living becomes completely outdated. And it is not their information that becomes outdated. Their process of learning becomes antiquated.

Part of the adolescent process of learning and becoming is believing that they/we "know it all" and our current knowledge is "true" and the most important and relevant. This process of arrogance is probably necessary to separate from what others have imposed on us. *And* this process is also exceedingly limited and limiting if it is maintained throughout one's life. Maturity demands that we become aware of how much we do *not* know and the limitations of our knowledge so we can be open to the possibilities of the process of the beauty of contradictions.

Take the old Zen master who said, "To learn more, we have to be willing to 'empty our cup.'"

Accepting That Choices and
Behaviors Have Consequences

THE VICTIM-PERPETRATOR DUALISM

*What we do with having been victimized can be one
of the greatest learning possibilities in our lives.*

Many of us have been victimized in one way or another.
And when we believe that we are victims, it is inevitable that we
will become perpetrators. Believing that we are victims justifies
becoming a perpetrator.

Most people who are on the victim-perpetrator dualism have
come to believe two things: 1) that they should not have any
consequences for their choices or behaviors and 2) that their
choices and behaviors are justified because they have been victimized. It is frightening to see the role that Western psychology
has played in setting up this victim-perpetrator dualism and how
destructive it has become as a belief system in our society. Some
therapists have gone so far as to tell their clients that they will
never heal until they victimize their perpetrator. My experience
in working with people and seeing the outcomes of the above
approach is that it never heals. The client is again "victimized"
by the therapist because when it does not work, the client feels
she/he too, in some way, failed. And the anger builds.

Remember: it is difficult for an approach that is built by
the system and integrated into the system to be able to heal the
wounds of the system.

Humility

KNOWING OUR PLACE

Humility is being sufficient, but lacking pride in sufficiency.
It is knowing grace—and knowing we did nothing to earn it.

— JOYCE SEQUICHIE HIFLER

So, then, when does humility start to emerge? It is not a manipulatable concept whose emergence into being we can try to determine. If it is not something we can control in ourselves and others, if it is not something that we can make happen, what is it?

Humility is that inestimable quality of essence that emerges when one is secure being a part of a greater whole. It emerges when we know beyond a reason of doubt that we belong to something much bigger than ourselves and we know that we do not and cannot run and control everything. Initially this knowledge of knowing for a fact that we cannot control our world or the world around us may result in fear and anxiety; that is only to be expected when our current paradigm has taught us that we *should* be able to manipulate and control everything . . . and we are always failing. Still, we cling to the belief that we should be able to. And clinging to the idea that we *should* be able to control our world has resulted in cultural feelings of failure, depression, and anxiety.

When one has humility, much of our cultural feelings of failure, depression, and anxiety evaporate.

Knowing and Being Known

REMEMBER OUR "SELVES"

In you is the accumulated knowledge of all who have gone before.
— CHEROKEE ELDER

Periodically we need to remind ourselves that we are on a lifetime journey of getting to know ourselves. This journey can be exhilarating, frightening, interesting, challenging, hilarious—pick out a positive adjective and it will apply.

The way the process of getting to know ourselves works is that as humans (who knows about the animals and the trees!), we have the wonderful ability to remember—the good and the bad and the indifferent. Our minds, bodies, and beings—even our DNA—hold on to all that we and our ancestors have experienced. Because of this marvelous ability, we have the opportunity to work through (and learn from) anything and everything that we/they have experienced. Few of us take advantage of this opportunity. And the current dominant paradigm does not value this opportunity very much, if at all. Yet once we recognize and remember that a big part of our responsibility as human beings is to heal, learn, and grow, we begin to see that this process of knowing and honoring all of who we are and what we have experienced is one of the greatest—if not *the* greatest—opportunities we have as human beings.

To ignore the importance of knowing ourselves is a lost life indeed. All of us have this opportunity. We need to embrace it with fervor and gratitude.

Everything Is Spiritual/Sacred

TREES

It took us a long time to decide where the trees and plants belonged (on the marae). We waited for the plants to let us know where they belonged. One day, I came over the hill and looked down on the marae. I could see every plant in its place. Then we could plant them.

— UNCLE HENRY, MAORI ELDER

Have you ever sat quietly on the ground and put your back against a tree and just leaned in to "take it in?"

How would our lives change if we let ourselves remember that trees are sacred and are to be responded to as if we knew that?

Trees give us so much. Not only do they provide beauty and shade for us, they provide us with food, housing, furniture, and probably most important, the actual oxygen that we breathe, which sustains all animal life on this planet. Trees are not just sacred because we humans need them. They are sacred and spiritual because they *are*. They are sacred and spiritual because they are part of creation. Trees do not, to our knowledge, suffer the kind of confusion about who they are and why they are here like humans do. They seem to have resolved that issue long ago, and are content to accept life on life's terms, which humans seem to have difficulty in grasping. What would happen with and in our lives if we began to see trees as sacred and spiritual? Would we think twice before cutting one down because it was "inconvenient" for us? If we did need to cut it down would we do it in another way if we remembered that it was a sacred part of creation and we lived out of that remembering?

Seeing everything as sacred and a part of the spiritual and not just created for human convenience could move one to living a major paradigm shift.

Wholeness

OUR EFFECT ON OTHERS

Wholeness is not a concept. It is a reality.

— CHEROKEE ELDER

Few people are completely cognizant of how much their decisions and behavior affect others. Most of us want to believe that we operate in isolation and if our decisions result in poor outcomes, only we are affected. This illusion of isolation and arbitrary, single-person functioning is just not so and is an illusion that has been strengthened by our scientific and cultural belief systems.

Slowly, very slowly, we are coming to see—and do not want to admit—that the waste of the industrialized countries is affecting everyone on the planet. We are beginning to see that not only do the decisions we make today affect the next seven generations—and more!—they affect the entire planet. It has taken our waste of natural resources and scourge of polluted air, water, land, and nature to begin to convince a few enlightened beings that we no longer can think in terms of ourselves alone and our selfish agendas or our country alone and its selfish agendas. Some of us are slowly seeing that when one person lifts a hand to scratch her/his head, another person is strangled.

We have thought in terms of self-centered individualism for so long as individuals and nations that in order to move into a workable paradigm, we must not only begin to think in wholes, we must begin to act out of a complete awareness of the reality that we are all part of the same creation, regardless of what this means financially.

Joy

FEELINGS AND EMOTIONS

Joy is inherent in our genes.
Why do we try to ignore it?

Feelings and emotions have become so suspect in today's world that people, in general, are almost afraid of them.

If we hope to learn to live a new paradigm, we need to learn to trust our feelings and emotions and realize that they are part of us and to be celebrated. Ironically, we have come to be as suspicious of joy as we are of anger or sadness. We have developed a world where *all* emotions are suspect. Yet in spite of ourselves joy is still there and bubbles up quite freely at the most surprising times. If we are going to learn to live a new paradigm, we need to recognize the naturalness of joy and the playfulness of just being joyful.

Seriousness is not smarter. It is not more "cool." It is not more impressive. Joy can be and often is contagious and even infectious. Yet, it is never dangerous in its "out-of-control-ness."

To be open to joy, we have to be reminded to risk the perhaps unfamiliar.

Emotional Intelligence

CONTEXT

Noticing is emotional brilliance in action.

An important aspect of emotional intelligence is a strong knowing that we live in context and being able to read, comprehend, and respect that context.

This means that we *notice*.

We notice what is going on around us and within us at the same time.

We notice the emotional brilliance of nature.

We notice the emotional brilliance of the animals around us.

We notice that the people with whom we interact are saying much more than their words are telling us.

We notice. And we do not interpret through our thinking!

All Is in Process

OUR FAMILIES ARE A PROCESS

*I discovered when I quit worrying about my kids
I had to shift into a whole new phase of my life.
What do I want to do with my life? That was scary.*

I recently experienced an incident that totally denied that people and families are a process. A 54-year-old man was going through a stressful phase in his life—mostly, I believe, because he refused to trust and live the process of his life. His father's approach was to e-mail another (male) family member and to try to elicit him to collude with him to control *his* son into doing what *he* thought his son should do. This was the pattern of functioning in this man's family of origin. Everyone in his current family was furious with the father's behavior. The father kept using the term *my* son, *my* son. Yes, the man is his father's son and will be always. And, if the relationship does not grow and change, what may have been acceptable at one point in their relationship becomes toxic. At this point, the son had several choices: He could go back to the control and illusion of stasis in his family of origin; he could ignore them; he could assess where he was in his own process of life and respond out of that. He chose the latter, saying, "I don't think I ever heard anyone in my family tell my father that she/he was angry with him before this." He had chosen the process of his own life and responded out of that in a kind and firm way. To try to make ourselves or our families static is always harmful.

Somewhere deep inside we all know that we cannot "static" our families (or anything) no matter how hard we, or they, try. Yet try we do.

Participation

PARTICIPATION AND WHOLENESS

Always leave any place you go better than when you came.

— VIRGIL WILLEY

Several years ago I observed that Westerners had a difficult time with meditation and did not approach it like Easterners or get out of it what Easterners did. It was not part of our culture.

Then I began to notice that we had developed our own kind of meditation that almost always included some kind of work and/or movement. Mowing the lawn could be a meditation. Washing the dishes could be a meditation. Working could be a meditation. Knitting and sewing could be a meditation. Cooking could be a meditation. Any activity that can be mindless and requires our presence could be a meditation, have the affects of meditation, be centering, and result in a more peaceful being. The key was in the complete participation.

Whenever one participated fully in a "mindless," nonthinking capacity, the doors were open for profound changes and new wisdom to emerge. Almost always the person doing the activity became more grounded on the material plane and more grounded on the nonphysical plane without trying to make this phenomenon happen. What a gift participation can bring to us!

Participation can be the embodiment of the process of wisdom.

Thinking

DISEMBODIED THINKING

Too much thinking leaves no room for wisdom to enter.

— CHEROKEE ELDER

It is important for us to be aware that much of the thinking—especially academic thinking—is based on disembodied concepts that have no basis in material-plane reality. This phenomenon is similar to the difference between spirituality, which is a participatory experience, and theology, which is thinking and theorizing about God.

Abstract and disembodied concepts have their place. They can be fun and we can move them around in our minds like pieces on a chess board. And they can never, never be the real thing. These thoughts, like our language, can only be approximations of our reality. They can be fun, entertaining, exciting, and certainly occupy our time—and they are disembodied abstractions. They have their place and some can be made into embodied reality at times. And they are not real. We need to be reminded that much of what we think is not tied to reality and not try to develop a new paradigm out of these disembodied thoughts.

If we want to create a new paradigm, participation in a process of being and operating differently will be more effective than disembodied concepts and trying to make it happen.

Beliefs and Assumptions

ARE WE STUCK IN A NATIONAL CHARACTER?

We are much more than our country of origin.

How much we resent it when someone says to us, "I don't like Americans," or "You are acting just like a German," or "Only a New Zealander would see it that way." Like it or not, the nation in which we are born and live has a tremendous influence on the beliefs and assumptions that we hold and the way we behave toward ourselves and others.

I so resented the term "ugly Americans" until I started traveling abroad regularly, and I cannot even count the times I have been embarrassed to see how so many Americans behave seemingly out of our unconscious beliefs that the world is or should be the way we see it.

When traveling, I have come to be able to identify the Germans, the French, the Americans, and the Australians at a great distance, mostly because so many of those who travel believe that the world is and should be as they know it. In working with people all over the world, I have had the experience that all of us, in order to become who we can become as human beings, absolutely have to deal with the national beliefs and assumptions into which we were born. We have to test them out and grow beyond them.

If we do not get clear about the beliefs and assumptions we unconsciously hold and the decisions we make based on them, we will never be free to develop and live a new paradigm.

Feelings and Emotions

FRIENDS OPEN DOORS FOR US

Life is so constructed as to be "unmanageable."

Our feelings and emotions are our friends. We need to remind ourselves of this fact on a daily basis. If we have repressed incidents, experiences, or events that we need to work through, heal from, and learn from (and all of us do), it is our feelings and emotions that will start knocking on our closed doors. Unconsciously, we may have come to believe that these doors are sealed or do not exist—and we are only fooling ourselves about this. We may find ourselves tearing up at strange times, or inexplicably feeling angry, or isolating, or . . . whatever. We need to remind ourselves that something good is happening. Something is coming up that we need to work on, work through, heal, and move beyond.

The good news is that our feelings will never signal us that something is there to work on unless we have reached a level of strength, a level of maturity, a level of awareness that we are ready and able to handle whatever is coming up for us.

Remember: when feelings and emotions start coming up for us, we are ready to heal whatever is behind that door.

Honesty

OUR NATIONS

Our nations, like all relationships, need our honesty.

Recently a woman whom I love very much and thought was a very close friend told me that as an Australian, she hated Americans "and everything American." She went on to say that most Australians hated Americans and thought it was an awful country. I was, as they say in Australia, "gobsmacked." She went on to say that her mother hated America and she was taught to hate Americans. After I wiped my tears away, I told her I was shocked and that I did not hate any country or its people. I went on to say that I was taught that all people and all nations have pieces of the truth and we are all trying to climb the same mountain to heal, mature, grow, and learn. None of us has all the answers and each of us has some of them; as we are willing to make our mistakes, learn from them, and to be open to others we will all benefit.

I went on to say that I loved America and thought that the tenets on which it was founded were based on the unalienable right of equality for all and the right of liberty and justice for all. This, to me, seemed a noble effort and was a great experiment and that no other Western nation had started out with equality for all. I also said that I took seriously the responsibility to challenge and question my country when it did wrong and needed to be more honest about itself and with itself. This responsibility is built into each citizen.

Without honesty in their citizens, our nations can never have the possibility to become what they can be.

Courage

COURAGE IS A PROCESS

*The ability to simplify means to eliminate the
unnecessary so that the necessary can speak.*

— HANS HOFMANN

Courage, like almost everything in life, is a process built on
the situational.

Courage does not just happen. It is built over a lifetime and
it is more linked to the unconscious than the conscious mind,
more linked with the unseen and the unknown than the known,
more linked to the spirit than our thinking. Courage is therefore, for some, quite a scary thing really. It is not something for
wimps. And none of us was born to be a wimp. Wimpdom has to
be learned. The good news is if it is learned, it can be unlearned.
If it has been conditioned, it can be unconditioned.

We can go back to the time when we knew that courage is a
given and wimpdom was an un-useful concept.

How peaceful it is to know that my courage is somewhere
there resting in my DNA and can be awakened.

Entitlement

GRATITUDE

*Being radical at this time on our planet can
be less frightening than not being radical.*

When we come to the realization that life itself is a gift and
no matter how wealthy (entitled) or not our family was/is, life
itself is a gift, it seems that an appropriate attitude and response
would be gratitude. Ironically, it seems that the people who have
the most in material goods are often the ones who have the least
gratitude. All too often, the response is to want more (entitlement), be fearful of losing it, and slip into trying more and more
to live out of an illusion of control.

When we stop to think of it, everything that we have is a
gift. All the material possessions we have are gifts from the earth.
Is one more entitled to these gifts than another? Indigenous people would say no and would feel embarrassed for people who feel
entitled. In that paradigm all the gifts we have been given are for
the betterment of the all. How radical is that?

To live a new paradigm, we have to be radical enough to
give up our illusion of entitlement and let ourselves experience
gratitude.

Accepting Our Humanness

NEEDING OTHERS

"We" overrides "me."

— HAWAIIAN PROVERB

If we accept our humanness and we see the limitations we have as human beings, it is clear that no one of us and no one group of us has all the answers. If there is a Satan, he probably is behind the illusion that we can or do have all the answers. Human religions seem to be particularly susceptible to this particular illusion.

Most native people believe that no one of us, or no one group of us, has all the answers and when we think we do, we are in trouble. Indigenous people know that as humans, we are all climbing the same mountain, on different paths, and each path holds different parts of the "truth." No one path is capable of having all the answers for everyone. Therefore we need the pieces of knowledge and wisdom from everyone and everything to gather more pieces to get a bigger picture for our understanding. This is why native people believe that we need to learn from other people and other ways and welcome them.

This is why we need to learn from the animals, the trees, the plants, the birds, the bugs and the earth. All have information we don't have. Refusing to accept our humanity is holding on to the illusion that we do or can know it all.

Respect

RESPECTING OUR ANIMAL RELATIONS

*The animals have more patience with our
slow learning abilities than we humans do.*

So many of my examples of learning about respect come from my early childhood that I fear that the person who wants to live in a new paradigm will begin to despair that if she/he does not learn to live out of respect as a child, she/he is doomed. If you're feeling this despair you may infer that living a new paradigm is hopeless. Not so! Anything that is learned can be unlearned. And anything we did not learn as children can still be learned. We just have to work at it. Anything is possible.

One of my earliest memories about learning to respect animals involves a little kitten. I was three years old. I had a little kitten and we were playing outside together. It had rained the night before and there was a little puddle in front of our big green house on the hill. The kitten had accidentally stepped in the puddle and would furiously shake its paws to get them dry. My three-year-old self thought this was hilariously funny and kept putting the kitten down in the puddle to see it shake its paws. My mother came out to see what all the commotion was. I now realize she was horrified.

She sat down on the ground and enlisted my help in drying the kitten's feet with her apron. While doing this, she patiently explained that the kitten did not like this and felt afraid. She asked if I knew how that felt and I did. She asked how would I feel if I were that kitten and did I want to be treated like that. Suddenly the whole thing didn't seem so funny anymore. She put the kitten in my lap and let me feel its purring. "Isn't that better?" she asked. It truly was.

To my knowledge that was my first lesson in respecting animals. There were probably others that I was too young to remember.

The Abstractualization of Life

RELATIONSHIPS

*You take people as far as they will go, not
as far as you would like them to go.*

— JEANNETTE RANKIN

Relationships are a process. They can never be manufactured by an idea or an image.

When we try to build our relationships on a preconceived image, they will be doomed from the start.

How many intimate relationships do we miss because we have forgotten that relationships emanate out of a process and are not built out of conceptual preconceived blocks? So many people have preconceived notions of what intimacy will look like. In reality, intimacy grows and is felt, not seen. The same is true of our lives.

In order to be ready and able to enter into an intimate relationship, we have to have someone who is not an abstraction to bring to the relationship. We are asking a great deal of a relationship if we are asking it to give us an identity. If we are doing this, we are probably asking it to fill in the pieces of our preconceived abstraction.

To live a new paradigm in relationships, we need to have the trust and openness to participate as honestly as we can and trust in the unknown and unseen, knowing that any and every relationship can facilitate our coming into being.

Being of Good Spirit

TOWARD OURSELVES

*A man begins cutting his wisdom teeth the first
time he bites off more than he can chew.*

— IRISH SAYING

Just as egoism, arrogance, and entitlement are built into the culture that we humans have created on this planet, so is self-judgment, denigration of the self, and self-hate. These polars have become part of the dualisms of our living.

Arrogance and self-hate go together. I have never met an arrogant person who was not also filled with self-hate. This dilemma demonstrates how deep our thinking has been conditioned to dualisms. If we expect and believe that we can be perfect, then we will always fail and then we will hate ourselves for it. It is just that simple.

We have been conditioned to think in dualisms, to compare and contrast. These patterns of thinking have distorted our souls and damaged our living out of a feeling of good-spiritedness toward ourselves and others.

So many people I know skate along the dualism of being arrogant versus feeling "like a piece of shit" and have no way to stop this swing between the two. The only answer is to get off the dualism and approach ourselves and others from a completely different option, an option of good-spiritedness that comes out of being a necessary part of the process of wholeness.

Dualisms have no place in a functional paradigm.

Domination Over and the Illusion of Control

PASSIVITY

The illusion of control comes in many forms.

Passivity can be a very deadly form of domination and control. When we think of dominating and controlling behavior we usually think of someone actively trying to dominate and control like a bully. Yet we can also try to control others through our passivity and nonparticipation.

When my son was in high school and started dating his first love, he shared with me what happened on his first date. He said that as they were driving toward the downturn from her house where he picked her up, he casually asked her what she wanted to do. "I don't know, you choose," was the answer. "Do you want to go to a movie, out to eat, drive around, hang out with friends . . . what? What do *you* want to do?" he asked. Again the answer—"Whatever you want."

At this point, he reported, he pulled the car over to the curb and said, "Look, if you are going to go out with me, you have to have an opinion. Say what you would like to do and let's negotiate." I was so proud of him! He told me later that that kind of passivity scared him. "It's so controlling," he said.

Passivity can be as controlling as actively *trying* to control and much more maddening, less honest, and more difficult to deal with. I have described passivity as akin to having a giant dead octopus on my head.

Humor

SOFTENING THE TRUTH

Humor should never be used as shaming or attacking.
Then it loses its effectiveness as a teaching tool.

— CHEROKEE ELDER

In indigenous cultures, humor is often used for teaching, especially with children and with everyone really.

I have noticed that when I want to give some pretty difficult feedback to someone, I often do it with humor in a loving way. It is like putting a sugar coating on a bitter pill. Native people do this all the time. Most native people are very gentle and compassionate with other people, especially strangers, and we also believe that it is our duty and responsibility not to let those near and dear to us get away with rude, violent, or disrespectful behavior.

I honestly believe, because of my own experience, that my ancestors were so appalled by the violence, dishonesty, lack of respect, and dishonoring behavior that the "newcomers" exhibited that they were not "stoic" as interpreted by the strangers, they were shocked into silence! They could not believe that these obnoxious behaviors had not been "nipped in the bud" much earlier by loving humor.

What kind of parent would not teach her/his offspring to be real, honorable, respectful people on this planet?

And what kind of parent would not use humor as a very effective teaching tool?

Wonder and Awe

CONSTRUCTED WONDERS

When we are open and ready,
feelings of awe and wonder are everywhere.

Probably the *feelings* of awe and wonder are much more important than what inspires these feelings. And, mentioning a range of possibilities is important as a reminder of what is possible daily as options—lest we forget.

I live in a beautiful, very simple place in Hawaii that is hidden away in a secret valley that many do not know exists. (This reality in and of itself is a wonder!) Whenever I leave my little space I am always eager to get back. This fact results in my not leaving too often. Why would I?

Just before I get to my turnoff, there is the most beautiful bridge. Just mentioning it fills my being with awe. It is a broad sweep of a bridge that spans a river and a beautiful valley. There are albizia trees on either side. The setting is beautiful, and it is always the bridge that catches my breath. Any old kind of bridge could have been built there, probably for less cost—and it wasn't. This bridge sweeps and soars in a broad breathing curve that fits and enhances its surroundings.

I have been over it thousands of times, and every time I feel wonder and awe, gratitude and thanksgiving.

Even human creations can elicit awe and wonder. We need feeling memories of awe and wonder to live a new paradigm.

Can Only Be Our Reality
Our Past and Our Future

Way to Undo Our Past

*e such healing power within us that
ds to be tapped for it to work its magic.*

When we are intent on undoing or denying our past, we can never own it. And only in our owning it with our entire being on every level and getting the learnings from it can we integrate it and experience the fullness of our being. Interestingly, what I have seen is that when people do their own work with past realities and traumas, the most important change that takes place is the change *within* them. People often find that with the information and working through the feelings, they feel more clear. With this work, we change the way we feel about it. With this work, we move into accepting our reality, and with this change our "reality" changes. We cannot think ourselves into these changes. The change has to take place at another level of consciousness.

Paradoxically, when this shift—this change—occurs, our past changes and we discover a new freedom. We cannot force or control this new freedom; it is a gift of the process of "going through." Then the past—or at least that part of it—loses its power to rob us of our present. Just as we cannot "think" ourselves into a new paradigm, we cannot think ourselves into healing on an unconscious level.

When we own our past at a feeling level, it no longer owns us or our present and future.

Walking in Beauty

ACCEPTANCE

Remember and think about the closeness of
Wakan Tanka (the Creator, Great Spirit). If you believe
in this wisdom, it will give you strength and hope.

— FRANK FOOLS CROW,
LAKOTA CHIEF AND SPIRITUAL LEADER

One who walks in beauty is one who walks with acceptance. Not resignation, acceptance.

There is no way that we can control and understand the issues we must face in life in order to learn the lessons we need to learn to grow spiritually. People who have resigned themselves to life, or given up, have a very different "feel" about them to those who accept the good, the bad, and the indifferent aspects of life, glean the learnings, and move on.

Those who walk in beauty have a gracefulness and an acceptance that breathes life into everything they do and all the processes of life with which they are confronted. Their heads are not "bloody but unbowed." Their heads are grace-ful, clear, and appropriately bowed and held high at the same time.

Walking in beauty is not an act or an event. It is a process. It is a way of being in and with the world.

Taking Time

TAKING ALONE TIME

Who am I not to believe that I need time alone?

Some of us will not take any alone time because we are so co-dependent that we have convinced ourselves that taking alone time is selfish. Let go of that idea right now! From what I have seen and heard, it is much more selfish and self-centered *not* to take alone time than it is to take it.

Since alone time is absolutely essential to remember how to live a new paradigm, we owe it to ourselves to take the alone time we need, even though we give ourselves all kinds of grief in the process. When we do not take alone time, we become irritable, testy, angry, and even a bit nasty—especially if we let this negative energy build up for some time. Also, there is no average amount of alone time that is "enough" or an "acceptable amount" or "what one *should* take." We absolutely have to gather this information for ourselves.

Our bodies and our beings will give us many warnings, *and* it is up to us to pay attention and do something about respecting what we need.

Taking alone time is absolutely essential to living a new paradigm.

A Belief in Healing

THE ROLE OF ADDICTIONS IN OTHER ILLNESSES

*It is difficult to see what is under our
foot when we are standing on it.*

— PROVERB

For many years now I have been trying to point out how many of our most serious illnesses are actually exacerbated or caused by our addictions. And I have found that few in the medical profession want to look at reality. They are willing to talk about the huge cost of health care and the immensity of the health problems in the U.S., for example, and they are not willing to see the direct correlation with addictions and the larger problems.

For example, nicotine addiction is directly related to lung cancer and a myriad of respiratory illnesses. Alcoholism is directly related to liver cancer, diabetes, kidney problems, and other major health issues. Work addiction is directly related to high stress levels, high blood pressure, and heart problems. Food addiction is related to obesity, digestive problems, heart problems, and endocrine problems. When we add in overeating and anorexia, the problems increase exponentially.

Yet the role of addictions still is rarely a regular exploration in a diagnostic medical workup.

Addictions are the secret causes and contributors to many of our health problems and our "healers" continue to be in denial about this reality.

Knowing and Living in Several Realities

FLEXIBILITY

Our best intentions may also be our worst.

People who get stuck in their earlier understanding of and belief in a level of reality tend to become rigid and inflexible with respect to their level of reality. They tend to believe that theirs is the only reality and that's it! When we build a rigid reality for ourselves and do not understand that as we grow and develop we are a process and that, hopefully, growth will bring us new options, and we will have the possibility to explore new and different realities and make choices, we are stuck.

Some people are so frightened that they do not want to let any new information in for themselves or others. I know a very intelligent woman who had had quite a wild time growing up. Then she "found" Christianity, married a "simple" young man and had two children. At that point in time, she decided to "static" her universe. Her first move was to quit her job as an excellent bookkeeper and to stay home and home-school her children.

When asked why she was doing this, her response was, "I want to make sure that they think like I do and are so thoroughly grounded in my beliefs and values that they will never stray from them. When I am sure I have accomplished this, I will let them go to public school and mix with others."

She was not preparing her children for life or giving them the skills they need to cope with the process of life.

To participate in living a new paradigm we have to have skills for participating in the unknown.

Being of Service

PASSIVITY

Plunging in has its own rewards.

How many of us have used passivity in order to protect and control ourselves and our way of life? How often have we told ourselves that we can't do something before we have even tried it or waited for someone else to come along who could "do it better"?

A woman told me recently how she still prefers to take a passive role around men whenever possible. Her excuse was that she was much happier when they did the heavy lifting, i.e., the "dirty work"—passivity as a manipulation. However, she is making progress. Her personality is changing. And her self-esteem soars when she just participates in whatever is needed at the time. Her passivity often was more about manipulation than it was about being of service. When she focuses on being of service, her controlling passivity seems to evaporate. When we plunge into being of service, our passivity is irrelevant—and oh so much less annoying.

We may get dirtier when we give up our passivity—and we sure feel better about ourselves.

Graciousness

TOUGH DOES NOT MAKE IT

*How lucky we are that we do not have to choose
between two great possibilities.
We can be and do both.*

Being gracious in today's world is much more difficult than being tough.

Oh, we have to be tough too. Being tough is not all bad and it serves us well sometimes, as does every aspect of our being. And being tough *and* gracious is a big order indeed.

We have already learned that getting beyond dualisms and dualistic thinking is absolutely necessary to learn to live in a new paradigm. So what happens if we embrace the idea that graciousness does not preclude toughness? Well, in a new paradigm, clearly the two are not mutually exclusive. We can see that to embrace the graciousness that makes us vulnerable requires a great deal of toughness, and not the kind that the current culture cares to exhibit and emulate. One has to be tough to stand up to the assumptions, practices, beliefs, and behaviors of the current dominant paradigm. It is not easy to be told that what another paradigm knows to be true is not only not real, it does not exist. To be gracious in the face of this kind of onslaught, not get defensive, and not fight back takes much more courage than pitching a fit.

Remember: always err in the direction of graciousness.

Moving Out of Our Comfort Zones

CONTINUING TO CHALLENGE HOW AND WHAT WE THINK

I just want to know!

If we are serious about living a different paradigm, we have to be willing to challenge not only *what* we think, we have to be willing to challenge *how* we think.

Most of us have learned to trust our thinking and the way, in our minds, we have constructed our worlds. When we find out that the conceptual world we have constructed may or may not have anything to do with the world around us and often is a figment of our disembodied constructs, we feel lost, confused, and alone.

This "lost-ness" is an important, necessary aspect of giving up what is not real or working. Feeling lost is not bad. Feeling lost is an opportunity, especially when we stop doing what hasn't been working that well. In our attempt to force our world into stasis, we have come to believe that stasis is real and possible. We have staked our lives on it.

Now, as we move into the lost-ness that is part of growth, change, and leaving old patterns behind, we believe our thinking that lost-ness itself will be a permanent state. We so believe our thinking that we have trouble shifting and putting our trust in the process and not clinging to our belief that stasis is and can be a reality.

This is the stage where faith in the process of the universe comes in.

Letting Go of What We Think We Know

JUDGMENTALISM

Make no judgments where you have no compassion.

— ANNE MCCAFFREY

Judgmentalism is part of the warp and woof of our culture, and repeatedly we have to be reminded of its uselessness. In the Bible it says, "Judge not lest ye be judged." Yet this seems to be one admonition that is easily forgotten (or dismissed). Part of the problem is that we seem, as a species, to have become confused between making daily judgments as everyone needs to do, and becoming judgmental.

Of course we need to make judgments. "I'll wear this today." "I like this food better than that food," or "This food is better than that food." "I feel good with myself when I am honest." "I don't like not being honest." Even "I just don't like that person." Judgmentalism comes in when we leave out the *I* in "I don't like that person," and the statement becomes "That person is bad" or "That person is unlike me so therefore evil."

Judgments facilitate the processes of our living and becoming. Judgmentalisms interfere with the processes of our growing and learning.

We need to be reminded on a daily basis that being judgmental limits our possibilities for learning, growing, and being open to new paradigms.

Accepting That Choices and Behaviors Have Consequences

STAYING ON OUR SIDE OF THE STREET

The only person I can change is myself.

— A.A. SLOGAN

The absolute most radical aspect of the 12-step program of Alcoholics Anonymous is the concept of staying on our own side of the street. There is no doubt that the 12-step program—especially the first 3 steps—is set up to facilitate a paradigm shift and the most radical and far-reaching process is that of staying on our side of the street. Let's see how it works.

First of all, the program itself is based on the knowledge that the only person we can change is ourselves. We may hate the way another person treats us, it may seem and be unfair. We often can see that we are being victimized here and it isn't fair. So what? That person will have to deal with what she/he has done. We have no control over what they have done or what happens to them. That is none of our business. The only person we can change is ourself. This attitude does not in any way take away that the other person is guilty of wrongdoing. That's none of our business.

What we need to look at is what we did or are doing with the situation. What is our side of the street now? Maybe we had some flashes and/or peculiar, uneasy feelings. Did we not trust them? What did we do and what have we done not to heal? What choices have we made not to go after healing?

If bad things happened to us or were done to us, what did we do in response?

Reminder: seeking out and finding our side of the street always empowers us.

Humility

HUMILITY EMERGES OUT OF OUR FEELINGS OF FAILURE

The clouds gathered together, stood still, and watched the river scuttle around the forest floor, crash headlong into the haunches of hills with no notion of where it was going, until exhausted, ill and grieving, it slowed to a stop just twenty leagues short of the sea.

— TONI MORRISON IN *TAR BABY*

In the old paradigm, our illusion of control has resulted in cultural feelings of failure, depression, and anxiety. It is not surprising that if we are led to believe that we should be able to manipulate and control people, places, and things—our whole world—we would fail. And constant, repeated failure will lead to depression, anxiety, and anger. What a relief it is to discover that we not only do not have to control and manipulate our entire world, we *can't*.

After working through the reality that we are not in charge, a great feeling of relief emerges.

If we are not in charge, we cannot be blamed for not pulling off this impossible feat. Of course, this means that beginning to open the doors for humility to emerge will be much more difficult for those who have been moderately or very successful in the current paradigm, as we can well imagine. This "success" has fed into the belief that manipulation and control are *possible*. I believe all our great teachers have taught this principle.

Didn't Jesus say that it would be easier for a camel to go through the eye of the needle than a rich man to enter heaven? So yes, being successful in the existing paradigm may make it more difficult to allow humility to emerge—and not impossible.

Knowing and Being Known

Exploring Our Selves

*Sometimes, we fail to realize that our
greatest adventure is within ourselves.*

Now let's go a little deeper into the Johari Window.

To reiterate, the most obvious self is our public/everyday self. This is the self we present to the world. The public self contains our masks and our cons. This self is who we think we are and who we want others to see. Many believe this is the real self. It is not!

Then there is the hidden self. This is the place we hide our "dirty little secrets." We hide our fears, our thoughts that we do not want exposed, and our fears about who we might really be. We may have some—perhaps distorted—awareness of this self.

The third self is that self that others see that we have no awareness of whatsoever. This self is our blind self. It is the self that we carry around like a sandwich-board advertising it and we do not know that others can see it. We need others we trust to learn about this self.

The fourth self is that self that is unknown to others and unknown to ourselves. It is filled with riches for healing, growth, learning, and maturing and some people never glean its rich learnings. This self is our unconscious. It is the self that bypasses our rational, logical mind and takes us to our connection with the wholeness of everything. It is usually only accessed through memory and feelings and may be beyond verbal. Our ancestral wisdom dwells in this self.

We need to remember that a big part of our journey is to increase our conscious (public) self and glean knowledge and awareness of our hidden, blind and unknown selves. This is a life work.

Everything Is Spiritual/Sacred

ANIMALS

*We often hate to admit that in our relationship
with animals, we are the students.*

Anyone who has "owned" (what a concept!)—or been privileged to relate to—a dog, a cat, a horse, or any animal, and is open to learn, is aware of what great teachers our four-footed, flying, swimming friends can be and how we need them in our lives.

In the current paradigm, with its emphasis on the world being a machine and the focus of a technological, materialistic, mechanistic science and worldview, we have moved toward the belief that everything is here to be used and abused and can be owned. As we relate less and less with the world around us and see it as existing to meet *our* needs, we seem to be losing the awareness that our lives are not only richer if we have other beings in our lives, we *need* other beings in our lives to help remind us that we are *part* of creation and not *above* creation.

Animals have more patience than we humans do with ourselves or with one another to help remind us that we are interconnected in a sacred, spiritual world. Sometimes our animals are the only ones we dare to have any intimacy with when we have retreated into our thinking, conceptual, mechanistic, non-living world too far.

When we trust the animals on this planet as a sacred part of creation, we learn something of the sacred in ourselves.

Wholeness

THINKING WHOLENESS AND LIVING WHOLENESS

*Nature is the storehouse of potential life
of future generations and is sacred.*

— AUDREY SHENANDOAH, ONONDAGA ELDER

Thinking in terms of wholeness is a big order for most of us.

We worry about ourselves. We worry about our own little nuclear families and, regardless of our spiritual knowings, we must put them first. We are concerned about our own small way of defining and trying to live out of our own spiritual beliefs and this requires of us that we set up a dualism of "us or them"—even if we have to annihilate them.

We really care about the principles and values of wholeness as long as it does not affect our status and financial security. We live with lofty concepts that are great, and one must, after all, be most concerned about *me* and *mine*. The chasm between the belief and action becomes greater and greater. So what does it mean to live out of an awareness that wholeness is our reality?

We no longer have the luxury to sit back and *think* about the reality of wholeness. To live a new paradigm, we need to learn how to *live* wholeness—one teeny step at a time.

Joy

A VARIETY OF EXPRESSIONS

Oh, listen! Hear sing with me, for I am joy.

— CHEROKEE SONG

There are many types of joy.

We all remember squeaking as a child when the unexpected happened or when we spied the Christmas tree surrounded by its bounty.

We all remember the birthday cake with its blazing candles waiting to be extinguished. Some of us may remember the trick candles that would not be blown out and the shocking giggles when we learned that we had been tricked.

We remember the thrill of joy with a new baby when that child first discovered its little hand and that somehow it was related to that hand. Or the first words and steps as a new being began to relate to and connect with its world.

We remember the rib-splitting joys and the quiet, tender joys with ourselves and others. And we also have noticed how difficult it is for some we know and love to give in to joy.

Joy has many moods and expressions. And they are at their best when they are in the driver's seat.

All Is in Process

OUR INSTITUTIONS AND ORGANIZATIONS ARE A PROCESS

How would we behave differently if we accepted that our organizations are and will always be a process?

For many years I worked as an organizational consultant. I was usually hired because the organization *said* that they wanted to change. In my experience, they truly *believed* that they wanted to change and, down deep, they revered and wanted stasis. This was the reason I left the field.

Most saw themselves as open and innovative. In the process of working with such institutions, I developed the concept of form as a fix. It seems that individuals and institutions are more comfortable with changing their form and structure than they are with being open to changing their process.

I did have the experience that with several organizations, I watched them make structural changes and feel quite happy about them. Then when those changes did not work, they would suggest making "new" structural changes that were exactly what they had been doing before. No matter what the *form* is or how it is changed, no *real* change will occur unless the *processes* change.

I see this same pattern in many of those writing about a new paradigm. They are completely oblivious to the importance of or existence of the process; they see form as a fix and already know what the new paradigm or shift will look like, which, of course, is impossible.

This kind of "knowing" is seductive and will never work.

If we participate fully in a process, we never know what the outcome will be. We can only take the next step and see what evolves.

Participation

PARTICIPATION EVOKES MEMORIES

Fate keeps happening.

— ANITA LOOS

Participation, without our realizing it, evokes memories of what we know deep in our psyches that we often do not remember. Hence, we need reminders.

It is amazing how full-focus participation opens the door for—what do we call it—our spirit guides, our unconscious, our inner wisdom, God, our higher power, the place where we are one with the universe—to seep in and feed us the information we need to take the next step in our process of evolving.

Most often these messages are not in the form of concepts, ideas, philosophical theories, or notions. These awarenesses may be in the form of body awarenesses, flashbacks, sensations, inclinations, and intuition. They are rarely the stuff of ideas and abstract concepts. When we participate in whatever our lives set before us our inner being/higher self seizes the opportunity to feed us the information we need to know to deal with whatever we need to resolve in order to move on with our growth and learning. It is important and necessary for us to remember that our inner process will never feed us something that we have not reached the maturity and inner wisdom to work through to heal and grow.

Our avoidance of participation may be because we are fearful and not trusting of ourselves and our inner process.

Thinking

AN EXAMPLE OF DISEMBODIED THINKING

Don't believe everything someone tells you or that you read.
You have the responsibility to check it out for yourself.

— MANILLA WILLEY

I mentioned before that I knew a woman once who was invited to write a book on a topic on which she had no real knowledge or experience. I suppose that this is not too unusual as probably many books are written that way. Yet, since I write only from my experience and my research, needless to say I was a bit shocked with the invitation and even more shocked when she accepted the invitation.

Then came the process of writing the book. She would have an idea and then, instead of researching the "idea," she would draw an idea from the idea and make some assumptions about the new idea—never test them out or research them. Then, she would put that on the first idea that had no substantiation at all and develop another idea. Since I was trained heavily in scientific research, validating hypotheses and testing them, I was shocked beyond belief. I was also uneasy with what I perceived as her lack of integrity. I could not believe that people believed her. I was incredulous with *what* she came up with and *how* she came to it. I was even more surprised that anyone accepted her information and conclusions as real.

I learned the very important lesson that just because someone says something or it is in print does not necessarily mean it is real. We also need to remember to distinguish between disembodied concepts (interpretations) and what is real.

We *know*—we need to remember that. Somewhere, down deep inside, we know . . . regardless of what someone says.

Beliefs and Assumptions

THE BELIEFS AND ASSUMPTIONS WE HOLD ABOUT OURSELVES AS A SPECIES

Who among us does not need the trees?

Having been raised as a Cherokee, I never cease to be amazed with some of the beliefs that Western culture especially holds about ourselves as a species. One of the beliefs that I continue to hear, again especially from the "scientific" community, is that we are the highest form of evolution—that evolution has culminated in the evolution of the human. What damage this particular belief has done to the environment and the planet! Believing that we are the epitome of creation gives us license to destroy nature and the earth. How arrogant!

For example, recently, there was a scientific study published demonstrating that animals have feelings! Where have we been? Anyone who has worked with animals knows that not only do animals have feelings, they often feel things we cannot.

When we destroy the rest of creation, we destroy ourselves! When we fail to learn from the animals, trees, and nature around us, not only do we avoid a possibility of great wisdom, we ignore that all creation is necessary and without all of nature and knowing we are a part of it and not above it, we cannot become who we are.

Our arrogance is fed by limited and outmoded beliefs and assumptions.

Feelings and Emotions

INTELLIGENT EMOTIONS AND FEELINGS

Words have great power and should be used carefully. Aloha, for example, should not be seen as just a frivolous tourist greeting. Alo means the bosom of the center of the universe, and ha, the breath of God, so to say this word is to appreciate another person's divinity.

— NANA VEARY, HAWAIIAN KUPUNA

Often it is our emotions and feelings that alert us that something subtle is going on that is important and needs attention.

For example, like all of us, I was taught by the culture not to trust or listen to my emotions and feelings. "There is nothing more unreliable than an emotional woman," was a mantra of the culture. So as any good student majoring in math and science, I attempted to make my main source of information my rational mind.

Luckily my mother and great-grandmother saw things quite differently, so rational, reductionistic, empirical science did not hold sway over everything. I was also reminded to trust my feelings, emotions, and intuitions. My mother often said, "Remember, it is the unseen that is the most important." And it is our feelings and emotions that hold the keys to the doors of the unseen, unknown, and not measurable. My mother and great-grandmother took their responsibilities seriously to see that I was made aware of and appreciative of the unseen and the unknown and how one gets there.

We all need tutors to remember what is important.

Honesty

WE NEED TO BECOME HONEST AS A PLANET

We need to learn to be stewards, not users.

We can no longer continue to delude ourselves about our necessity to take care of this planet and to lie about this reality.

Personal dishonesty, national dishonesty, corporate dishonesty, and our dishonesty about the reasons we are not willing to work together with all creation is fast destroying this planet that has been so good to us. One level of dishonesty that we perpetuate about the planet is to ignore that it gives us everything we have. Being Native American, I was raised with this truth.

I remember years ago when I was pondering why it was said of native people that we worshipped the sun, the moon, and all earth. I knew that was not true. In fact, I questioned if "worship" is not really something peculiar to the revealed religions. Like a bolt of lightning hitting me, I realized that absolutely everything we have comes from the earth with the help of the moon and the sun. Why would we not be truly grateful for such gifts? Honest gratitude is not worship!

At the same time I was astounded with the systemic dishonesty about this fact that everything we have comes from the earth and we are using it up. If we keep perpetuating this lie about the earth's not providing everything we have, we will no longer have it.

Courage

LOOKING BACK

Courage breeds courage.

It is good for all of us to look back over our lives with a perspective of our job being to heal, grow, and learn. From the perspective of the paradigm out of which I live, life is, quite simply, about healing, growing (especially spiritually), and learning. It's very simple really. If we have the courage to do our work and not frither away the opportunities of this life, we are presented with everything we need to heal, grow, and learn. It is up to us what we do with these opportunities.

For example, none of us had perfect families, *and* whatever was presented to us in our families we could use to learn what we needed to heal, grow, and learn. Everything, no matter how "bad" or "good" it is, can be used for our healing, growing, and learning. It is up to us what we do with the circumstances we experienced in our families. Our family experiences may be the earliest proving ground that we have to kick-start our process of growing into courage.

We may not have had the courage to face our family dynamics as children—*and* the choice to do so as adults may be the door for our courage development.

Our human process of growth and development is very conservation minded. Nothing need be wasted.

Entitlement

FROM GRATITUDE COMES HUMILITY

*How frustrated we get when we do not know
how to get something we cannot make, buy,
or cause to be brought about.*

Humility is another one of those elusive processes that we cannot *think* ourselves into or force upon ourselves.

In fact, there is nothing more amusing than someone who is *trying* to be humble. The term *false humility* did not come out of thin air. It was developed to describe a real phenomenon.

Humility, like most of the truly precious things in life, cannot be bought, earned, deserved, or controlled. We cannot be entitled to it. Humility is a by-product of genuine gratitude. Isn't it just amazing how so many of the very most important aspects in life are by-products of a process?

No matter how much we try, we cannot make ourselves "humble." Indeed, from my experience, true humility seems to be in very short supply these days and I have found that it is most prevalent in Native elders.

Humility is not a commodity to be bought, sold, traded, earned, or garnered through entitlement. It only creeps up on those who are otherwise occupied.

Beware of those who say, "I am very humbled."

Accepting Our Humanness

OUR SENSES ARE LIMITED

*Is it so difficult to see that other creatures,
other cultures have gifts that we do not have?
Wisdom comes from valuing differences.*

When we accept the limits of our humanity, we are forced to admit that our senses are limited. We have a good set of senses and they probably are able to feed us as much information as we can handle. *And* our senses are very limited.

Our eyes give us wonderful information (if we do not clutter it up too much with our thinking) *and* our eyes are not as good as the eagles' and many other of our animal brothers and sisters.

Our ears have an amazing range of hearing and we can't hear what our dogs hear.

Our sense of smell can save us in a burning house and our cats and dogs are usually onto the problem long before we are. Our animals sense an earthquake long before we feel it.

Native peoples have accepted outsiders because they "knew" they could learn something from them. It is a story of disaster on this planet that those who invaded did not believe they had important lessons to learn from those already there.

Remember the story of a young Ojibway girl asking her grandmother, "Grandmother, when the strangers came, there were more of us. Why did we not kill them? Why did we let them stay?"

The grandmother sighed and with tears in her eyes said, "Because they needed us."

Perhaps they "needed us" to form a new society, a new paradigm.

Respect

RESPECTING THE ANIMALS—MORE

Our teachers are all around us all the time.

I could probably write a whole book on learning respect from the animals and respecting the animals. My mother would like that!

My mother chose to practice her medicine mostly on animals. My great-grandmother made sure that she had a complete education in using our medicine with humans, and my mother found her calling to be working with animals. I believe she thought that animals were the far nobler species at that point in the evolution of the human race so that is where she put her energy.

Many who adhere to the practice of respect, I believe, will probably agree with her.

When I was five years old, my babysitters were a black border collie and a big Orphan-Annie's-Sandy-like dog called Shep.

The three of us spent hours alone together in the woods. One could not have wished for better teachers and my mother always admonished me to take care of them and learn from them, which I did to the best of my ability.

Our house and yard were always filled with strays and animals in the process of healing.

All were family and worthy of respect. Their teaching was gentle, respectful, and ever-present. They taught me respect and responsibility.

The Abstractualization of Life

HOMES

*For me, there was always a sense of contentment in feeling a
rhythm beneath my feet. The heartbeat of the land. That season would
follow season and that the rhythm would never alter. Knowing
this brought me peace like no other I had known.*

— WITI IHIMAERA, MAORI

Our withdrawal from participating in the world around us
has been concretized in the way we have built our homes.

The ideal home or apartment is one that prevents and keeps
us from dealing with nature. As a result of this withdrawal from
nature, our bodies have lost much of their ability to deal with the
change of the seasons and the world around us. Our living has
physically become abstraction.

Now don't get me wrong here. I am not suggesting that we
all need to go back to living in huts in the wild. And I am suggesting that if we do not find ways to make a living reconnection
with nature, we will suffer and so will nature.

The more abstract the process of living is the more
ungrounded we become. To re-ground ourselves, we need to recognize how ungrounded we have become and see it as a problem.

Being of Good Spirit

THE WONDERS OF OUR UNCONSCIOUS

*Remember, Elizabeth Anne, we never really know what is
going on inside another person to make them act the way they do.
Try to understand that they have their reasons.*

— MANILLA LONGAN

Being of good spirit does not necessarily imply being happy about everything all the time. We are humans. Trying to be happy all the time would require a great deal of denial. Denial requires a large dumping of all kinds of negative stuff into our unconscious. It is inevitable that when "stuff" is dumped into our unconscious it will come back to bite us and others at some point.

One of the beautiful aspects of being human is that we have memories and our memories store the good and the bad in the wonderful vault of our unconscious. All this "stuff" waits there until we have reached a level of maturity, insight, strength, and awareness that allows us to deal with whatever it is, heal, and learn from it. This storage of material in our unconscious is such an amazing phenomenon that it gives us an option (if we take it) to work through anything and everything and free ourselves to be more whole.

This opportunity for healing is such an amazing wonder that to approach it with anything other than good spirit would be absolutely stupid. And we don't want to be stupid now, do we?

Domination Over and the Illusion of Control

COLONIZATION

When we start justifying our behaviors,
we know that we are in big trouble.

Colonization is a form of domination that has been practiced by most countries in the Western and the Eastern worlds except Ireland and those who had indigenous cultures.

Colonization is systemized domination and control, whether it is under the guise of spreading a "true" religion, or modernizing, helping, or "developing" another person or country.

Colonization is always about killing off the existing culture and raping the land and the people. It involves physical, emotional, psychological, and spiritual annihilation. It assumes that mass destruction of a people and a way of life (and the wisdom inherent in that way of life) is justified because what we have is "better" and more valid.

We will never be able to live out of a different paradigm as long as we have a shred of justification for colonization in our hearts, minds, beings, or souls.

We are losing vast amounts of wisdom, knowledge, ways of being, information, and healing when we act out of domination over and the illusion of control—no matter how and when we practice it. Any "new" paradigm must include letting go of the illusions and behaviors of colonization.

Humor

LAUGHING AT AND LAUGHING WITH

Where I come from, we only tease those we love.

Native people rarely, if ever, laugh *at* someone. We laugh *with*.

This approach to humor is much easier for native people because of our firm belief that we are all family and are all connected in and through the whole.

There is an old saying among the Irish, "There are no strangers here, only friends we have not met yet." I would, from my teachings, say, "There are no strangers here, only *family* I have not met yet." And part of being family means that we already "know" all our relations, we just need to get acquainted.

As I have worked with people throughout the world, I continue to be shocked that many people do not know that we are family. This lack of knowing also has extended to my having to learn that there are many cultures that are not filled with humor and in which people don't tease one another. It took me many years to learn (and I have to keep relearning this) that when I believe I am laughing *with* someone over their human foibles, they are experiencing being laughed *at*.

People I work with are often making amends to me for resentments they have held for years because they misinterpreted my loving them through teasing. I can't remember ever laughing *at* someone.

Wonder and Awe

MY SECOND BIRTHING

We can even experience wonder and awe
when we have "no time" for wonder and awe.

When my second child was born, I was a little wiser than I had been at the birth of the first one. Even though I had attended births and worked in the hospital during my premed training, actually birthing a child is something different from knowing about it intellectually. At one point, in the birthing of my first child, I decided I "didn't want to do it" and informed my resident/friend of my decision to reabsorb the fetus and "do this another time."

He laughed lovingly and said, "Well, that is an interesting idea—and, quite frankly, you have no choice. That baby is in charge, not you." And so it has continued.

With my second child, I discussed this whole process with my new ob/gyn. He too laughed and said, "Don't you know that when you feel the pain you are describing to me, you are birthing? There are usually only ten or twelve of those pains and you are done." I felt blank and then said, "No problem, I can stand ten or twelve of anything." I so "participated" in that birthing and pushed so hard that I had black eyes from breaking the blood vessels in my eyelids. I was awestruck from both births and so gratefully in wonder that the second doctor guided me in full participation.

We need to remember that we have more wonder and awe in any task when we participate with all our body, mind, and spirit.

The Present Can Only Be Our Reality
if We Own Our Past and Our Future

THE CUSHION OF OUR PAST

*If most of us realized how much work
we have the option to do as a human being,
we probably would decide not to be born.*

As we become comfortable with our personal past and all our personal traumas and issues, we have the opportunity to look at bigger and bigger spheres of influence in our lives.

All of us are affected by histories of our families, our institutions, our nations, our cultures and our species. For example, when I first started working intensely with the German people, almost 40 years ago, I was a bit shocked, impressed, and touched by the lingering impact of the Nazi era and the effect it had and still has on German society. Clearly, even though many of the people I work with were not even alive during the Nazi era, their lives are still deeply impacted by what their grandparents and parents did. Some of the older ones "remember" the trauma they personally experienced. All of us have racial memories.

The more work I do on myself, the more I physically, emotionally, and spiritually "remember" what has happened to my people—the Cherokee, the Irish, and the British—and what they themselves did.

My work of owning my past and healing my past has involved the healing of my ancestors and of their past. Their past is in my present, alive and often not so well. All of this is my work to do.

Walking in Beauty

THE UGLY

You mean, everyone isn't as happy as we are?

— TSERING DOLMA, LADAKHI FARMER

To walk in beauty is to accept the ugly and not become contaminated with it.

We have all known and seen people who live their lives in denial and need to force everything into being "good." These people are not walking in beauty. They usually are walking in denial. For one who walks in beauty, the ugliness and the pain of this human existence are never denied.

To deny the ugly would necessitate not seeing the beauty that can come out of the ugly and the horrible. For walking in beauty requires that we accept the whole of all creation and the inherent beauty of the lessons to be learned. The violent, the mean, and the ugly just teach us that as human beings we have a long way to go and need to be open to all the learnings that are put before us. To accept the violent and the ugly means that we will then have the opportunity to do something about them.

Walking in beauty relieves the pressure of the immediate.

Taking Time

Fear

Fear is a close companion of the illusion of control.

One reason that we do not take the alone time that our beings and our bodies are telling us that we need is that unconsciously we are afraid. So many of us fill our lives to overflowing because we have no skill and little or no experience in being alone. When we are alone may be when the information we have been trying to keep unaware of for years will take advantage of the situation and resurface. As long as we keep terribly busy, those old thoughts and memories that we still don't believe we have the strength or ability to cope with might escape. Also, when we surround ourselves with space and silence, who knows what will come up?!

Exactly!

We are stuck in a nonfunctional way of being in the world at least partially because we will not let our wisdom of another way of being in the world creep into our conscious mind. We may have to do something.

How we humans long for and try to create some kind of stasis even when we are offered something that is so much better.

A Belief in Healing

THE ENVIRONMENT AND HEALTH

I do wish others would change their lifestyles.

Our denial about the role of addictions in disease and the inadequacy of the mechanistic medical model to address these issues is secondary only to our denial about the role of our lifestyle in creating an environment that cannot and will not sustain life on this planet.

We acknowledge pollution, and we completely refuse to do much about it if it interferes with the bottom line—commercialism and consumerism. Ultimately we, at this time in our evolution as a species, are not willing to take a serious look at anything that will sidetrack the inevitable "progress" of mankind. The almighty dollar (or pound or Euro) is justification for any and all methods of approved destruction.

There are many who believe that when the environment is unhealthy all the planet is unhealthy. And fewer are ready and willing to act on this recognition, which will require a process of complete paradigm shift.

We don't need wars to decimate life on this planet, we are willing to do it with our lifestyle.

Knowing and Living in Several Realities

TRAINING IN MULTIPLE REALITIES

*We learn the most important/subtle learnings
slowly through participation and experience.*

As I look back over my life, I can see very clearly how the circumstances of my life have taught me about different realities and prepared me to recognize the existence of several realities simultaneously.

For example, I was raised and educated in a world dominated by white Western thinking and approaches to life. Simultaneously I was raised as a traditional Cherokee in a Cherokee Women's Healing line. Both "realities" were part of my reality. Neither was "right." Nor were they separated out, named, or delineated. They just were.

This combination was my life and seemed to function very seamlessly in our household, although, as I look back, I realize my mother and great-grandmother seemed to have more tolerance for my father's Western scientific reality than he did for their fuller Cherokee reality. There were times when my mother and great-grandmother were labeled "superstitious." Yet, I believe, because they were strong women and "knew what they were talking about," what became very obvious was that they just knew some things in areas where my father's heavy education in science and math had failed him.

Growing up in multiple realities is a definite asset in being open to other paradigms.

Being of Service

DEPRESSION

*Humor is the sense of the absurd which is
despair refusing to take itself seriously.*

— ARLAND USSHER

I have noticed that depression is an increasing "problem" in the paradigm of Western culture. Depression tends to feed on itself and is so imbedded in the current Technological, Mechanistic, Materialistic culture as to be epidemic and endemic.

From my experience, one of the best antidotes for depression is to get busy helping others. In the 12-step program of Alcoholics Anonymous, which can, I believe, be viewed as steps toward a paradigm shift (i.e., recovering from our Addictive System/TMM culture), sponsors often suggest that we cannot recover without selflessly being of service to others. In the very physical act of being of service, something begins to change inside the person. The chemistry changes.

Self-centered persons do not want to be of service to others. It's difficult (but not impossible—self-centered persons are very, very tricky) to be of service and maintain an active self-centeredness.

In living a new paradigm, being of service is a natural state of being.

Graciousness

GRACIOUSNESS REQUIRES HUMILITY

*Oh Great Spirit, who made all races, look kindly upon
the whole human family and take away the arrogance and
hatred which separates us from our brothers and sisters.*

— CHEROKEE PRAYER

True graciousness cannot exist without humility. And humility—genuine humility—is our door to our spirituality. False humility abounds in a dysfunctional society and there are many people who will readily tell us how humble they are. True humility is a kind of quiet seepage from the soul, which waters and restores everything it touches. Like our breath, which can only actually be seen on rare occasions, it is quiet and essential for living.

True graciousness, then, is a by-product, which can only emerge as an afterthought. We cannot think ourselves into true graciousness. It must seep and flow from a place deep inside of us without our noticing or controlling its passage into the light of day.

Graciousness is an outer expression of an inner essence not controlled by our conscious mind. Indeed, it must be unconscious to work its true magic and humility is its creator.

We, as humans, are so fortunate that some of our most valuable assets are not under our conscious control.

Moving Out of Our Comfort Zones

FINDING NEW COMFORT ZONES

*The word "possibility" is one of
the most beautiful in the English language.*

If we truly want to find a new paradigm of living with this planet, we have to see that the artificial comfort zones of stasis we have built with our minds need to shift. They need to shift from solid, unchanging illusions to the reality that all is process and in process. We need to get comfortable with "I don't know" and "All I need to do is participate."

Not only will this awareness result in relief, it can result in a peacefulness that underlies all we do and think.

We can stop standing back and trying to control our world and we can begin to participate in our world without having to know what the outcomes will be.

We can begin to move beyond this solid, static world we have constructed with our minds into a world of process and possibilities, which do not need to be controlled by *us*.

We can move into possibility.

Letting Go of What We Think We Know

JUDGMENTALISM IS TOXIC

Judgmentalism is and creates more negativity.

We have explored and reminded ourselves of the necessity to let go of our use of judgmentalism if we wish to learn to live a new paradigm. And judgmentalism and the need to move beyond obviously deserve a good amount of attention. No discussion of the role that judgmentalism and negativity play in our lives would be complete without a discussion of how toxic they are. It is toxic to the one who is judging and to the one judged.

For the one who is judging, that judgmental process literally distorts our perceptions so that we lose the ability to see clearly and be objective. It "colors" not only the way we perceive the world around us, it distorts and blocks some information from being available to us at all. Being judgmental results in our filtering out any and all information that comes our way if it does not fit into our bias. Judgmentalism constricts and narrows our world, and most of all, it makes us mean. It destroys the possibility of hope and feeds whatever tendency we have for negativity, which will grow exponentially when it gets the chance.

Judgmentalism and negativity distort our insides and result in our being twisted, angry, narrow people. Judgmentalism also sends tons of negative energy to those judged and out into the atmosphere in general. It's bad stuff.

A daily reminder of the destructiveness of judgmentalism and negativity to ourselves is absolutely necessary if we want to live a new paradigm.

Accepting That Choices and Behaviors
Have Consequences

TAKING BACK OUR POWER

*Think of yourself as an incandescent power, illuminated
perhaps and forever talked to by God and God's messengers.*

— BRENDA UELAND

Often it is very difficult to see our side of the street if we have
been victimized. Sometimes we have no control over being victimized. We *do* have a choice in becoming a victim and accepting
the choice of being a victim.

When we become victims in our own mind and we represent ourselves as victims to ourselves and others, we *will* become
perpetrators. Yet the even greater loss to ourselves is that each
moment we accept a role as victim, we are giving away big pieces
of our personal power and resenting others for having it. We may
have been victimized; that happens. *And* we make the choice
to *be* a victim. *And* that choice results in a seeping away of our
personal power.

For example, someone may have stolen some money from
you. Yes, that was wrong—no doubt about it. Then, if you begin
your work on the issue, you may realize that you left the money
in the car, unprotected. Of course they should not have taken
it, that's not the issue. You can't do a thing about that. And, if
you can see that it would not have been stolen unless you left it
there, then your personal power begins to return and you move
on with the lesson learned. And you feel more powerful.

Reminder: when we take ownership of the choices we make,
we begin to feel our personal power returning and we find ourselves shifting out of an archaic victim-perpetrator paradigm.

As we affirm who we are, we become who we are.

Humility

RELIEF

Water has to return to the sea
just as I have to return to me.

What a relief it is to "get" in the depth of our beings that not only do we not need to run our world and the worlds of others, we can't.

Relief is such a cleanser, especially when it comes out of a soul-recognition of reality and not out of one's thinking, concepts, and human-made belief systems. What a relief it is to begin to see that our illusion of control and manipulation is just that, and not only do we not *need* to control ourselves and others, we can't! This relief is like a drink from a fresh, clear, life-giving spring that has been flowing all along and we just had not discovered it. It is refreshing to know that not only do we not have to manipulate and control, we cannot. It is just not possible.

We can participate in our own and others' lives, we can participate in the life of the planet, and in no way can we control anything.

We have the possibility to experience the relief of knowing that we are not in charge. We can influence through participation. And, we are not in charge.

Knowing and Being Known

EXPLORING AND SHARING OUR HIDDEN SELF

*As awareness increases, the need for personal
secrecy almost proportionally decreases.*

— CHARLOTTE PAINTER

As we grow and mature, we become aware that many of the secrets that we think we have kept hidden are not that hidden, aren't nearly as big and important as we thought they were, or have lost the reason for keeping them hidden.

If we are, indeed, growing and maturing in our personal selves, we come to a place where we would rather spend our time and energy in healing, growing, and learning about ourselves than we would in keeping huge areas of who we are hidden. We realize that keeping aspects of ourselves hidden, and the concomitant energy it takes, could better be spent somewhere else.

Indeed, we may discover that intimacy—true intimacy—with others and ourselves is just more exciting and interesting. So we begin to come out of the closet. We seek out people we can trust with the self we have tried to hide. We want to connect.

The process of sharing who we are is a lifetime process, and as we do it, our perceptions change and our worldview begins to shift.

Everything Is Spiritual/Sacred

NOTHING IS DEAD THAT LIVES IN NATURE

Given the proper incentive, no mountain, it seems, is too high to climb, no current too swift to swim, if one is a Cherokee.

— GRACE STEELE WOODWARD

In our dualistic thinking in the current dominant paradigm, we have developed the tendency to divide our world into the living and the dead, the sentient and the nonsentient, the sacred and the nonsacred. What an exercise in futility!

When we make this division in our minds, we force ourselves into an illusionary reality. Who is to say that a rock is not alive? The Zen Buddhists have a saying: "Rocks are people who have sat Zazen for a very long time."

If you know anything about rocks at all, you know that some have come into being under pressures that are not even conceivable to us humans and they have wisdom that is thousands of years old. Within them is information, knowledge, and wisdom. They do not have to be made into "sacred objects" by people. They are sacred objects in and of themselves.

Have you ever had the experience of holding a certain rock and feeling calmer? Have you ever felt relieved to come home and see a favorite rock or stone waiting for you? These rocks and stones are not dead, inanimate objects. They embody a quiet sacredness that is often difficult for us even to imagine.

Whenever I forget that everything in nature is sacred and has a possible spiritual teaching for me, I am in trouble. I need to remember and live this awareness to enter the process of shifting into a more living paradigm.

Wholeness

ACTING OUT OF OUR CONNECTEDNESS

The welfare of the people was what was important.
In ceremonies held early in their lives, children were taught
to think of what was best for the tribe as a whole.
Being selfish or thinking only of oneself was unheard of.

— ABORIGINAL WISDOM

Growing up in a family that lived out of our Cherokee traditions, I had the opportunity to experience wholeness in my daily life.

I was born during the Great Depression and there were always people coming to our door who were hungry and asked for food. Regardless of who they were or how little food we ourselves had, they were never turned away. My grandmother and mother always knew that they had the same light of the Creator in them that we all did and our sharing what we had was feeling our oneness. They always said that we should be grateful that we had anything to share.

At some very deep level, they conveyed to me that they knew that all any of us had came from the same source and was meant to be shared. If we but stop to remember, we will realize that we *know* about this connectedness, this wholeness, even if we have trouble remembering at times.

Down deep, it is a natural state to know that we are all part of one creation. We have had to work at forgetting this truth and, for some of us, we have not been successful.

Joy

AWE AND WONDER

If grains of sand can become a reflection of the divine,
just think what can happen to the human being.

— THE DALAI LAMA

Letting ourselves experience the awe and wonder of the world around us and the life we have has the potential to be a very quiet, refreshing joy.

When we let ourselves experience the awe and wonder of natural beauty like the Tetons or Yellowstone Falls, the sun setting into the ocean, or a simple birdsong, our joy contains a peace that passeth understanding.

To experience the joy of feeling at peace is soothing indeed. Rarely does our being have the opportunity that it has with the experience of a peaceful joy.

We cannot manufacture a peaceful joy. It is a pure gift that flows over us in spite of ourselves. Awe and wonder are gifts of being human. The joy of experiencing awe and wonder is also a gift of being human. Quiet joy is a gift of being human.

We need to remind ourselves that there are many quiet joys available to us as human beings and that we do not need excitement, adrenaline, and explosive entertainment to feel joy (or something at all!).

Emotional Brilliance

OUR RATIONAL MINDS

How can I become emotionally brilliant?
By getting out of my own way.

One of the most important aspects of being emotionally brilliant is that we do not let our rational minds run amuck as they sometimes want to do. Emotionally oriented people are very good at noticing and then sitting with the noticings before they plunge into what could be a disaster.

Our rational minds are always frantic and in a hurry. When they notice something about themselves or others, they want to rush to a conclusion. They want to *know*. They especially want to *interpret*. They want to *understand*. Our rational minds do not realize that the most important aspect is not "understood" in abstraction and concepts.

The most important has to be "waited with" for comprehension at all levels.

To live a new paradigm, we need to avoid the temptation to rush to interpretation at all costs.

All Is in Process

OUR NATIONS ARE ALSO A PROCESS

*Not my country, right or wrong—
my country righting its wrongs.*

No student of history can deny that our nations are also a process bumbling along as best they can. This fantasy is partially because most nations, especially the more "developed" nations, are founded on the illusion of control—for ourselves and others. Historically, it is interesting to see the process of how we came to nation-states.

In the history of the human race, whenever we manage to get leadership that has some inkling of process and operating in a process way, they are quickly tied up by the illusion of control and manipulation and are eliminated. Every nation has a "character" that is perpetuated by its beliefs and assumptions and the structures of those nations are designed to perpetuate the "character" of that nation. A big part of our growth as individuals is to outgrow the static beliefs and assumptions of our country of origin. Only in the process of seeing and growing beyond the assumptions, beliefs, and structures of our national heritage and seeing them in context will we be able to become the people we have the potential to be.

If we choose to jump in and participate in the process of change, trusting the outcome will be something that we could never have thought of, there is a great possibility that it will be better than anything we ever could have imagined. Even if what we experience is bad or difficult to deal with, we have the opportunity to learn something that we might never have learned otherwise.

Participation

THE UNCONSCIOUS USE OF NONPARTICIPATION

*All of a sudden a gate shuts down
and I want to be left alone.*

Nonparticipation can be used in ways that are destructive to ourselves, others, and the ongoing process of the universe, often unconsciously. All too often, we humans use nonparticipation as a way to feed our illusion of control. We can, for a number of reasons—fear, anger, punishment—simply withdraw and refuse to participate in our own lives and with others. When we do this, we and everyone around us suffer the loss of what we have to offer. The person who refuses to participate withdraws more and more into a self-imposed prison and there is nothing that anyone—except the person who is nonparticipating—can do to change the situation. In a negative way, nonparticipation can be very powerful and a way to halt the natural processes of a life or lives. It is quite amazing how powerful doing, sharing, contributing nothing can be.

Even when we do not realize it, the choice is ours. We always have choices and the choice *is* ours. The choice not to be a part of the streaming force that is the process of life is a powerful choice indeed.

Sometimes we forget how important participation is—for ourselves and others. We need daily reminders.

Thinking

THE ROLE OF WORRY

Worry gives a small thing a big shadow.

— SWEDISH PROVERB

No discussion of our thinking would be complete without mentioning the role that worry plays in our day-to-day living.

If there were ever a disembodied thinking process, worry should qualify. Worry is generated by the "what ifs" of our lives and comes directly out of the delusion of control that is so prevalent in our culture.

I asked a woman who often paralyzes herself with her worry about her grown children why she worried so much about them. She had two responses: 1) "If I don't worry about them, how will they know that I love them?" and 2) "Yes, they are doing fine *because* I worry about them" (simple cause and effect in her mind). She wondered why I couldn't see and respect that belief. No control issues here!

When I have something coming up like a possible health issue, people will say to me, "Aren't you worried?" My answer is always "No!" I don't pre-worry. If there is something that comes up, I will deal with it. Until then why would I miss the time to participate in my life?

Worry and pre-worry are almost always related to the illusion of control and can be excuses for nonparticipation in our life which we, of course, can never really control.

Beliefs and Assumptions

THE ROLE OF RELIGION IN STATIC ASSUMPTIONS

When we concretize our perceptions,
we are participating in theological idolatry.

— NORM JACKSON

When one looks at the role that beliefs and assumptions (conscious and unconscious) play in our attempts to stay static and not grow as humans, nothing surpasses the role that religious beliefs play.

I approach this topic with fear and trembling because, historically, more wars and violence have resulted from religious differences than from any other cause (except in more modern wars where economic power and money—the new religions—are outdistancing traditional religions).

It is curious to me that trying to examine religious beliefs and assumptions is a reason for death and destruction. I remember years ago when one of my friends said that she was fearful and praying for me because she was afraid the Christian church would kill me. My response was, "Why would they do that? I'm a practicing Christian."

"That has nothing to do with the church," she replied.

It is not the teachings that are at fault. It is the rigidity with which some hold these beliefs and assumptions. Most religious founders taught peace and equality.

Why would a static God create a universe that is in process?

Is trying to make God and God's teachings static heresy?

A wise man once said to me, "When we concretize our perceptions, we are participating in theological idolatry."

He was a Native American professor at a theological seminary.

Feelings and Emotions

TRUSTING INFORMATION OTHER THAN THE RATIONAL

Don't listen to friends when the friend inside you says, "Do this!"

— MAHATMA GANDHI

As I came to grips with my cultural training to worship the logical/rational mind, I became more and more aware that there were other sources of essential information that I could trust.

I began to notice and gradually trust information my body continually gives to me. For example, I had just returned to the country and decided to catch up with current affairs, so I was watching one of the candidates for the United States presidency on TV. As I sat there, my solar plexus became more and more agitated and almost "painful." I said to myself, "He's lying." The awareness was so strong that I totally believed it. So I did my research and learned that my solar plexus was a very accurate indicator of when I am being lied to. My rational, conscious brain wants to believe the person (or not) and I have come to trust that my solar plexus—if I listen to it—will reliably tell me when someone is lying. I usually do not know what she/he is lying about *and* I know that there is something I cannot trust about what is being said to me. If I can trust that I am picking up a lie, it is my job to find out where and what the lie is. I can trust that somewhere there is a lie.

Needless to say, knowing when we are being lied to is important information. Our mind is not reliable; our solar plexus (or somewhere in the body) is.

Honesty

LIES WE TELL OURSELVES ABOUT THOSE UNLIKE US

Everything the same; everything distinct.

— ZEN PROVERB

One of the dishonesties we humans have convinced ourselves of is that differences are a threat. We have come to believe that sameness means safety and in service of this belief have tried to homogenize our world. In order to perpetuate this belief we have tried to force others in one way or another, some subtle and some not so subtle, to all be the same.

Colonization has attempted to destroy those who come out of another paradigm instead of learning from them. And in our dishonesty we have convinced ourselves that our way is not only the better way, it is the *only* way and we are helping them by colonizing them. In trying to perpetuate this illusion we have wrought destruction on cultures and the planet.

We can let go of the lie that differences are a threat and begin to see differences as an opportunity for growth, seeing how the lies we tell ourselves limit our possibilities.

Courage

COURAGE GROWS

Do I have the courage to speak up?
Do I have the courage to be quiet?
Do I have the courage to wait?
Do I have the courage to act?
Living fully takes courage.

As an older woman of 82, when I look back I can see the process of my developing the courage to stand up for a new paradigm coming out of the wisdom of my ancestors and their women's wisdom. Everything, absolutely everything, in my life has contributed to where I am now. The path is zig-zagged, and there is a distinct path. I can see my courage and wisdom growing. I can also see that each stand I took prepared me for the next.

I can see that my playmate and uncle who was five years older than I, was one of my early teachers in my process of becoming courageous. I never would have experimented with so many methods of getting up in that old sycamore tree to play Buck Rogers if it hadn't been for him. We did what no one thought we could do and what most told us not to do. It took courage and helped me believe in myself.

When I was in first grade, the little girl in front of me was afraid to ask to go to the bathroom and wet her pants. I helped clean it up and when the teacher took her to the bathroom, I told everyone in the class not to tease her or make her feel uncomfortable or I would beat them up. (I'm sure I learned this from my uncles—not a good solution. Yet it was courageous.)

Our courage is like a tapestry on which the incidents of our lives weave into our strength—or not.

Entitlement

THE VALUE OF ENTITLEMENT

Illusions are more difficult to ignore than reality.

Entitlement only seems to be valued by those who blindly seek it and believe they have it. Others don't seem to be so impressed by the phenomenon and, indeed, seem a bit disgusted by it. Why, then, is entitlement sought after and valued by those who believe that they possess it?

The answer is simple: Because the world is dominated right now by a system that is built on illusions, and entitlement is one of those favorite illusions. It is right up there with the illusion of control, the illusion of intimacy, the illusion of the meaning of money, and the illusion that we are not all connected and part of a larger whole and that oneness and wholeness are our reality.

If we are to participate in the process of building a new paradigm, we have to see our most treasured illusions for what they are—illusions.

Accepting Our Humanness

THE HUMAN QUEST FOR STASIS

*Life comes in clusters, clusters of solitude,
then a cluster when there is hardly time to breathe.*

— MAY SARTON

One of the limitations of the human race is that we believe in stasis and try to enforce it upon ourselves and others.

I have often told the story of how at different points in my life I have wished I could just make my world stop right there as it was. How many of us could relate to the title in that old Anthony Newley musical *Stop the World, I Want to Get Off*? I can remember times in my life when I wanted it to *stop right there*. I was happy. My children were healthy and happy. My marriage was good. The house was just the way I wanted it. I was at the peak of my work as I saw it at that time. I wanted to deny life, my humanness, the reality that all is process and just keep everything the way it was. Luckily I was only human and could not do that.

I was only human and did not have the imagination, the brain power, or the ability to dream how great it could be beyond my dreaming. As I have participated fully in the unknown process of my life, it has been so far better than anything I could have constructed.

At the moment, I am sitting on a ship getting ready to spend some time in Tahiti. See what I mean? Who would have suspected that accepting the limitations of my humanity could have resulted in such a wealth of experiences?

Respect

RESPECTING NATURE

Begin to care for nature and nature cares for you, in unsuspected ways.

— BILL NEIDJIE, ABORIGINAL AUSTRALIAN

There is nothing that puts us in our place better than nature.

Nature is so big, so powerful, so everywhere, so steady, and so present that not to respect her would be absolutely stupid. Obviously we need her so much more than she needs us.

When I was a child, my mother and I used to sit on the porch to watch those magnificent thunderstorms that Arkansas produces move across the valley. They were beautiful, fierce, and awesome. "Remember, Elizabeth Anne," she would say, "nature is so powerful, much more powerful than we are. We need to respect that power and not be arrogant in relation to it."

One day when it was really hot and muggy, we had the front and the back door open to get a breeze through the house. Mother was at her sewing machine and I was playing on the couch across the room. The lightning was crashing and banging outside.

Suddenly a ball of lightning rolled through the front door. With great command in her voice, Mother said, "Stay where you are!" as the lightning rolled through the front door and out the back. The whole incident lasted only a few seconds, and my mother's many admonitions to honor and respect the power of nature were emblazoned in my being that day.

Who am I in the face of such power?

The Abstractualization of Life

MEDITATION

*Getting out of our heads and doing
physical work helps a lot.*

At one point, I noticed what seemed to be hordes of Westerners flocking to Eastern religions and meditation.

After spending some time in India to experience and learn about ayurvedic medicine, I made some interesting observations.

I noticed that Westerners differ radically in the way they handle gurus and meditation. In general, Westerners handle both as an abstraction, whereas Eastern cultures participate.

For example, my companion there was a medical doctor. He wanted to *understand* ayurvedic medicine. For the people of India I met, ayurveda was a way of life. It was not a belief, an approach, or a method. It was a way of participation.

And when we were there, ayurveda was in a process of change. In the "old" ayurvedic, the "doctor" did all the treatments so he/she could be a part of the entire process. When I was there, they were trying to move to a more Western model of the doctor working with abstractions and using technicians rather than staying with the traditional ways. They wanted to make it acceptable, to sell it. I can see the effects of Western culture on this transition, which compromised some of the basic tenets of ayurvedic healing.

I also noticed that in India, gurus were a normal part of life, like garbage collection, and meditation was not a technique, it was part of life.

I came to believe that Westerners do not know what to do with gurus in our abstract hierarchies. We need movement and concrete processes—washing the car, vacuuming the floor, gardening—to get beyond ourselves, to ground us.

We need the earth to ground us.

Being of Good Spirit

THE ROLE OF HUMOR

Humor is emotional chaos remembered in tranquility.

— JAMES THURBER

So many of those concerned with the need for a new paradigm are now recognizing that indigenous people may have a key to a new way of living with this planet. Indigenous people have been telling our white brothers and sisters that a time will come when our knowledge will be necessary to save the planet and that time is now.

One of the "disconnects" that is so obvious between indigenous and nonindigenous people is that nonindigenous people approach this transition through their thinking (abstractions, ideas, and concepts) and indigenous people approach these changes and life in general through the process of *living*.

Inherent in the living of this new/ancient paradigm is the role of humor. Indigenous people laugh a lot. We laugh at ourselves a great deal. Often when we do something stupid, we are the first to laugh and tell the incident over and over, laughing heartily at our "mistakes"—for mistakes are an opportunity for learning. We also laugh heartily at others' mistakes and foolishness. Others' mistakes are also an opportunity for laughter and teasing.

And do we tease one another. Teasing is never mean-spirited or shaming. It is a time for group hilarity and fun. It is a great opportunity for all to let off steam and share being of good spirit.

We only tease those we already love. Teasing someone we don't know well could be harmful.

Domination Over and the Illusion of Control

OUR MINDS

The idea of strictly minding our own
business is moldy rubbish. Who could be so selfish?

— MYRTLE BARKER

We are living in a phase of colonized minds. Some have called this colonization of our minds the homogenization of the world.

There is more and more pressure to believe that one or another of the "revealed religions" developed by man (men!) is the one true religion and we have used this belief as an excuse to kill, dominate, and control. Killing off those who differ is the ultimate form of domination and control, whether we do it by disease, actively, or ideologically.

Indigenous people believe that we have different people and different ways because as human beings, no one group of us has or can have all the answers, so we need as much diversity as possible to put as many pieces of a puzzle for which we will never have all the pieces together. In being open to the wisdom of all the pieces, we will have a fuller perspective, we can become more whole, and one with the all. Diversity is not just an abstraction of a good thing; it is a reality of more pieces. Domination and control limit the number of pieces so we do not have what we need for a better grasp of the wholeness.

What if in every new situation we put ourselves in the role of an open-minded student who needs to learn?

Humor

HUMORLESS PEOPLE ARE DANGEROUS

*Beware of people who never laugh at themselves
or with others. They cannot be trusted.*

People who are too serious or serious most of the time seem to have squeezed much of the life out of themselves. That is bad enough and, unfortunately, they seem to want to squeeze the life out of others as well. Humorlessness is a kind of creeping deadness. It is like a pall that falls over everything slowly squeezing the life out.

Many years ago when Mount St. Helens erupted, I was traveling through eastern Oregon and Washington as I have many times. On this particular drive, I found myself in shock. The usual green fields of alfalfa were gray. The blacktop road was gray. The houses and barns were gray. Even the cows were gray, and there were little piles of snow-like gray along the highway where the roads had been plowed. My usual world of bristling life and color had suddenly become a monotone gray. I wept.

This is what humorlessness does to its world. It takes a world bristling with life and covers it with a gray ash, suffocating the life out.

It is difficult to get a full breath around humorless people.

Wonder and Awe

EXCELLENCE

*Expertise of any kind needs to be recognized
before we can deal with it—
the good and the bad and the indifferent.*

I have learned to respect excellence in many forms because excellence itself is awe-inspiring.

Years ago I visited a graduate program in clinical psychology. I was teaching in such a program myself, and with my lifelong habit of always collecting new data and doing "research," I asked if I could sit in on some of their classes. It was the beginning of the year and I sat in on a class that was an orientation session for new students. I chose this particular class because the teacher was very well known and had the reputation of being an excellent teacher. I was eager to know him.

Since I had worked with groups and group dynamics for many years, I very quickly picked up on what was happening in the group. One of the new students, an older man, immediately began to hijack the group. He revised the agenda, took over the group, and generally created havoc. I watched the well-known professor wilt before my eyes. I did not feel it was my place to intervene, and then, well, I just could not help myself—really, I could not. This fellow was one of the best group saboteurs I had seen. The group was in chaos and he was definitely in charge. The professor was bewildered.

I started laughing and clapping. "Bravo!" I said. "I love excellence wherever I see it. You're good! And if you and the others in the group want an orientation to this place, you better back off."

Order was restored.

Sometimes, when we refuse to feel awe and wonder with the awful, we can never be able to make the move to fix it.

The Present Can Only Be Our Reality
if We Own Our Past and Our Future

WE CANNOT ESCAPE THE
PAST OF OUR SPECIES

Being responsible for does not mean being blamed for.

When we assume that we are all connected and all parts of a process of a living, pulsating whole, we begin to experience the enfolding of the all. The words of this phenomenon are a bit confusing. The experience is as real as the table before me. This said, it is also our responsibility to take responsibility for the actions of our ancestors and heal them and the consequences of their actions.

This process of healing does not mean that we are to blame for all things and everything they did. It does mean that once aware, we have the amazing opportunity to own our/their reality and take steps to heal; in so doing, we can heal the future for ourselves, our ancestors, our nations, the human race, and the planet. This opportunity, when we experience the reality of it, is not overwhelming—it is exciting and hopeful. It implies a whole new order of functioning and possibilities for the human race and all creation.

To live a new paradigm, we need not to limit our possibilities before we start.

Walking in Beauty

Mr. Beck

Best friends come in all shapes, sizes, and ages.

When I was five years old, our family decided to leave our home and my father's work to go gold mining in California. It was a bold move to leave a job in 1939!

We would move to the Klamath River in Northern California (we had friends there), live in a tent with and among the native people there. One of the old-timers, Mr. Beck, had first come to the Klamath at age 14 and driven the first supply wagon over the mountain to bring supplies to the miners. He married a Karuk Indian woman and never left. He was 95 when my five-year-old person first met him. He was to become my best friend during our stay on the Klamath.

Even though he was a tough old geezer, Mr. Beck walked in beauty. He loved the land—his land. He loved the people of the Klamath—all the people. He loved the life he lived on the Klamath. And he loved me. And I loved him.

Our days spent together were filled with teachings, learnings, stories, and most of all, silences. How I cherished those silences we had together.

People who walk in beauty are often silent for long periods of time, yet never noncommunicative.

Taking Time

JUST BEING QUIET

*I am suddenly filled with that sense of peace
and meaning which is, I suppose, what the pious have in mind
when they talk about the practice of the presence of God.*

— VALERIE TAYLOR

Quiet alone time. Thank goodness it is not an issue to be dealt with that often. Everywhere we go there is "background" music. TVs are blaring, people are talking, talking, talking, our minds are making lists of things to do, people to call, bills to pay, commitments we have made that need to be kept.

People won't leave us alone even when we are in the bathroom.

When *will* these kids go back to school?

Perhaps it is time we admit to ourselves that no one is going to arrange for our quiet time alone except ourselves. We can have a million excuses and our quiet time alone is up to us. The reason our families think that they have the right to interrupt us is quite likely because we have given them the message that they can. How difficult it is for some people to teach themselves that just because the phone is ringing does not mean it *has* to be answered.

Phone messages and e-mails can wait. How important do we think we are, anyway?!

A Belief in Healing

BELIEVING THAT HEALING IS POSSIBLE

All I have to do is my part—
nothing more, nothing less.

To live the process of a paradigm shift, we have to believe that healing is possible.

When I was a little girl accompanying my great-grandmother on her "healing rounds," I often felt overwhelmed with the suffering that some individuals and families were experiencing.

"Grandma," I would say. "It is so hopeless. Why do they try?"

"Shush!" she would reply. "Who is to say what is hopeless? We don't know everything, now do we?"

She would go on, "There are forces operating in this world that are much bigger than anything we can know or understand. You can see them everywhere if you are willing to see." Grandma always seemed to know more than anyone else who talked to me.

"You see, Elizabeth Anne, we each have a part to do, a role to contribute, and all we have to do is that—no more, no less. If we each do our part, something will happen. We don't always know what. We don't always know how. We just do our part."

When she said this, I could begin to imagine that something beyond our understanding *could* happen.

Knowing and Living in Several Realities

WOMEN'S ADVANTAGE

When one has to live in several realities,
it is easier to believe that there is more than one.

In my book *Women's Reality*, I wrote about several systems in which we live. I described the dominant system in which we live in Western culture as the White Male System (WMS). I called it that because the power and influence in that system were held by white males and it was designed by white males (with the rest of us passively supporting that system).

Then I described what I called a Reactive Female System, which, again, had been built and defined by the WMS and was what the WMS needed it to be to support its functions and beliefs. I called it RFS because it was not a natural system for women. It was one that had been designed by the WMS to support its assumptions and goals and was "unnatural" to women. Yet women had passively accepted the RFS as a way to operate in the world because they believed it was the only way to survive.

Then I described another system or reality. This reality was emerging with the feminist voice of women as we sought to define ourselves and our reality. I called this reality the Emerging Female System (EFS).

I share all this because in the process of seeing and recognizing other realities, I became progressively open to see and accept different realities. I came to know that we can participate in new realities that are coming into being.

Being of Service

PITFALLS

All the beautiful sentiments in the world
weigh less than a single lovely action.

— JAMES RUSSELL LOWELL

Being of service is not a new concept and in the current paradigm it has become skewed in many ways.

For example, giving money to worthy causes and issues we believe in is a very, very good thing to do. And, when we demand a tax credit for doing it, well, that sort of taints the "being of service" aspect, doesn't it? Or when we want money (tax breaks), or recognition, or praise, or adulation for being of service, well, it just does not seem anywhere in the same ballpark as really being of service. Or when a nation gives money to another nation or its people, money that nation needs in order to have clean water and more importantly be indebted to the first nation, well, this type of "giving" is not what is meant by "being of service" in the new/old paradigm, now is it?

To begin to shift into living a new paradigm, we need to be willing to challenge all these positive gestures that have been incorporated into the current destructive paradigm because they may feed our illusions. We need to find ways to redefine, clarify, and act out of a core of being of service that our cells and our DNA remember. We have the opportunity to quit fooling ourselves with the distortion of what once was or could be "good."

Start small.

Graciousness

RESPECT

Don't steal, don't lie, don't be lazy. Let's just respect each other.

— PERUVIAN WOMAN SPEAKER

For graciousness to be genuine, it must emanate from a deep pool of true respect for all creation. We cannot tap into our wellspring of true graciousness unless we have a deep honoring and respect for everything. Who are we to say that one aspect of creation is better than another? Who are we to say that one race of people is better than another? We may like one group better than another. We may know one group better than another. We may feel more comfortable with one group than with another. But to truly believe that one group is *better* than another is pure folly and stifles any hope of the flow of graciousness and true respect. Those who live out of partial respect for others are incapable of wholeness in themselves and certainly cannot create fullness and wholeness around them.

Graciousness flows from the respect of the whole. Carefully chosen, meted-out graciousness is a manipulation, not a flow, and feels exactly like what it is—a con.

Moving Out of Our Comfort Zones

Trusting in "I Don't Know"

What we anticipate seldom occurs;
what we least expected generally happens.

— Benjamin Disraeli

Moving out of our comfort zones affects every area of our lives because this paradigm we have built as humans in Western culture permeates every area of our lives.

One of the dualisms our minds have set up is the dualism of chaos and control. As a Western culture we have believed that chaos or control are our only options and we have opted for the illusion of control as the best option. Putting our faith in the illusion of control has not proven to be very healing or helpful.

And, when our minds tell us that dualisms are reality and the only option we have to be safe is to control everything—ourselves, others, and the universe—our minds do not see or feel other options. We are struck between (dualisms) something that isn't working and something we fear more than what we have in the present, which we believe will be chaos.

There is no comfort zone! Except the beauty of "I don't know!"

Having no comfort zone that is working can be the absolute most positive and creative point in our existence because it can force us to be open to possibilities that are as yet unknown to us.

Wanting stasis in a process universe has not proven very effective up to this point in our evolution as a species.

Letting Go of What We Think We Know

JUDGMENTALISM IS TOXIC

*Life has taught me that it is not for our faults that
we are disliked and even hated, but for our qualities.*

— BERNARD BERENSON

We have looked at how toxic judgmentalism is to the one doing the judging; now let's take a quick look at the poisonous effect it has on those being judged.

When one is judged, in any way, that judgment results in that person feeling unappreciated, not valued, worthless, and meaningless. Often this dynamic results in resentment, anger, hostility, and a wish for revenge. When one is the recipient of relentless judgmentalism, maintaining a modicum of self-esteem is difficult, if not impossible. Feelings of worthlessness creep in which also, at a very deep level, result in anger and depression.

When one is an ongoing recipient of judgmentalism, it is difficult to have hope for the future or even to envision a future. Indeed, the most frequent unconscious reaction to judgmentalism is an instinct to retaliate and destroy those who judge.

It is important to note here that all of the above is true for those who are judged, including when we judge ourselves. Judging ourselves is equally as toxic to ourselves as judging others is.

Refusing to accept ourselves and others as we/they are is toxic to all involved.

In living a new paradigm, judgmentalism needs to become an idea and a way of being that can no longer be tolerable. The antidote is acceptance and humility.

Accepting That Choices and Behaviors Have Consequences

THE LEGAL SYSTEM

*If corporations are people, they should be restrained
by the same laws as people, including tax laws.*

In our present legal system, much of the focus—especially of corporate law—is to prevent individuals and corporations from taking responsibility for their choices and behaviors.

Whether it is the pollution of the planet, a rape, or an automobile accident, the accepted role to the defense team—through whatever means possible—is to see that people, institutions, and corporations do not have to take responsibility for their choices and their behaviors. We are sent a loud, clear message that it is good to "win" and not take responsibility for what we do. Children, when they break another child's toy, get messages that it is okay to let it go or to let some adult take care of it. Lawyers who defend corporations from class action suits glean large earnings, while those who were wronged have to deal with the consequences. What has happened in society that convinces us that victimizing the victim is acceptable if they can "legally" get away with what they have done?

Just because something is legal does not mean that it is all right or good for us. At what cost are legal battles "won"?

Humility

OUT OF RELIEF

*Though a tree grow ever so high, the
falling leaves return to the ground.*

— MALAY PROVERB

Have you ever noticed that people who have let humility
into their life have a sense of calmness about them? Out of the
relief of knowing that we really cannot manipulate and control
anything, this sense of calmness emerges. There is no pressure,
no need to make anyone or anything unfold in an order pre-
determined by ourselves. The anxiety and frustration of trying
to *make* anything happen has been replaced by a trust of the
unfolding process. This trust results in an openness to options
as yet unthought and unheard. We can again become explorers.

Our agendas no longer rule our lives and we have room for
creativity and the unknown. The unknown no longer is to be
feared. It can be welcomed and an expectant openness begins to
emerge.

As humility starts to emerge, a soul-felt relief of calmness
and creativity is possible.

Knowing and Being Known

EXPLORING OUR BLIND SELF

Don't try to be such a perfect girl, darling.
Do the best you can without too much anxiety or strain.

— JESSIE BERNARD

How much we hate the thought that there is a part of us that is hanging right out there in public that others see and we don't! How frightening it is to discover this reality when we were so sure that we were doing such a good job of presenting to the world just what we wanted them to see and nothing else!

Well, we might as well get used to the fact that we have not been able to carry on the great masquerade that we thought we had and others see something in us we cannot and have not seen in ourselves.

We need others!

We come to a place where we need others to help us see ourselves. And because of the myths and beliefs in the dominant paradigm which we have bought about the unknown self, we will have to make some adjustments in our belief systems to realize that even in our self-journey, we need others and must depend upon other people. I say other *people* here because in the dominant culture the setup is that the only acceptable source of this information is a spouse, close friend, or guru. *And*, these three sources are not enough.

This kind of information is best gleaned in a group of others who are also seeking to heal, grow, and learn. We need to remember that in order to heal, grow, and learn as human beings, we need others.

Everything Is Spiritual/Sacred

PROCESSES

*May our Mayness become all-embracing. May we see
in one another the All that was once All-One become One.*

— LAURA RIDING

All the processes that swirl around us all the time, even those unrecognized and unseen, are sacred in nature.

It is as if we are standing in the middle of a swirling, rushing stream with breezes all around us and all are trying to remind us that we are part of a world that is spiritual and breathes the sacred into us whether we know it or not.

So, not only are all the objects that surround us sacred in their very nature and are to be treated as if they are, so are all the processes that present themselves to us as we pass through life. No matter how good or bad or indifferent a process that presents itself to us is, there is always something in that process for us to learn and that will add to our awareness and wisdom.

I have often said to people that at some level it does not matter what has happened to us in this life. Whatever has happened to us is our reality. We can choose to be victims of that reality *and* that position does not get us very far. The real issue is not what has happened to us or what we have had to deal with. The real issue is what we have learned from whatever an experience was, and how we can heal, learn, and grow from it.

It is up to us if we will let ourselves remember that healing, learning, and growing are the sacred parts of everything that has happened to us.

Wholeness

THE ADVANTAGES OF
OPERATING OUT OF WHOLENESS

*Spiritual energy brings compassion into the real world. With compassion,
we see benevolently our own human condition and the condition of our
fellow beings. We drop prejudice. We withhold judgment.*

— CHRISTINA BALDWIN

One of the major side effects of acting out of our awareness
of wholeness is that compassion accompanies the process.

Most of us believe that compassion is a good thing. Developing a true compassion *is* a good thing. Yet, like humility, compassion is not something we can think ourselves into. We cannot decide that compassion is a good thing to have and being compassionate makes us a good person and just do it. This kind of compassion does not ring any truer than false humility.

Compassion, for it to be true compassion, is a by-product of knowing about, believing in, and connecting with our absolute experience that we are connected with everything and everything is connected with us. We are all part of a whole that is beyond our understanding and yet known by us all.

Some would say that we come from the wholeness and it is to the wholeness we return.

To act out of wholeness is the practice of being who we are and where we come from.

Joy

DISCOVERING SOMETHING NEW ABOUT OURSELVES OR ANOTHER

When one's heart is glad, he gives away gifts. It [the potlatch] was given to us by our Creator to be our way of doing things, we who are Indians. The potlatch was given to us to be our way of expressing joy.

— AGNES ALFRED

For those of us who love the experience of healing, growing, and learning, there is such joy in discovering something new about ourselves.

When we are on the trail of some new awareness that has been triggered by something in our present lives, that trail can be like a treasure hunt into ourselves. And when we discover something new about ourselves, regardless of whether it is painful or difficult or happy, the excitement of just getting some new awareness that makes other pieces of our lives fall into place can be beyond belief in the joy of awareness it creates in us.

Just to learn something that has been affecting our lives and bringing it out into the open can be so wonderful for us.

As I work with people throughout the world, I have found such joy and excitement when they uncover a hidden gem about themselves. Even when this gem is difficult, I can rejoice with them as they shake off the shackles and constrictions of their past that are keeping them from being who they can be.

The joy of the revelations of self-awareness is the joy of freedom.

Emotional Brilliance

BEWARE OF YOUR THINKING

Emotional brilliance is inherent in us all.

People who are emotionally brilliant may not be filled with information.

In fact, for many, information and technological expertise may be barriers to accessing emotional brilliance.

Or, perhaps, those who choose to excel in information and technology may have greater difficulty accessing their native emotional brilliance, may be afraid of it, may have had it suppressed by their environments, or may not have been encouraged to develop it.

We all have the capacity to be emotionally brilliant and some may have to work harder and be open to it.

Not everyone takes to calculus immediately and most can learn it if they do not think too much.

Thinking too much can be a real problem in living a new paradigm.

All Is in Process

THE HUMAN RACE IS IN A PROCESS OF EVOLVING

We are not alone in this together.

As we look back over our known history as a human race, we see a species bumbling and lurching toward—who knows what? We have, in much of our time on this planet, been focused on the material plane. We have become quite expert in exploiting the material assets of our planet. And if we stand back and assess our "progress" with an open mind, we might accept that our spiritual, emotional, and psychological development as a species has not gone so well.

As an Australian elder once said to me, "You white people, centuries ago made the mistake of focusing on science and technology and they will destroy the planet. We hope that you realize it before it is too late. It's not that there is anything wrong with science and technology, it is just that you had not matured enough spiritually to develop a science and technology that will not be destructive to the planet and all creation."

Clearly the development of the science and technology we now have is not *the* science and *the* technology. What we think of as science and technology may have been the best we were capable of in our process of becoming more fully who we can be as humans. *And* we have yet to see what we can do and be with sciences and technologies that evolve out of the processes of the creative wholeness.

A process science and a process mathematics will probably look quite different from what we now have based on our illusion of stasis and control.

Participation

PARTICIPATING OURSELVES INTO A NEW PARADIGM

What can possibly exist that I can't imagine?

— HUMANS

We cannot think ourselves into a new paradigm.

Many have tried to do just that and are still trying, and the truth is that a new paradigm will only emerge if we *participate* ourselves into it.

In an addiction-driven culture, the goal is to shut off feelings, awarenesses, and intuitions and to control, control, control. If we are participating fully in our lives, the lives of those around us, and the process of the universe, we have to be willing to let go of the illusion of control. Our participation alters the process and the outcome of every situation in ways that we can never predetermine. This alteration can take an infinite number of directions including some that we could never have imagined in a million years.

As we participate, the situation is altered, the outcomes are altered, and we are altered. At some very deep level these alterations are necessary for us to grow into being and for our entire species to grow into being.

We need to remember that it is probable that being what we can be has possibilities we have never imagined.

Thinking

THE TYRANNY OF THINKING

*When we try to control our controlling,
we are in deep trouble.*

I recently read in a book that our thinking (mind) is the one thing over which we have complete control. My experience in working with people is that the exact opposite is true.

I know that some people who come out of a paradigm of control and do meditation in order, in their minds, to have some relief from the tyranny of their own thinking. And they see this *relief* as control.

I have a different perspective. From my experience in Zen Buddhism, the purpose of meditation is not to control our minds, the purpose is not to be distracted by them. The practice is about nonattachment to the thoughts as they come. And come they will. In the practice of not attaching to our thoughts when they come, we have the potential to empty our minds and be available from the deeper planes within ourselves which the chatter of the mind drowns out. We also have the inestimable possibility to tap into information that is available to us from other planes of validity.

It is not that we *control* our minds. It is that we are not as distracted by the white noise they continually produce. When having complete control of our minds is our goal, we are probably on the wrong track.

Beliefs and Assumptions

THE INTERDEPENDENCY OF OUR "ISMS" AND OUR BELIEFS AND ASSUMPTIONS

For some, questioning their beliefs
and their "isms" is beyond possibility.
Some in the new generations see it differently.

So many of our -isms that are divisive to any wholeness that we might try to achieve in living a new paradigm come out of our conscious and unconscious beliefs and assumptions.

Sexism comes out of a belief that women are not as good as or as important as men. There is a belief that men's work is more important and valuable than women's work and that the decisions about how the world is to be run must be left in the hands of men.

Racism comes out of a belief that some people of God's creation are "better than," "smarter than," "more important than," and therefore should have power and control over those who are "less than." The assumption is that not only are those who are more than more intelligent, they have superior ideas about how the world should function and the role of those who are less than is to carry out the wishes of those who are more than.

Some, if not all, of the people who are stuck in these -isms believe that their superiority is not only God given, it is also reasonable and the way the world is.

In this system of -isms, it is not only *what* the superior beings think that is important, they believe that it is also their *way* of thinking that is the most important. They believe that no other way legitimately exists.

For us to live a new paradigm, we have to remember to step back from these beliefs and refuse to participate in a world of isms.

Feelings and Emotions

THE RICHNESS OF FEELINGS AND EMOTIONS

For years I have endeavored to calm an impetuous tide—laboring to make my feelings take an orderly course. It was striving against the stream.

— MARY WOLLSTONECRAFT

People who are devoid of feelings and emotions or who try to hold them in check all the time are not very interesting. Indeed, they are not very full people. They are not very happy people.

People who are not in touch with or dealing with their feelings are also people who are not very trustworthy because the more they suppress and repress their feelings the more of their "junk" is being dumped into their unconscious and will come out in unpredictable and even destructive ways. Suppressed and repressed feelings are there for a reason and need to be acknowledged and worked with.

Perhaps this is one of the reasons that people are so afraid of their feelings and emotions. The unconscious *will* find a way to get noticed.

Our feelings, ultimately, are our friends.

Honesty

RELATING TO OTHERS

We need relationships.

Because of the personal and cultural lies we have told ourselves, we are losing the ability to form deep and meaningful relationships.

Lies, by their very essence, are an escape from intimacy and result in a lack of intimacy with ourselves and others. When we have no intimacy with ourselves, it is impossible to have intimacy with others.

How can we possibly have a relationship with the unseen and the unknown when our science has taught us to lie about their existence and we have agreed to do so?

To relate we have to quit lying to ourselves about ourselves and others.

We can approach everyone as equals. We may have different cultures, different educations, and different amounts of money, and as human beings we are equal.

We can approach everyone as part of the family and the family of creation—at least until they prove that they are not ready to be "family."

We can assume that because of who they are and their life experiences they know things we don't.

We can approach everyone as being part of creation and deserving respect.

We can assume that we, too, know some things and don't have to prove our worth or impress.

We can assume that our job is to learn what others have to teach us.

It's just that simple.

Courage

THE COURAGE TO CHANGE

How exciting is the potential that we have the possibility to help humankind to move to a better way of being in and with this planet! Participation builds courage.

Each situation in our lives offers an opportunity to heal, grow, and change. We are not static. Our lives are not static. And we will only change when we are ready. We usually take little steps, and as we get stronger, if we do, the steps become bigger and bigger. Our personal courage to change is the foundation of what we can do in the world. As personal changes free us from the baggage of putting our energies into holding down and denying old hurts, they also are building processes that allow us to take on larger and larger issues. If we are fully living the process of our life, it presents us with more and more opportunities that we probably would not have seen before.

For example, for years I have been advocating for the need for a *paradigm shift*. Then, at some point, I realized that that idea itself was old, dualistic, static thinking. I needed to see that paradigms themselves—in spite of the dualistic thinking of the scientists who developed the concept—are not a shift from this to that. They are an ongoing, unknown process. A shift would be easy; participating in a process that may never end and has no definition—now that takes courage.

Do we have the courage to participate fully when we don't know where we are going or what it looks like?

Entitlement

RESIGNING FROM THE WHOLE

*Our illusion of entitlement actively removes
us from our place in the wholeness of the all.*

Even though we do not recognize it, this removal results in a desperate feeling of alienation and loneliness. It produces a sadness and depression that can't be "fixed" by any pills, therapy, drugs, alcohol, work, or accumulation of those things to which we think we are entitled. We can try to fill this endlessly craving cavity with any number of things and nothing works because the problem is never really addressed.

No one has brought this feeling of loneliness on us. We have brought it on ourselves in the process of removing ourselves from our place in the equality of the whole. In this respect, humans seem to be the dumbest creatures on the planet because we are "entitling" ourselves out of the whole.

Participating in the wholeness of all creation feeds us much more than trying to be above it.

Accepting Our Humanness

NONACCEPTANCE—A PARTICULARLY HUMAN TRAIT

*What do you mean you don't accept where
you are? How will you ever get anywhere else?*

As I study and learn from all of creation, I have come to wonder if the nonacceptance of our being human is a particular human trait. Clearly I do not know the answer to this question, and I do see that all the nature around me teaches me again and again to accept life on life's terms. To me, this has not come to mean to capitulate, to give in passively, and not take part in life. This concept has come to mean to participate fully in my life and not believe that I can control the direction it will take or that I somehow know better what path it will take or should take. Part of my responsibility as a human is to participate as fully as I can and trust what is next.

The gift of our humanness is not to try to make ourselves and our world static by feeding our illusion that we know best. So many people are trying to do this with what they call the new paradigm. They believe that they know what it should look like and how to get there.

That's the old paradigm in new clothes.

To be human means that we fool ourselves a lot. Knowing this truth really helps.

Respect

RESPECT HAS MANY ELEMENTS

Many religions have been brought to this land.
And the way my religion is, they teach me, and they taught me,
and told me to respect all religions. When someone else believes
what his Creator is, we can stand and pray together.

— HORACE AXTELL, NEZ PERCE ELDER

Living with respect is not linear or simple. There are many nuances to respect and many levels of respect.

Respect is being realistic and filled with awe at the same time. Respect is the practice of a subtle and quiet honoring based upon the reality of our existence. Respect is not a slavish worshipping. To be truly respectful one has to see and honor one's place in the natural order of the universe while participating fully.

There is no one up/one down in respect. There is the recognition of a basic equality in having our place in the workings of the universe while accepting that all have their place and have different gifts and strengths. Respect means that everyone and everything has something valuable to teach us if we are smart enough to be open enough to learn from anyone, and everyone and everything. Nothing is too big to teach us something and nothing is too small to teach us.

None of us is too important or too big or too busy to contribute something to the whole. This is why we are here. It's that simple.

Who am I to choose my teachers when the universe has presented me with such great ones?

The Abstractualization of Life

EDUCATION

*We can never learn what we are not ready to learn
and when we are ready to learn, no one can stop us.*

We are depending more and more on an education that is becoming increasingly distanced from our real life while refusing to admit the reality of the unknown and unseen. For indigenous people, education is not divorced from life nor is it wholly dependent on the abstract. In fact, the abstract is intimately tied to the everyday.

For example, everything, every day, in every way is an opportunity for learning. Learning is not isolated from living and is ongoing (or before, as in the case of the Australian Aboriginals) birth to death. Learning is not isolated and ascribed to a classroom or a degree. Everything is a possibility for learning. Mechanics are not abstracted into a course or a particular object. Each object is to be studied in and of itself, and as we do that we begin to experience and participate in the principle. The principle makes sense. The principle is not taught abstractly first as a disembodied "fact." It is discovered through participation with it.

Principles discovered through participation are never abstract and never leave us.

How we learn is much more important than *what* we learn. If we get the *how* we can learn in any situation. We need to be reminded about the value of the many ways of learning.

Being of Good Spirit

MORE ON TEASING

Those who don't know teasing are handicapped.

I have spoken previously about the role of teasing and the importance it plays in indigenous cultures, where it is always good-spirited and has loving energy attached. This reality is often difficult for people in the dominant culture to understand because their experience has been so different. Either there was absolutely no teasing in their cultures and they are teasing "virgins," or teasing was used to bully and shame and was a form of violence. It's also possible that teasing was a way of asserting domination or control, which has no place in living a new paradigm.

From the perspective of indigenous people, anyone who wants to live a different paradigm will have to come to terms with teasing.

Usually, indigenous people start slowly and carefully with the teaching of teasing because in the feeling of being good-spirited, we know that it will take time to learn to be teased and to be a good teaser. Yet we also know that learning to deal with teasing and humor is an integral part of remembering to live another way.

The most important things can only be learned in the process of living them.

Domination Over and the Illusion of Control

CHANGE

The only thing we can change is ourselves.

— A.A. SLOGAN

What a powerful concept this is.

Another aspect of this impressive fact is probably one of the most radical practices in the world today, which is a corollary of changing ourselves. That idea, process, way of being, as we said earlier, is staying on our own side of the street.

The time we spend focusing on others is essentially wasted where change is concerned. It is good to see and name the problem; naming is a powerful and necessary tool. Blaming is not.

After we have named the problem we are facing, the next step is fearlessly and honestly to look at our side of the street. It is so tempting to look at the other's side of the street and point a finger. (Isn't the old saying that if we point one finger at someone, the other three are pointing back at us?)

When we stay on our side of the street, we do not ignore what the other has done or how bad it is. We just do not focus on it because that is a waste of time.

We see how we are contributing to the problem and we do our work and quit supporting the problem with our time and energy (including blaming).

This change in process is what we are attempting to do in this book. What is my part in each issue and what do I need to change in me and the way I am doing life?

Humor

CHANGING A MOOD

Humor is an affirmation of dignity.
— ROMAIN GARY

I have been a group facilitator for most of my life. I was trained as a group facilitator back in the early 1950s and since then have worked as a group facilitator in one way or another— therapy groups, consciousness-raising groups, organizational consulting, church groups and classes. Working with groups large and small has been an integral part of my life and I continue to be fascinated with the myriad of ways groups function and what can happen in groups that could never happen in work with individuals. More than 35 years ago, I started working only with groups for healing and learning. They are just so much more powerful and the amount of experience, knowledge, resources, alertness, and wisdom is multiplied a hundred times more than what can be possible with one person. (That is, of course, if one is open to admit wisdom and experience other than one's own!)

What I have noticed over the years is that humor can change the mood and direction of a group naturally. I tend to believe that techniques used as "techniques" are disruptive and destructive to the spirit of the group. And when a group is getting tired, for example, if something funny is said, a person teased, or a quip blurted out, the whole mood of the group changes and it is again open for more learning.

Spontaneous humor is a great game-changer.

Wonder and Awe

THE CREATIVITY OF THE UNKNOWN

*I share Einstein's affirmation that anyone who is not lost in
rapturous awe at the power and glory of the mind behind the
universe "is as good as a burnt-out candle."*

— MADELEINE L'ENGLE

With our ingenious minds we have the ability to learn a great
deal about our world. In Western science we have been very good
at focusing on and understanding the workings of the material
plane. We have a firm grasp of the material/mechanical and we
have used this knowledge to "make our lives easier" and create
an unworkable paradigm. We have done well for ourselves on the
material plane—perhaps.

And on the spiritual plane we are a bit constipated.

We have so focused our minds and our explorations on what
we can know, measure, and control with our mechanistic minds
and science that we have lost the wonder of the belief in what we
cannot know with our minds and science.

We have dismissed huge areas of wonder and awe from
our reality because we do not have the tools, techniques, or
approaches to predict, measure, and control with the tools now
at our disposal. Morris Berman called it *The Disenchantment of the
World* in his book of the same title.

Wonder and awe—the feelings of, the experiences of, the
wonder of—cannot be measured, controlled, or predicted.

We need daily reminders that wonder and awe are necessary
components of the human experience.

The Present Can Only Be Our Reality
if We Own Our Past and Our Future

HOW DO WE OWN OUR FUTURE?

*Look behind you. See your sons and your daughters. They are your
future. Look farther and see your sons' and daughters' children and their
children's children even unto the seventh generation. That's the way we
were taught. Think about it—you yourself are a seventh generation.*

— LEON SHENANDOAH, ONONDAGA ELDER

How do we own our future? This is a good question not
answerable with today's common paradigm, and yet we are infi-
nitely able to respond to, with, and beyond our being.

We often hear native people say that we have to think in
terms of the next seven generations. Western cultures have
latched onto that statement and, from my experience, like it a lot
and at the same time, from my experience, have a very limited
concept of what it really means in a process universe.

Yes, when I do not recycle I am injuring the next seven generations. And this way of being in the world is much more than
that because time is not linear.

Yes, our polluting our planet is destroying it for generations to
come. That is the simplest linear understanding of what is really
meant, which is that we must live in such a way as to be concerned
and responsible to the next seven (and more) generations.

In order for us to own our future so that we are living it in
the future, we need to see that the next seven generations are
now and we are affecting them now and have already done so.

We need to keep time linear, as Einstein said, "so that everything doesn't happen at once." And we need to be aware that in
spite of our linear minds, it already is.

Walking in Beauty

THE QUIETNESS OF WALKING IN BEAUTY

May the great mystery make sunrise in your heart.

— SIOUX BLESSING

In my experience, people who walk in beauty are silent a lot.

Perhaps their main form of communication is not concepts, words, and abstractions. Perhaps they are the original conservationists and they do not want to squander words when they don't need to. It's not that they are not saying something when they are not speaking. They are. They are communicating volumes.

Their sacred information is often not the kind of information that has to go through our five senses. Indeed, those "senses," especially when they have to go through the human brain, may distort the essence of the messages that are emanating from those who walk in beauty. People who walk in beauty are communicating something much more complex than information that can be registered by our sense organs and computed by our brains.

Can living in beauty be measured, calculated, or predicted and controlled?

I don't think so.

Taking Time

THE RELIEF OF ALONE TIME

*And when is there time to remember,
to sift, to weigh, to estimate, to total?*

— TILLIE OLSEN

What a great relief it is when we finally entertain the idea that not only is it all right to take alone time, it is necessary for our health and well-being and also for that of those around us.

Then, when we actually expand the idea of taking alone time and realize that there is absolutely no way we can become who we can and need to become without it, the need for alone time becomes painfully obvious. There is no way we can take our spiritual journey without quiet alone time. With it, our lives begin to fall into place.

How fortunate are those who have this realization before all those that around them die off because they too can benefit from our taking that time alone.

All of us are here to grow spiritually. We cannot possibly grow spiritually unless we have alone time. We owe it to others to take alone time.

Our time alone may well be the most important contribution we have to make to the culture and the future. It definitely is essential to participate in evolving a more humane paradigm.

A Belief in Healing

CIRCLES OF REALITY

*How wondrous it is that there is always
another circle of reality—just beyond my reach!*

Every time I began to focus on one circle of reality as a child, Grandma would very gently push me just beyond my limits to a new circle of reality.

Maybe "push me" is too strong. I never felt pushed. It was more like a door was being cracked and I could choose to peek through it if I felt up to it. Sometimes I did and sometimes I didn't.

In the process, the important issue was not what was behind the door. The important issue was the process of knowing that there was always another level just beyond my reach and if I just kept growing and doing my work, I could probably see it—and then there would be another.

A belief in healing works that way. It is not that we can heal everything at once or that we even know what needs to be healed.

Yet we can believe from experience that there is always more healing possible than we could ever have imagined. Our imaginations are just not that thorough or that big.

Knowing and Living in Several Realities

Moving in Other Realities

The problems I worry about don't exist. There are some problems that I hadn't thought of. It's clear to me now that I was living in a false reality when I was worrying.

— Peter Sidley

As I mentioned earlier, I grew up in several realities, and my work in the women's movement certainly facilitated my recognition of and comfort with "other" realities.

I also recognize and am very grateful for my experience in the civil rights movement in the 1960s and how it prepared me for the women's movement.

I now see that I went into the civil rights movement as a Cherokee. We Cherokee are very strong on fairness and equality. We share a general recognition that all creation is to be honored and valued equally and this not only includes humans, it includes all creation.

For a Cherokee, it would be unthinkable that I, as a human being, am more important than a tree, a coral reef, or a polar bear. In my Cherokee reality, we are all different and we are all equally important. So in my reality, not to recognize the basic truth of all equality would be like spitting in the face of the Creator.

This means, where inequality appears, step up and take responsibility.

No good Cherokee—or human being—would spit in the face of the Creator.

Being of Service

SIMPLICITY

*I'm just glad that now the sun does rise and the days
are warm, so that I can listen to the birds singing happily,
and the animals munching away at their food.*

— DAVID GULPILIL, ABORIGINAL AUSTRALIAN
ACTOR AND WRITER

Being of service was not even named by the native people of this planet.

Being of service was not thought out or thought about.

Being of service was a way of being that made sense. This way of being did not have to be taught in institutions because it was experienced in every facet of one's being and acted upon in every interaction.

Being of service was not extraordinary. It was so ordinary that entire societies believed that it was a normal way of being for the human organism until these people encountered other people who had not learned and did not practice this way of being with one another and the world.

In the early writings about the indigenous peoples' reaction when they first encountered the "newcomers," one can hear the shock in the words when they discovered that this way of behaving was not core in the newcomer's being.

The response was often, "We need to pray for them." They did—and still are.

Being of service is a way of *being*, not a way of *doing*.

Graciousness

GRACIOUSNESS DENIES HIERARCHY

*Graciousness, true graciousness, is an
unconscious, active denial of hierarchy.*

A belief in hierarchy breeds judgmentalism and separation. If we truly believe that the human species is better and more important than the other aspects of creation, if we truly believe that some people are better than others, if we truly believe that we are more important and contribute more than the tree standing in our front yard, we are in big trouble. This kind of belief in hierarchy breeds contempt, smothers humility and the natural flow of graciousness.

Graciousness cannot take root in contempt and hierarchy requires contempt of anything we perceive as being beneath us—or above us.

A world built on the illusion of hierarchy is a world built out of the false world of human-made and developed thinking, which will tumble with the slightest breeze of truth.

Hierarchy is a construct, not a reality. Hierarchy cannot breed the humility that will result in true graciousness. Down deep we know this reality. We, as a species, have moved so far away from what we know deep inside that we need to be reminded of what is there.

Moving out of Our Comfort Zones

WANTING LEADERSHIP

We need to arrive at new ways of leadership.

As a species, one of our comfort zones has been to choose leaders, imbue them with the power we feel that we don't have . . . and then be disappointed. And, then, we look for new leaders.

What if those of us who realize that the paradigm we have created is just not working give up the search for the new "perfect" leader? What if we recognize that there are no perfect leaders and anyone who would want the job is too arrogant and unrealistic to get the job done anyway?

What if we came to realize that in giving our personal power away, we have not become more powerful through a leader, we have become less powerful individually and collectively?

What if our comfort in not taking responsibility is a major piece of the problem itself? What if our willingness not to take responsibility as individuals has not only weakened us, it has weakened the human race?

What if our power is in participation and not in giving our power away or holding onto it.

The current Western paradigm has not proved to have very healthy ideas about leadership.

Letting Go of What We Think We Know

A PROCESS OF CONTINUAL EMPTYING

*Was this what Jesus meant when he said
we should become like children?*

If one truly *lives* this life, is open, and is eager to learn, one of the realities that begins to emerge is the difference between what we think or thought we knew, how little we really know, and how much is unknowable yet felt.

In order to "empty our cup" as the old Zen master recommended, we have to broaden our understanding of knowings, beliefs, and facts.

In cultures dominated by Western mechanistic science, this domination has resulted in a cultural belief that the only true, real knowings that are possible are those that can be empirically proven. Literally nothing else is "true." This belief has, for some, fallen into the same category as religious belief, even though many of the proponents of empirical science would be upset to see this in print.

This belief in the complete trust in empiricism is just that, a belief.

Beliefs are necessary and important to all human beings. At many points in our lives they sustain us and give us pegs on which we "believe" we can hang our lives and try to stop that which is a process.

If each of us wants to have the opportunity to grow into our full potential and not just think about *living* a new paradigm, an ongoing process of challenging and testing our beliefs is a necessary component of being open enough to see another way and the value of that way.

Our scientific beliefs, our religious beliefs, and our cultural beliefs can all hold us back from living a new paradigm.

Accepting That Choices and Behaviors Have Consequences

REMOVING THE BEAM IN OUR OWN EYES

Blame keeps wounds open. Only forgiveness heals.

— WILLA CATHER

There is an old Bible story in which one person is focusing on the mote in the other person's eye and ignoring the beam in their own. Who among us does not have our own beam in our own eye? Who among us would not rather focus on what the other person is doing wrong and ignore all the mistakes we are simultaneously making?

Who among us could not benefit from staying on our own side of the street? And who among us has not given our personal power away by the bucketful rather than admit to our bad choices and behaviors?

Who among us does not need daily reminders to be willing to accept the consequences of our choices and behaviors and work through those consequences?

Personal healing can lead to societal healing. Societal healing can lead to planetary healing.

Humility

NOT HAVING TO HAVE THE ANSWERS

*Today would be a good day to recognize the role that
others have played in our lives, our heritage, and the support
we have been given. It's good humility training.*

As humility begins to emerge, we begin to know that we do
not have to know it all. We do not even have to *be* it all.

We have only to be what we are at that moment as honestly
as we are capable of being.

Whenever we slip into arrogance or knowing it all or having
it all, we have opened a crack for our humility to tap us on the
shoulder and say, "You have come this far, do you really want to
detour back again?"

The emergence of our humility in its gentle way can remind
us that we are at the beginning of living a new paradigm and
how dysfunctional the old one had become.

Do we really want to regress? Remember, we no longer *have*
to have the answers. Participating in our own lives and with others who know that they do not have to have the answers could,
just could, result in something better than any one of us could
have come up with on our own. What's wrong with that?

Perhaps, just perhaps, the emergence of humility has not
only taken off the pressure that was destroying us and our
planet—perhaps humility has opened a deep door to oneness
and participation that would not have been possible if humility
had not emerged.

Knowing and Being Known

DISCOVERING THE UNKNOWN IN OURSELVES

What I do not know (in me) will hurt me.

All of us have unknown selves. There are large parts of our being which we simply did not have the strength and awareness to deal with when we were children, or memories hidden in our DNA, or experiences our thinking minds have twisted, to which we do not have access. On some unconscious or semiconscious level, we have not been ready to work through this information, so it is buried deep in our unconscious.

Just because it is buried does not mean that it has no effect on us. In fact, it has a great effect on us and unconsciously influences decisions we make and the way we live our lives. Indeed, this unknown/hidden/unconscious self may, in some of us, have more control over our lives than our conscious or hidden selves do.

In a world based on the illusion of control, it has become part of "human nature" to be wary and fearful of anything we think we cannot control. Of course, there is very little we can or need to control, and awareness of this inability seems to be in short supply in the current paradigm. Other, more ancient paradigms were fully aware that the issue of living was not to control. The issue was to participate and live in the process.

Only as we let ourselves remember another way of dealing with the world will our unconscious selves be more accessible to us for healing, growing, and learning.

SEPTEMBER 28

Everything Is Spiritual/Sacred

OUR MEMORIES

Memories are our wealth—
the good and the bad and the indifferent.

We need to remember that our experiences and memories are sacred to us and thus *are* sacred.

As mentioned earlier, some years ago I heard that medical scientists were working on a "forgetting pill." Their theory was that if we had experienced traumatic events in our lives, we would be better off if we had no memory of them. So much for mechanistic science and medicine!

We can see how far our attempts to "forget" our histories and experiences culturally have gotten us. Why would we want to do that as individuals?

Only in our remembering can we really heal. Our memories are sacred and an integral part of our spiritual beings.

We need our memories to heal, learn, and grow. Anything that suppresses, represses, or takes our memories away from us is robbing us of the potential for spiritual growth and awareness.

If nothing else, our memories help us remember what we do not want to be like and what we do not want to do to ourselves and others. They help us return to the sacred.

Our memories hold a special place in the sacred for us. Storytelling is a form of the sacred if we but take the time to listen.

Wholeness

WHOLENESS IS SECURITY

Wholeness is not something we, as humans,
can create. It is something available in which
we can choose to participate.

When we settle in to knowing that we are all connected and we are part of a much greater wholeness, we experience a celestial sigh of relief and we feel secure. No matter how much money, power, or influence we have, none can produce a genuine knowing of security.

Security comes from somewhere deep inside of us. Security comes from knowing at our deepest soul level that we are connected with the all that is and nothing can sever that connection.

We may have stretched that connection thin with our self-centeredness and our grasping for icons of external security, and only we can do that. We are the ones who retreat from our connectedness and awareness of the wholeness of all creation.

No one else can break that connection/participation and no one else can open us to it. That connection is always there. We are the ones who turn the other way.

Almost all of us know when we feel and act out of that connection. Something shifts and we can accept "whatever." When this shift happens, we find ourselves seeing and being in a new world in which we gratefully have no control and have the option to participate fully.

We feel relief. We feel secure.

Joy

ALLOW JOY TO BLOSSOM

*In our world, joy, like spirituality, was
never talked about. It was just understood.*

— CHEROKEE ELDER

We cannot manufacture joy nor can we make it happen. We can, however, ignore it and keep it out of our consciousness, not allowing it to flow freely.

Joy has a life of its own and is blessedly not under our control. It is a prerogative of our spirit and is always there to burst forth if we get out of the way.

The current paradigm does not encourage joy nor do people living out of that paradigm experience it that often. There just is no room for joy.

Joy needs a lot of room to venture out. It is too smart to show itself to people who will not notice or value it. In that way, joy is very conservative. Why waste its time on those who aren't interested?

Rarely do we think of joy as wily, yet it is.

Even when joy has been ignored for years and years, it still hangs in with us. Is that not a miracle?

All Is in Process

OUR PROCESS AS HUMANS AS PART OF A WHOLE

Aroha is: Unconditional love that is derived from the presence and the breath of the Creator. Aroha is a quality that is essential to the survival and total well-being of the world community. It is a pillar of life from Io Matua (the Godhead, the Divine Parent). Aroha is not to be talked about. It is only meaningful when actioned.

— RANGIMARIE TURUKI PERE, MAORI WRITER

One of the mistakes we have made as a human race is to try to separate our process as individuals and as a human race from the process of all creation.

We have happily fed our illusion that our process is the ultimate process of evolution and therefore the most important, ignoring that the whole is the all. All the processes of creation are intertwined and necessary for all to become.

When we eliminate a species—plant, animal, or culture—we are handicapping our own possibility of the process of becoming who we can be.

The truth is that everyone and everything contributes in some way in each and everyone's process of becoming. With parts missing, that process becomes more difficult.

Whoever it is, whatever it is, we have the opportunity to learn something from it. If and when that opportunity is taken away from us, our process of becoming suffers.

As we participate in our process of life, it is often difficult to discern what is most important. Only by participating in the process do we have the possibility to find out.

Participation

HIERARCHY

Why waste our precious time?

Believing in and perpetuating the illusion of hierarchy is a way to not participate.

When we buy into the illusion that we or others have more power, more influence, more education, or more money and are therefore more important and that that is "real," we have fallen into a form of nonparticipation.

It takes a lot of time and energy to maintain a one-up or one-down position and many have devoted their lives to just that belief and stance. Preserving a one-up or even a one-down mentality requires a great deal of time, effort, and energy, leaves little energy for anything else, and is thus a form of nonparticipation.

Few of us realize how much energy it takes to try to know and understand everything, always know what to do, and always be right. Very few admit to themselves how much energy it takes to maintain a position of one down. Ask any woman or any person of color!

It is important to remember what a thief of time and energy we are when we try not to participate by being better than or less than.

Thinking

NOT THINKING

*Emptying our minds may be
a bigger job than we expected.*

Many years ago when I was learning about the addictive process, I had been participating in 12-step meetings in Hawaii. I had learned that one cannot "know" why it works without participating. During that time, I had peeled off many layers of nonparticipation, standing back and observing/judging and the general woes of so-called objectivity. I still held on to the belief that those coming from California seemed a bit snobbish and thought they knew more. I had stopped "sitting back and evaluating" the meetings and had come to know that what I would get out of a meeting was directly related to how open I was and up to me. At that point in my peeling off layers of the addictive culture, I went to a meeting and there was the usual "Californian." Sigh. Then he said one of the most important things I have ever heard at a meeting! (So much for snobbishness and judgmentalism!) He said, "I have been in recovery long enough not to trust anything I think."

Wow! That was it! In this culture we are all involved in a thinking disorder. We all believe what we think. We believe that if we *think* it, it is *true*. And, as one Cherokee elder told me, "We can think ourselves into anything." (Or out of anything.) Have we looked at how many of our difficulties as people, as nations, and as a species are generated by our thinking?

Thinking is not all bad. Not all thinking is bad.

We just need to be careful with it.

Beliefs and Assumptions

THE DIFFICULTY OF LETTING GO OF OUR BELIEFS AND ASSUMPTIONS

*Our beliefs and assumptions are so entrenched
that even to question them, for some of us,
feels like evisceration.*

How difficult it is to let go of our beliefs and assumptions when we believe that they are real and law!

How difficult it is to let go of our beliefs and assumptions when we have built our lives around them!

How difficult it is to let go of our beliefs and assumptions when those around us are holding on to the same beliefs and assumptions!

How difficult it is to let go of our beliefs and assumptions when so many of them are unstated and unconscious!

How difficult it is to let go of our beliefs and assumptions when one of our major beliefs is that they have provided the framework around which our lives have been built! Without this framework, we fear that we would be like a jellyfish or even worse, not exist at all. Indeed many of us humans have reached such a level of terror about our beliefs and assumptions that we are ready to kill or go to war to protect them. We cannot live a new paradigm unless we are willing to step back from our beliefs and assumptions and evaluate and reevaluate them again and again. How easy it is to concretize them!

I remember, when I had been in college for a while, saying, "My Sunday-school God is too small for me now. I need to grow into another."

Feelings and Emotions

BALANCING OUR BRAINS AND BEINGS

Sameness is not always balance.

We need to be reminded of the simple fact that we have right and left brains and the connections in between for a reason, and that reason is that we actually have much more brain capacity than we usually use.

Isn't it just logical that the more of our brains we use the better off we will be? Then, if you add connecting to the other aspects of the body, it is easy to see that the more information we have available to us at all times the better off we will be.

As human beings, balance is very important. In order to evolve and build a new paradigm we will have to take a world and beings that are very unbalanced and try to find a way to create more and more balance.

Our own evolving personal balance is essential to our being open to a new paradigm and creating new options for us all.

Honesty

WE HAVE TO BE HONEST ABOUT OUR PLACE IN THE SCHEME OF THINGS

God Almighty has made us all.

— RED CLOUD, OGLALA SIOUX LEADER

Over time, we seem to have forgotten that the human race is a part of creation and not above creation. Every day we hear that we are the highest form of evolution or the most important and elevated form of creation. How lucky that the trees and the plants have not come to believe this lie or we might not have any oxygen to breathe and sustain our life on this planet.

Perpetuating this lie about our place in the scheme of things has resulted in an arrogance that far surpasses any ever seen before on this planet. Unfortunately, arrogance probably will have no place in living a new paradigm.

Almost every spiritual practice recognizes the role that humility plays in our spiritual growth. Arrogance and humility are not compatible.

If we persist in our illusion, our lie that we are the pinnacle of creation, we can expect a lessening of our spiritual growth and an inability to live a worthwhile new paradigm.

Courage

EVERYDAY COURAGE

Courage, true courage, is often very quiet.

I am always struck by the courage it takes a woman to carry a child, birth it, and face the terrifying challenge to raise it. No man will ever know what it feels like to have a somewhat alien being taking over our bodies, changing them, pressing on our already fragile bladders, seeing an okay body become something that we don't know at all, and then working harder than we have ever worked in our lives with more pain than we have ever before experienced to bring forth a being that will take over and change our lives forever. This whole process is a practice of participating in courage.

Yet books and films mostly portray what is considered male-like courage and heroes. So we as women have to find our own form of courage.

Unfortunately, the male form of courage has led us into some terrible disasters.

Perhaps a new paradigm will be a process of acknowledging a new kind of courage that has nothing to do with power over another and the illusion of control.

Do we have the courage to evolve new ideas and practices of courage?

Entitlement

OUR HUMANNESS

I will not be involved with the dreams of angry men.

— HMONG VILLAGER

Our humanness does not give us special gifts that put us above all other creation, feeding our egos and making us better.

Our humanness gives us particular challenges and tests our ability to deal with the illusions we feed ourselves and try to live out of.

If the universe were created in a hierarchical fashion, we humans might be at the bottom because we cause so much trouble, are not very adaptable, and create illusions out of which we try to live and grow. A redwood tree has it much easier and does not create so much of a problem for itself. Perhaps a redwood tree had to go through being a human to get where it is now. Who knows?

Of course, speculation is irrelevant. The real issue is what is relevant *here*? What is relevant *now*, to each of us, today?

A little humility would be nice.

Accepting Our Humanness

WE ARE NOT ALL BAD

Perhaps our lives would change significantly if we accepted that we humans are here to entertain God. How much damage do we do by taking ourselves so seriously?

At one point in my life, I was participating in a discussion of why God created humans. (At that point I truly believed that I *knew* something!) The thought occurred to me that God created humans for entertainment. When you look at it, this idea seems quite reasonable. We can really be quite dear at times. And we are very entertaining.

There is a saying in the 12-step groups of Alcoholics Anonymous that goes, "If you want to make God laugh, make plans." We certainly do invest a large amount of energy and pain in making plans and trying to make sure they happen, regardless of the evidence that our carrying out the plans causes a great deal of sturm and strife.

Our trying to deny the limitations and the possibilities of our humanness is certainly one of the best shows in town.

Respect

RESPECT FOR THE PLANET

Probably our most important learning is our accidental learning. Never underestimate it.

I almost feel embarrassed writing about the obvious need to show respect for the planet because it seems so self-evident that I should not even have to mention it. Yet so many of the things that were self-evident to our ancestors seem not even to be in the consciousness of humans at this time in our evolution as a species.

In fact, I am appalled by how easy it has become for many of us who are writing about the need for a new paradigm to not remember to practice what we preach, myself included.

Hence, the need of a little book of "reminders" to help us remember what we really know—that we cannot only change the way we think or our consciousness, we have to be willing to change everything, simply everything. And we have no idea what that will mean or how we do it. One thing is very clear, however. We can no longer "have dominion over" and destroy the planet while we are preaching a new paradigm.

Simple respect for the planet may teach us more than we are prepared to learn. Yet learning respect for all nature and the planet is beyond being a necessity in all its facets—even if we can only take one step at a time.

The Abstractualization of Life

PARALYSIS FOR LIVING

You're calming down enough to be in your world.

— NANI, HAWAIIAN KUPUNA

The more we live in our heads, the less we participate in our lives.

Many of the people who seek therapy or end up going "mad" are people who are "living in their heads." They have lost their grounding. Often they are so fearful of what *might* happen that they cannot let *anything* happen.

Everything that is going on in their minds is an abstraction. Worrying is an abstraction and is often "pre-worry." Yet to the person who is doing it, the abstractions that are the focus of the worry are real, very real. These worriers are always *thinking about*, not *doing*.

If we truly want to live a new paradigm, we need to see the ways that we use our abstractions and concepts to remove us from us from living and paralyze our participation.

How delightful it is to relate to someone who lives realities. We can simply ask the question, "Is this real?" If not, we may want to get on to something else.

Being of Good Spirit

THE RHYTHMS OF LIFE

I couldn't understand it then, but nothing was done unless there was a karakia [prayer]. It was just a whole way of life in those days, to pray.

— MIHI EDWARDS, MAORI ELDER

The rhythms of life teach us about being of good spirit.

Did you ever stop to think how reassuring it is that the sun rises every day? The process of the sunrise assures us that we are surrounded by a feeling of good-spiritedness. Regardless of how much science we know and how much we "understand" what the universe is and how the earth rotates around our sun, the experience of the coming of the day, if we stop to take note of it, is emotionally and spiritually very reassuring.

Our brains can rest awhile. We *feel* reassured. We *experience* the good-spiritedness of the new day. (Of course, only if we take the time to let ourselves experience the subtleties of the goodness.)

My people always went to the waters to bathe at sunrise to wash away the night and welcome all the goodness that is available to us. Each day was the beginning of a new possibility.

What will change in us if we welcome each new day with a feeling of good-spiritedness and gratitude? It only takes a *little* time.

Domination Over and the Illusion of Control

CHANGING MY BEHAVIOR

*Only when I see the big picture
can I live the small picture.*

I have always been a person who has stated my opinions and observations and spoken out about them. This behavior is not new for me. I've spoken out on human rights. I've spoken out on women's rights. I've spoken out on all rights—and still am. I speak out whenever I can and on whatever I can. That is just the way I am.

Imagine my shock and confusion during the George W. era after September 11, when I found myself being afraid and quiet. I had never been afraid to speak out in my country because I was taught that one of the mandates of being an American is that we have to be willing to take a stand for "freedom and justice for all," even when it is unpopular or suppressed.

This time of unconscious, self-imposed silence was a painful and horrible time for me as I have always been proud of my willingness to speak up and was a bit disdainful of those who do not speak up. I felt lost, confused, and frightened.

Then, I turned to my side of the street. Instead of riling against Washington, what was I contributing to the situation at hand? I devoted several years to this process of cleaning up my side of the street. One of the major learnings I had in this process was that when I focus on others I give my personal power away. This is not my domination over others or my controlling. I *give my personal power away* when I focus on others and then I resent others for having it!

When we have our personal power, we have no need to dominate or control. We have other, more important things to do.

Humor

WE ARE A FUNNY LOT

The only way to conquer the pakeha (white people) is to marry them.

— DAME WHINA COOPER,
MAORI ELDER AND STATESWOMAN

That woman had a sense of humor.

As we have said, we are a process, life is a process, all is in process.

How amusing it is to watch humans trying to plan their lives and others' lives down to the smallest detail. It is even more amazing to see that we actually *believe* those plans and are sure that we can make them happen. Our current paradigm lives out of this illusion. How funny and dear we are as we try to control anything and everything in our lives. Do we really believe that we can make our children turn out just the way we want them to? How amusing is that? Do we really believe we can choose a partner, get the relationship all nailed down, and then forget about it? How silly is that? How silly do we appear as we are trying to *make* life happen when it is happening all around us anyway?

Probably the most successful thing we have ever done as humans is to provide amusement for everyone and everything around us, including God.

Living with God and all creation is a different thing entirely.

Wonder and Awe

OPENING TO WONDER AND AWE

The center of the universe is everywhere.

— HEHAKA SAPA (BLACK ELK),
OGLALA/TETON SIOUX

We live in a world in which an important aspect of "wealth" is the ability to have the money to pay for riskier and riskier and more and more "unique" experiences to try to feel something—anything. "Making it" means that we have enough to skydive, swim with the sharks, shoot big game, travel in outer space, or seek more and more ways to destroy the planet to get a thrill or generate more adrenaline. We wear out our adrenal glands seeking busyness and extravagance. Our thrill-seeking does not leave us the time or the energy for the peacefulness from which wonder and awe spring.

Wonder and awe are not adrenaline based. They come from the quiet knowings that emerge when we stop trying to manipulate them. Wonder and awe are gifts. We cannot manufacture them. We cannot make them happen.

We can only stop long enough to let wonder and awe emerge and seep into our consciousness, for they are already there within us.

The Present Can Only Be Our
Reality if We Own Our Past and Our Future

THE ROLE OF CONTROL IN NOT OWNING PAST AND FUTURE

You kinda have to work with what you got and accept what you get.

— HURRICANE SURVIVOR

Isn't life difficult enough? How can we possibly own the past and future of our own selves, let alone that of the human species?

The answer is easy: We can own the wholeness by admitting all of our reality and healing it. As we own all of our, our ancestors', and humanity's past, we gain the wisdom to integrate a process of owning and changing our future. If we want to pre-plan it, it will not work because control and the illusion of control have no place in this process. We simply are not smart enough and aware enough to make whatever needs to happen, happen.

What I do know is that we cannot indulge in denying the past or worrying about the future while we are being realistic about the present (as well as the past and the future). We cannot indulge in and waste our time in the "if onlys" and the "what ifs." To focus on these only distorts the "what is." Our only choice is to heal the past when it comes up, participate as fully as we can in the present, and trust the future to unfold.

To live a new paradigm requires a high level of trust in whatever.

Walking in Beauty

A STATE OF BEING

Walking is what I need to enjoy the most.
Walking, you take in everything and enjoy the scenery.

— GOODWIN SEMAKEN, SR.,
INUPIAT/KOYUKON ELDER

Is walking in beauty dependent upon the material plane? Do we have to have full bellies to walk in beauty? I think not. Do we have to be surrounded by material beauty to walk in beauty? Not at all.

Do we have to be a certain race to walk in beauty? No, that has not been my experience.

Do we have to be a powerful person to walk in beauty? Not in my experience—and, if we seek power, it seems to be more difficult to walk in beauty.

This issue is very similar to the situation of a person who wants to be wise. She/he will probably never make it in the eyes of those who "know." He/she may fool some people along the way or even her/himself. Those who really matter—they will know.

So we are pretty much saying that it is not really possible to "con" walking in beauty and those who want to probably won't.

Walking in beauty springs from our inner beings. It is beyond thought. It is a by-product.

Taking Time

ALONE TIME IN NATURE

Nature is always right on time.

Nature always offers us the opportunity to take alone time. We not only get exercise for our bodies, we get exercise for the quieting of our minds.

Nature offers one of our best paradoxical experiences of being completely alone and also simultaneously surrounded by the abundance of life teeming around us. Coming to a place in which we are comfortable being alone with nature and knowing that the two of us together is enough is very healing.

I remember a time when I was privileged to do a 10-day Hawaiian cleanse with the respected and renowned Hawaiian kahuna Aunty Margaret Machado. Just being there was so special; we had bodies draped all over the place practically on top of one another for those 10 days.

At some point, I had had enough "togetherness" and I wandered quite a ways down the beach and sat on the rocks. I just needed some alone time. Then, I looked up. The first whales of the season were just "sounding" very close to shore. I cried with gratitude.

The whales were the company I needed right then. Nature has a way of being right on time, without appointment.

A Belief in Healing

BELIEFS IN TRANSITION

The new space has a kind of invisibility to those who have not entered it.

— MARY DALY

For all of us, if we do our work and continue to heal, learn, and grow, there comes a time for moving from belief to knowing. We may not even know what we know—and we know. We do not have to explain what has happened to us. Indeed, we probably cannot. Yet we know. We know that healing is possible. We have been so focused on the need for healing to be on the physical plane that we have almost forgotten that there are many levels of healing and many planes for healing.

At this point in our development of our awareness and knowing, we know that we do not have to know what we do not know. We know that healing is always possible and can take place on many levels of reality one at a time, together, or in the wholeness, and that we are a part of those larger and larger levels of healing.

The burden gets lighter as our belief in healing gets stronger.

Knowing and Living in Several Realities

EXPERIENCES IN THE CIVIL RIGHTS MOVEMENT

Right action has a reality of its own.

I was young when I first got involved in the civil rights movement—very young, in fact. My first experience that I remember was in Arkansas in 1938 when I was four years old. We lived in Fayetteville, in a white neighborhood on the edge of a black neighborhood. It was a "safe" neighborhood and I had permission to roam, which always was important to Mother and me.

One day I came home with a bouquet of flowers for Mother, roots and all! Instead of pure pleasure, Mother responded in a mixed way. "That's sweet, Elizabeth Anne, I appreciate that you want to give me flowers, and these are not our flowers and you pulled them up by the roots.

"Let's go make this right," she said, as she grabbed a trowel from the gardening basket. I took her to the place where I had picked the flowers and she had me knock on the door. An elderly black woman came to the door.

Mother explained that I had picked the flowers. They were beautiful flowers and we wanted to replant them. Clearly the old woman was a bit uneasy at that time in the South with a white woman and white child knocking on her door. "That's okay," she said. "She didn't mean any harm. It doesn't matter."

"Yes, it does," said Mother.

We replanted the bouquet and had tea with Miss Adelade—I was instructed to always address her as Miss Adelade, as she was my elder. We became fast friends, Miss Adelade and I.

In Mother's reality, everyone deserved respect. I knew that my friends' parents would have responded differently. I liked the reality we lived out of.

Being of Service

ACTION—NOT THINKING ABOUT

Actions speak louder than words.

— PROVERB

Just like as a young psychologist I could not learn about the 12-step program of Alcoholics Anonymous by observing others, reading about it, and asking questions, there is no way to learn about the power of being of service without actually doing it. And it destroys the entire learning if one is doing it to learn about it or has a hidden agenda.

One has to practice selfless being of service to experience being of service. This is another one of those situations when our thinking will not get us from one paradigm to another. We have to participate. We cannot think ourselves into it. Our scientifically trained and conditioned Western minds are just not going to get us there.

We can *want* to shift. We can have a great deal of information. We can even watch others and try to emulate them (which can be helpful). And the very moment we try to *think* it into being we lose!

Being of service is a kind of knowing that can only come from practice. And when we are really doing it without noticing it, we feel so good.

Graciousness

Invitation into Remembering

Sometimes we need reminders to remember.

Erring in the direction of graciousness is a way of reminding ourselves to remember what we know and have had a tendency to forget in the society that we have created as a human species.

Deep inside, hopefully, we still have a flame of remembrance of graciousness. Unfortunately, there has been less and less in our daily existence to fan that flame. We have created a society that would love to extinguish this flame completely. Fortunately, our cells (our DNA) have such strong memories of the potential beauty that we have in our very essence, that these tiny flames are not easily extinguished.

Somewhere, deep inside, we remember. We *remember*. How glorious is that! We even remember things that we do not know how we remember.

We need our memories. We are a compilation of centuries of memories and out of that past will come healing and hope for all our futures.

Our true graciousness will help us get where we have the opportunity to go as a species.

Moving Out of Our Comfort Zones

REMEMBERING

For every clever person, there is a person more clever.

— MEXICAN PROVERB

Embedded deep inside of the DNA in all of us are memories of another way of being on this planet. These ways may not have been perfect in their functioning, and they may have had valuable pieces and processes that we can put together to form something new that works. We can only respond to these reminders if we can let go of our cherished illusions and venture out of our supposed comfort zones to remember what is hidden deep inside of us. For example, some of us have learned that raping the planet for material comforts will probably not fulfill our needs. Some of us have learned that giving our power away to those who will accept it has not proved to be very useful. Some of us have learned that wealth, prestige, recognition, power, and celebrity do not seem to meet the needs of the complexity that we humans have created for ourselves.

The revealed religions appear not to have been able to teach us how to live peacefully and in a fulfilling way with all levels of our being. Even our comfort zones have become uncomfortable.

Maybe, as a species, we are ready to learn from our mistakes and live and be another way on this planet. And, to do that, we need to move out of our illusionary comfort zones.

Letting Go of What We Think We Know

BEING OPEN TO OTHER KINDS OF KNOWING

Knowing is a process, not an event.

If we truly want to live a new paradigm or live into the *process* of living a new paradigm, we need to be able to explore a variety of processes and ways of knowing that might challenge our beliefs of how we know what we know.

I have always loved epistemology. I not only wanted to find out *what* people know, I wanted to find out *how* they learned what they learned. As a young school psychologist in the 1960s, I discovered that some students learned visually, some learned auditorily, some learned kinesthetically, and some just knew things they had "no way of knowing." I was always fascinated with them all, and the latter group especially, because according to the culture, they had no way of learning what they knew, *and* they knew it.

A Lakota elder once told me that we cannot always trust what our brains teach us or tell us. He said it was because we can manipulate and control our brains into thinking whatever we want to think. He said we need to trust what our hearts tell us.

In this culture, we are taught to trust our brains. In his culture they were taught to trust their hearts. Probably neither can be trusted completely and both need to be checked out. We need to listen to and consider how we learn the process of balancing these two with other information.

Options generate options. Options are our wealth.

Accepting That Choices and Behaviors Have Consequences

CAREFUL CHOICES

Yes, I have doubted. I have wandered off the path. I have been lost. But I always returned. It is beyond the logic I seek. It is intuitive—an intrinsic, built-in sense of direction. I seem always to find my way home.

— HELEN HAYES

One of the ways not to get in so much trouble with ourselves with our choices and behaviors is to stop and consider what we are about to do before we do it. Rather than be in a constant state of cleaning up our messes, it is so nice to stop, take a breath, and see if what we are about to do makes sense. Of course we can convince ourselves that we really *want* or *need* to do something. And yet, do we? A hesitation can save a lot of grief. There is an old saying in Al-Anon: "When in doubt, don't."

Sometimes we have no idea why we should *not* do something or should *do* something, and there is just something there that does not feel right. We may get on a roll on some new ideas about a new paradigm and have little awareness about how those "new" ideas are just thinly disguised old paradigm tricks. Often when we are going to make some serious choices, it helps to run it by some people who know us and our blind spots or a group who knows us well.

None of us has to do anything alone and it always helps to have trusted people who clearly know our tricks.

We are, after all, most easily fooled by ourselves.

Humility

LOSS IS GAIN

How lovely it is to be surprised by humility.

Can it possibly be that as we let go of our illusion of control, our arrogance, our self-centeredness, and our need to know what is next, that we have greater serenity and more personal power?

Can it be that in not having to be "special," "in control," and in just being "a part of," we have regained our personal power in our connectedness?

Could it be that in our letting go of our need to be special we have become more special in a "belonging" way?

If our humility emerges as a by-product of doing our work, is it possible that our belongingness and participation become more rewarding than our illusion of control ever was?

As we have lost the illusion of what we *thought* we needed to exist happily on this planet, is it possible that what we *thought* was important may be a long way off the mark?

Humility is a by-product, not a target or destination.

Knowing and Being Known

REMEMBER INTIMACY WITH OURSELVES

There are two rules for living in harmony.
1. Don't sweat the small stuff.
2. It's all small stuff.

— RICHARD CARLSON, QUOTING DR. WAYNE DYER

Only as we recognize the various aspects of the complexity of our beings will we begin to remember the joy and excitement of intimacy with ourselves *and* others.

We now live in a culture that not only does not support intimacy with ourselves and others, it actively militates against such intimacy. In fact, we have developed a culture where the focus is to escape intimacy with ourselves and others.

Our addictions are very effective in shutting off our awarenesses, feelings, insights, and knowings. I have said many times that this paradigm/culture not only supports addictions, it *requires* them in order to tolerate the culture we have built.

We *have* to shut off our awarenesses and knowings in order to watch the evening news, ignore our longings for intimacy with ourselves and others, and tolerate what we have created within ourselves, with one another, and in our culture.

We need to remind ourselves daily that escaping from intimacy with ourselves, others, and our world is not a healthy state of being for the human organism or any part of creation. We need connections.

Everything Is Spiritual/Sacred

THE SEASONS

*Whilst feeling compassion for you in the sweetness
of our repose, we wonder at the anxieties and cares
which you give yourselves night and day.*

— GASPESIAN-MICMAC CHIEF

Sometimes we forget how lucky we are that we have the seasons to remind us of cycles, rebirth, and possibilities. The changing of the seasons helps us remember that life has cycles and the very fact of the existence of these cycles helps us remember that we too have cycles, are part of cycles, and can participate in the cycles of life.

Spring reminds us that there is always rebirth and renewal. No matter how bad things get, we can remember that change is the only constant and rebirth occurs out of the darkness. We have the opportunity to see the trees come alive again, the bushes grow tall, the flowers bloom, and the earth giving birth to new life. We see the trees that looked dead burst forth in new foliage and we know and remember that cycles are our reality. The summer eases forth with long days and short nights and we have time to relax, be in nature, and play—if we will let ourselves. Fall is a time for savoring the harvest and is a very good time to remember and reflect. Winter is a resting time and invites us to slow down, settle in, and experience the quietness of the sacred.

We need to remember that the seasons are sacred and spiritual, and give up pretending that we are not part of them and that we don't need them.

Wholeness

REALIZING CONNECTEDNESS

Remember! We are never not connected,
even when we try to ignore that connection.

Some time ago I realized that I did not live out of an abstract concept of wholeness. I actually *knew* that everyone and everything was family to me. This was quite a revelation to me because I had always thought that it was a nice concept. Yet I realized that in the depth of my being, everyone I encountered was family to me. I approached them as family and was open to them as family. As I grew older, I realized that many did not return the feeling of openness and sometimes I was hurt in the process. Then I realized that after I got to know some people, I really did not want them as close family members *and* they were still family.

Over the years I have come to see that this attitude of mine taught to me by my Cherokee family is not shared by many, if any, people in Western culture. I have been hurt when I treated other people's children as part of my family and my children did not receive the same courtesy from their families. And I have come to believe that seeing all creation as family is a very good way of being.

When we know all creation to be connected and we know that we are a part of the all that is, it is a very good thing. We can relax a bit.

Joy

LETTING NATURE IN

Children can teach us about joy.

If joy has been a stranger to you for some time, try letting the beauty of fall into your being.

Take a walk in the woods, drive out into the country, take some time off, add a drive down the Appalachian Trail to your bucket list and do it, or reacquaint yourself with the beauty of the aspens in this season of their quaking glory.

See if you can not only take in the beauty around you; see if you still have the capacity to let nature reawaken the beauty within you. See if you can tap into that capacity to know on every level that you are one with nature and that the separation has been from and within you. Reconnecting and being a part of can release so much more joy than trying to be "above" anyone or anything.

Joy is very simple. It is a process within us that may have gone underground for a while and is still there within us to tap into whenever we get out of the way.

Emotional Brilliance

Experiencing Our World with Our Whole Being

Traditionally, Halloween is more than trick or treat.
Forgetting the meaning does not mean
that we have lost the meaning.

According to many traditions there is one day a year when the souls are free to roam the earth.

Halloween is a day when we are given permission to rest from our rational-logical viewpoint of the world, dress up in costumes, and be relieved from the rational/logical.

On this day, we are open to other realms of being and to the idea that we have other realms of being.

Just for a second in the many seconds of our year . . . perhaps there is something more.

To live another paradigm, we have to *know* there is something more. We may not know what it is, and yet most of us know there is more than our present paradigm has admitted.

All Is in Process

THE BIGGER PICTURE

Everything in its time, remember, everything in its time.

— SEÑOR CASTRO, GUATEMALAN ELDER

It is so wonderful to be 82 years old and have the opportunity to look back over the process of my life and see that it was and is a process. And also to see that this process has led me to greater and greater understanding of the events that contributed to my overall growth and awareness.

As I've said, there were many times when I was younger that I was so happy that I just wanted to stop the world and keep my life that way forever. My house was the way I wanted it, my children were lively, beautiful, and happy, my relationship with my husband was peaceful and happy, and my professional life was full, challenging, and successful. What more could I want? If I could just keep it that way forever. If only . . . and I couldn't. Thank goodness.

Luckily, early in life I realized what a horrible mistake it would have been if I had been able to "stop the world." I realized that I do not have the knowledge, wisdom, or imagination to have created the wonderful life I have lived thus far.

All I had to do was trust the process of my life and participate as fully as I could, be ready and willing to see the doors that were presented to me, peek in, and, if I wanted, walk through them and participate. Not all the doors revealed something pleasant, yet all—every one—presented me with something that contributed to my growth, learning, and healing (if, and only if, I was open to it).

To be open to the process of our lives is the greatest gift we can give ourselves. We need reminders to remember this reality.

Participation

GRATITUDE

Our own life is the instrument with which we experiment with truth.

— THICH NHAT HANH

How often have we stopped to feel grateful that we have the gift of this lifetime to heal, grow, and learn. It is quite amazing when we shift from seeing something as a burden to seeing it as an honor and a privilege to be treated with great care and tenderness.

Regardless of what the tasks and opportunities are that are placed in our path, there is always something that we can (and probably *need*) to learn. And if we do not learn them the first time around we will probably be given the opportunity to learn them again—only in a more difficult version.

Why not plunge into the opportunity the first time they are presented to us? This jumping in can be so efficient. Why not take advantage of the opportunities our lives present to us and participate in them?

It is amazing how an attitude of gratitude can contribute to our participation in our lives and the situations the process of our lives present to us.

Thinking

THE GIFT OF THINKING

My mind is here for me to use, not abuse.
It can be a great spiritual ally.

Although we have spent time looking at the way we misuse our thinking potential and how this misuse can stifle our possibilities, we truly need to remember that our minds and our ability and possibility of consciousness are truly great gifts.

There is little in our culture that supports our utilizing these gifts except in linear, rational, and controlled ways.

Yet when we trust our process and participate as fully as we can in the lives and opportunities we have, our conscious and unconscious minds and beings find ways to come together and work together with realities beyond us that contribute to new levels of information and learning.

It seems appropriate to be grateful for the possibilities our thinking and our minds have in store for us and to make some amends to them and ourselves for abusing them so we can see the prisons we have built around both.

Beliefs and Assumptions

LETTING GO, REVISING, REBUILDING

*We will never run out of the beliefs and assumptions
that we need to challenge in order to be more whole.*

What beliefs and assumptions are holding you prisoner and inhibiting your blossoming into who you can be? Are you holding on to a belief that there is only one way to see and understand the world and therefore all others have to be false? Are you ready to see that there are many paths to truth and not all have to be put through our same old filters?

Are you ready to move beyond nationalism ("My country, right or wrong!") and see the good in your society and also the glaring limitations? Are you willing to learn from those you have believed to be inferior to you and less than you in order to gain a more realistic perception of the whole?

Are you willing to see bias for what it is—limiting—and challenge your own biases about yourself and others, your nation and others, your race and others, your religion and others and see and experience a larger whole?

Remember: Growth is a process that continues (hopefully) throughout our lives. There is always some assumption or belief we have just begun to look at or that is waiting for us to explore.

Feelings and Emotions

OUR CHOICES WITH FEELINGS AND EMOTIONS

*Remember our "doors" to our depths are
many and varied. Our job is to see them.*

I have learned that my feelings and emotions are not only essential for my liveliness and well-being, they make my life fuller and richer and carry information that I cannot access through any other means.

So many people are afraid of their feelings that they hold them in until they are about to burst and then, in one great explosion, they "puke" them over anyone and everyone in sight. This behavior confirms to them that feelings are bad and need to be held in at all costs. Not true! We need to be reminded not to get stuck on old dualisms like holding our feelings in or puking them out indiscriminately. These are not our only choices with feelings and emotions. We can learn to feel them fully and see where they take us. I "go to the mats" to do this. Then if I need to tell someone I am angry about something, it can be expressed in some good and not so harmful way.

Never, never puke your feelings on anyone. That is participating in the old paradigm. On the other hand, feeling intense anger over an injustice, be it personal, cultural, or paradigmatic, can feel like a celestial enema and is not to be missed if wholeness is to be achieved.

Honesty

A CULTURE OF DISHONESTY

*I have refrained from speaking the truth
and have just gone along with a lot of things.*

— MARION COHEN

We need to recognize that not only have we developed a culture of dishonesty, in the process we have almost lost the ability to recognize honesty and be honest. The culture of dishonesty has not only become accepted, it has become acceptable as normal. Though dishonesty may be statistically normal, it is not healthy for human beings or the planet as a whole.

Being dishonest actually makes us physically sick. It initiates a kind of tension in the body that results in tight muscles. Tight muscles result in a blockage of blood flow and the normal flow of our endocrine system. This tension progresses to chronic tension and chronic tension results in physical dysfunction. So being dishonest literally poisons us physically, emotionally, and spiritually. And we are not even aware of this progressive disease process.

Quite literally, our dishonesty is a killer. And, quite honestly, keeping track of our lies is exhausting.

Courage

A NEW PARADIGM OF COURAGE

If our hearts are open, courage is an instinct.

Perhaps the process of bringing in a new paradigm of courage will be a gradual process of refusing to participate in the old paradigm, one process at a time.

For example, over the years I have noticed that my family and I are changing. I'm not sure when, how, or why it happened: we have become avid recyclers. We recycle almost everything. Since we live far out in the country, it is not easy. When we make our few necessary trips to town, we always take our well-organized recycling. Courageous? Maybe. Necessary? Yes!

Our diets have changed. Less meat. More vegetables and a few fruits, all fresh. We are growing more of our food. Was this a conscious decision? Not really—just an awareness that we needed to change.

One that still startles me is with my retirement. As most good Americans do, I set up a retirement fund. That was good. For a while I was happy in being with an investment firm that did not invest in alcohol, tobacco, or war production. Then I became uncomfortable in having my money in stocks. So just before the market hit a positive run, I took my money out.

"But your money's not working for you? That's terrible!"

"I know," I said. "I just can no longer feel honest or good about participating in a system that is built on the necessity for poverty and scarcity and supports materialism, greed, and gambling (the stock market). I just can't do it anymore."

As Martin Luther said: "Here I stand. I can do no other."

Courage? Necessity? Spiritual integrity?

All, perhaps—or none.

Entitlement

GRATITUDE

Back to basics.

— A.A. SLOGAN

How, then, do we begin to deal with the sneakiness of our feelings of entitlement?

Perhaps we can try to practice gratitude. A combination of big gratitudes and little ones might be nice.

Of course, it is important not to delude ourselves with a mechanistic gratitude con (mechanistic things and processes are less than useful with the important things).

How about starting each day with something you can be truly grateful for?

Don't fool yourself.

No "fake it until you make it."

There's too much at stake here.

Let's start with little things.

Do you have good teeth?

Are you grateful for them?

Do you have bad teeth?

Are you grateful for them?

Bad teeth may teach us more than good teeth in the long run.

If we find that we genuinely cannot find a truly grateful cell in our body, great!

What can we learn from that on our road to dealing with the illusion of entitlement?

In some ways illusions are like matter: Once here, they can never be created or destroyed. They can only be changed.

Accepting Our Humanness

THE SPREAD OF AN ILLUSION

And they believe what they are doing is real.

— PETER SIDLEY

How can we possibly participate fully in the process of moving into a new paradigm if we are trying to carry into that process the old paradigm illusion of the possibility of being suprahuman?

How can we move into a new paradigm if we insist on the illusions and assumptions of a paradigm that cannot work and is not working?

If we cannot accept the strengths and limitations of ourselves and others, how will we ever let go of the resentments we have built up because others are not perfect? Once we have accepted that all of us are human with the resultant mistakes and soaring moments of grandeur, how much easier it is to see and forgive their (and our) mistakes as necessary elements along this path of learning. Recently I was sitting with a person who had not forgiven his parents for a feeling of rejection he felt in the womb! This was more than 60 years of holding a busy, confused, first-time parent hostage for not being perfect.

Only as we accept our and others' humanness in all its ramifications can we be ready to live another paradigm.

The next time you get worked up about something, stop to ask whether the issue is real or not.

Respect

FIGHTING EXTINCTION

People are more than the worst thing they have ever done in their lives.

— SISTER HELEN PREJEAN

Before we let the process of living out of respect become extinct as we are letting so many species of plants and animals become extinct, we need to remember and relearn how far-reaching an attitude of respect is. We need to see what the implications are of this wonderful reality of living that previously was in plentiful supply.

For example, respect may start small, like treating our food with respect when we buy, pick, prepare, and eat it. Indeed, in spite of ourselves, we need to learn to respect plants and fan the seed of gratitude that exists in the center of our beings and our spirits, even when we do not realize it is there.

Whoever thought of gratitude as a by-product? As we practice respect, gratitude—genuine gratitude—will creep up on us before we know what is happening. Also, respect is asexual and nondiscriminatory. Anyone and everyone can indulge in it regardless of race, sexual orientation, social status, or nationality. Some may find it harder than others, and the practice of an attitude of respect is available to everyone.

Although at this present time in the evolution of humankind, if you practice respect in all that you do, you may become conspicuous in a crowd.

The Abstractualization of Life

GETTING OUT OF THE ABSTRACTUALIZATION OF LIFE

*It is far better to take things as they
come along with patience and equanimity.*

— CARL JUNG

One of the best antidotes I have seen for dealing with the temptation to abstract everything is gratitude. When runaway abstraction is beginning, it is useful to stop, take a breath, and simply ask ourselves, "Am I all right at this very moment?" Usually the answer is yes and the present is all we have to deal with at that moment. Being in the present and being grateful for that present seems to have a magical way of bringing ourselves back to reality.

Gratitude almost always brings us to the concrete and the real. Gratitude shifts our attention. Gratitude, for it to be useful, has to be a *feeling*, not an abstraction. For example, it rarely helps for us to *think* we should feel grateful. What a difference we experience when we actually do *feel* grateful.

Sometimes we have to be reminded that gratitude is a natural state for human beings.

Being of Good Spirit

THE EXAMPLE OF THE EARTH

Go to your mother, the earth.

— PHIL LANE, SR., YANKTON SIOUX ELDER

If ever we wanted a good example and teacher for being of good spirit, we have only to look at the earth.

How generous the earth is with us! It is no wonder that she is called our mother because everything we have except life itself comes from the earth. And she sustains the life we have been given. An old Lakota uncle of mine once said to me, "Whenever you are confused or hurting, go to your mother, the earth, press your face against her breast, and she will comfort you and heal you." Just writing these words brings tears to my eyes. I can always return to the earth no matter where I am or what happens to me and I will be cared for.

The good-spiritedness of the earth is all around me all the time, whether it is the water that rocks me, the trees that sustain me, or the ground that holds me, I know the goodness of spirit when I take the time and let it in.

Sometimes when I am in a big city and I begin to feel overwhelmed by the concrete and steel, I will find a tree growing in a small plot of earth surrounded by concrete and asphalt. When I stand in that little plot of earth, I feel better.

The earth helps me recover my goodness of spirit.

Domination Over and the Illusion of Control

FREEDOM

Freedom is not trying to be who we aren't.

Few have seriously looked at the consequences of giving up domination over or the illusion of control, individually or as a nation. Yet there is much to be gained and learned by moving toward a different paradigm than the current one in which we are operating.

It is very stressful to try to dominate and control others. It is exhausting, in fact! How much wiser we will be if we focus on letting go of trying to dominate and control.

We believe that we have to be alert. We have to be on duty more than 24/7. We have to know more than they do and be in a position of proving it on a moment's notice. We have to be stronger, smarter, more agile, more cunning, and more deceitful of ourselves and others. We have to be and *stay* more powerful, no matter the cost to ourselves, our relationships, or others. We have bought the illusion that we have to know more than any human being could possibly know and we have to know it faster, deeper, more extensively, and better. Is it any wonder that we are exhausted, angry, unhappy, or as they say in the 12-step program, "restless, irritable, and discontent"?

There is another way and it has worked very well for many people for centuries.

Humor

THE HUMOR OF CREATION

We have been hoping and waiting for you to come to your senses.

— FRANK FOOLS CROW,
LAKOTA CHIEF AND SPIRITUAL LEADER

Native people would say that if we look around us we have to admit that God—the Creator—has a good sense of humor.

How creative is creation? Who could have imagined a porcupine, an elephant, and a hippopotamus? Creativity and diversity are inherent in all of creation.

How perverted are we to want to homogenize all that diversity into the dullness of what we would create? Now you have to see the humor in this whole belief in homogenizing all creation. How ridiculous it is to have a world with all shades and forms of human beings who bring different pieces of the truth to the table and want to make them all the same! Do we honestly believe that we know better?

Older wisdoms on this planet will find these ideas and the attempt to bring them to fruition laughable if it weren't so serious, especially at this point in the evolution of life on this planet. This is why many native people have come to believe that it is time to speak up.

We seem to have quit laughing at our seriousness, and that is extremely dangerous if we want to change.

Wonder and Awe

THE CREATIVITY OF OUR INSANITY

*Boast is always a cry of despair except
in the young, when it is a cry of hope.*

— BERNARD BERENSON

We will never be able to build a new paradigm of living in respect, honor, and wholeness on this planet unless we are able to step back and see how immensely creative we have been with our insanity in relation to living with one another and the planet.

It would probably be more appropriate to devote several books to this subtopic, and many of us have. Yet we need to and are exploring the role of wonder and awe in the process of learning to live a new paradigm. For example, I am in complete wonder and awe of the tolerance we have developed for dishonesty and lying. Our ancestors could never have predicted how deceitful we have become.

What kind of species with consciousness would be so addicted to material gain that we would be willing to pollute the very air we breathe, the food we eat, and the water we drink? How insane is it to destroy diversity in nature, peoples, beliefs, and thinking when none of us has the whole picture? How crazy is it, if we stand back and look at it, to believe that people of one skin color are better than those of another, or that we don't need the innate wisdom of both sexes, or that people with more money know more?

Really now, incredulity, shock, awe, and wonder are normal responses (initially) to such audacity; our minds are *amazing* to have come up with such idiocy.

The Present Can Only Be Our Reality
if We Own Our Past and Our Future

BUILDING TRUST FOR
PAST, PRESENT, AND FUTURE

*Each moment of every day can build trust
for the future—if we let it.*

How do we build trust for knowing and healing our past, living in the present, and owning our future?

One very reliable process that helps is gratitude. It is truly amazing how gratitude—free-floating gratitude for everything, even the negative—changes our planet.

I have seen this phenomenon in native people. Nonnative people look on in horror and say, "Look at their situation. Who could be grateful for that?" The truth is that they are not necessarily grateful for "this" or for "that." They live out of an attitude of gratitude.

Those who do not live out of an attitude of gratitude will never understand it because it is not understandable. There are many, many things that are not understandable, and recognizing that they are not is the first step toward not getting hung up with them. They just *are*.

I remember when I first became aware of addictions. I was doggedly determined to "understand" them and kept butting my head against a very solid brick wall. One day I realized that understanding addictions was not possible because they (I don't mean the chemicals here, I mean the *process* of addictions) are *not* understandable. They don't make sense. My work with addicts became much easier at that moment in time. I was grateful for my change in attitude.

Walking in Beauty

NATURE

We see God in Water, Sun, Air—everywhere.

— GEORGE GOODSTRIKER,
KAINAI (BLACKFOOT) ELDER

Sometimes nature can help return us to a familiar desired state when we are having trouble getting back there. Concrete, asphalt, and man-made houses and cars seem to have an adverse effect on walking in beauty. The seasons of nature are very supportive to our remembering what it means to walk in beauty.

Nature, however, in the extravagance of her seasons, can help call us back to what we already know. I have found that fall is especially good at calling us back. Down deep, we *know* what it is, what it feels like, and what we are like when we are "back" and words do not prove too adequate.

Walking through the leaves when the woods are a riot of greens, yellows, reds, and deep purplish browns against the white, brown, black, mottled, smooth, and rough barks help us to return and remember.

Somewhere down deep in all of us, our ancestors have planted a seed of remembrance of walking in beauty. We have only to rediscover it.

Taking Time

GRATITUDE

I need quiet time every day. It's just like vitamin C;
my body and my being can't store it up.
I need regular doses.

I grew up as an only child. My uncles were always around and we always, as my mother said, "took in strays" and had someone living with us.

I also had great gobs of alone time. At one point in my life, my favorite place to be alone was to climb up in the old sycamore tree and sway with the wind as I "unconsciously" sorted out . . . whatever.

I do not remember having any specific thoughts when I sat up there swinging in the breeze with my legs wrapped around the trunk, sitting on one of her big comfortable limbs with my face pressed against her.

How grateful I am that my family did not think this behavior strange and had no worry about my climbing so high in that big old tree!

How wonderful they were to realize that the relationship I had with that tree enhanced me and my relationship with them.

Gratitude for alone time is so sweet.

A Belief in Healing

GRATITUDE FOR THE WAY WE HEAL AND LEARN

Stress is an ignorant state. It believes that everything is an emergency.

— NATALIE GOLDBERG

If we are truly living and participating in the process of our lives, slowly—very slowly—we come to realize that we do not have to get or understand everything all at once.

If we believe in healing, if we are doing our work with dedication, honesty, and sincerity, we will come into our knowings as we need to and are ready to.

We do not have to heal everything at once. We may even learn more from what cannot be healed at that time.

All we need is a belief in healing: that healing is possible, that it comes in many forms, and almost always does not look like what we thought it would.

We can be grateful that all these unknowns can contribute to what may be a very shaky humility.

When our humility is shaky, we need to be humbly grateful for the gift of healing.

Knowing and Living in Several Realities

MY ASSUMPTIONS GET ME BEAT UP

Racism has many, many layers.

As I have said, being a Cherokee and being raised as I was, as I now look back I can see that it was inevitable for me to get involved in the civil rights movement. How could I not? When I first got involved, I assumed that my black brothers and sisters were coming from the same reality, and I was shocked when they did not always welcome me with open arms.

It was not until a black man, who was being what I considered arrogant and discounting with me as a white man would be, taught me a lesson. I confronted him with how he was treating me and said, "What's the matter with you? I'm here fighting the same cause as you—inequality. We need to join forces." He visibly stepped back and said, "Are you kidding? I don't want to be down there with *you*, I want to be up there with *him*." Another reality. As a visibly white, liberal woman, I had made my "elitist assumptions" without any awareness of doing so. I had assumed an equality. He did not. His male "reality" was more important to him than my human equality.

Later, two black men stuck with me as I moved to learn about other realities. I had grown up with white privilege—even I did not know I was Cherokee as I grew up in Cherokee territory. The truth was I passed for white. I had a white-trained mind, white privilege, white assumptions. I was a white liberal. These men loved me enough to keep confronting me until I got it.

I could never know the black experience or reality. I *did* have white privilege. Only when I realized that truth could I begin, painfully, to face the reality of my racism.

Being of Service

OPPORTUNITIES

*I am in a state of being of service
when I am present to the moment.*

The holiday season offers so many opportunities for *institutional* "being of service." It is easy to confuse these institutional outlets with real, personal, paradigm-shifting "being of service." So beware of yourself and others. You have been wanting to learn to live a new paradigm for almost a year here. Don't lose the plot now.

One of the most beautiful things about the month of November in the United States is that, thanks to the native peoples of this land, we lean toward being thankful and grateful this month.

Just to help us along in a paradigm shift for the rest of the month, let's try a little activity. Every time you think of something you want or want to do for yourself (eating, wanting to buy something, wanting to indulge yourself) try being of service to someone at hand. It does not have to be big. It does not have to be significant. (Holding a door, waiting for someone without getting grumpy, respecting an elder—something very, very simple. See how you feel. See if something shifts.

See if you can glimpse a new paradigm.

Graciousness

GRATITUDE

*Acceptance of the gifts we already have
is graciousness in action.*

How lucky we are that each of us has buried deep inside of us everything we need to learn, heal, and grow and that this ability has never left us. The ability to heal is so much a part of who we are as beings that we rarely stop to think about it, much less feel gratitude for this marvelous ability.

Indeed, just having this ability built into our beings is, itself, an act of graciousness. And being genuinely gracious is such an act of healing for us all. Nothing feeds our spring of graciousness like gratitude does. The very act of gratitude is the soil out of which graciousness grows. Erring in the direction of graciousness feeds our equality with all creation.

All creation moves in circles. Our ancestors knew that creation moves in circles and this wisdom is hidden in our DNA. We have but to access it. We have only to stop burying this knowledge under a barrage of disembodied, human-created concepts for it to bubble forth.

If we want to shift from this paradigm that is destroying the planet and all life on it, feeding our pool of graciousness could be a good thing to do. Gratitude for what we have been given to us in our DNA is a good start.

Moving Out of Our Comfort Zones

BEING GRATEFUL

There are times when we need our comfort zones.
There are times when we need to outgrow them.

How lucky we are as human beings to be able to look at the mistakes we have made collectively and individually, to learn from them, to forgive ourselves and others and move on, hopefully, to something better.

This kind of movement, however, is not possible unless we are willing to move out of our comfort zones and look back at our mistakes with perspective and gratitude for the learnings they provided.

How powerful it is for us humans to move out of our comfort zones and our usual ways of processing only to find that we are still alive and have gleaned some precious learnings. How silly we have become when we think that there is only one way of doing and being on this planet and that way is ours. What a gift we have been given when we come to the awareness that none of us has all the answers and we need one another—even those we have called enemies.

What a great gift we have that we can participate in a process in which the outcomes cannot even be imagined by the human mind as it is now burdened by all our different "comfort zones."

A good start would be to remember gratitude that we have possibilities.

Letting Go of What We Think We Know

GRATITUDE FOR OUR SENSES

*Why hold on to what we think we
know when we can learn so much more?*

There is no question but what we live in a world culture that
overvalues the rational/logical/scientific and generally denies
and disdains other forms of thinking like intuition, knowing,
and feeling.

The paradigm in which we are now living—that many are
coming to recognize is destroying not only human life and
potential, *all* life and *all* potential—needs to change significantly.
When we stop to look at what we "think" we know, it is important that we stop to feel and have gratitude for all we have been
given.

Clearly this current paradigm has caused a great deal of
destruction to all creation. The *what* and the *how* of the way we
live and think as a species may be shortsighted and based on a
very narrow form of what is possible in math, science, and reality, and we need to ask: Does it incorporate the higher levels of
our spiritual beings? We need to see that we as a species are in
trouble.

When we begin to view ourselves and our world from a
broader perspective, we can feel gratitude for the wanderings,
good and bad, that have brought us to this place.

Yes, we are in trouble. Yes, we need to let go and change—no
doubt about it. And . . .

Yes, we need to be grateful for where we are so we can move
on. We have to be where we are so that we can see the need to
be somewhere else.

Accepting That Choices and Behaviors Have Consequences

GRATITUDE

*Why in the world would we not want to have
consequences for our behavior? We're not stupid.*

One of the most beautiful things about growing older is the possibility to look back and be grateful that our decisions and behaviors had consequences. If we look carefully, we can see that facing the consequences resulted in much more growth and learning than getting away with whatever it was would ever have.

After all, do we really ever get away with anything? We know! And we have, in addition, compromised our precious personal power. Was it worth it? Ever!

Regrets can be useful when we learn from them. And wallowing in regrets can produce the same old, same old. We may not have liked the consequences at the time *and* if we grow and use them wisely, they have always been for our own good. A world that is seeking to be without consequences for dysfunctional behavior is not good for the human race and the planet. And both are suffering right now.

We need to be reminded that consequences are our friends and used properly can facilitate our growth and help us blossom into wisdom.

Humility

GRATITUDE

Gratitude is the partner of humility.

In a month of gratitude and Thanksgiving, can we allow ourselves to be grateful for:

- Not having control of people, places, and things?
- Not being in charge of our lives?
- Not knowing the answers?
- Being able to trust the process?
- Recognizing that we are part of a greater and even wiser whole?
- Our mistakes, for they have been our teachers?
- That our greatest teachers may be a rock, a waterfall, or someone who has nothing whatsoever in common with us?
- That we need the wisdom of people we formerly hated or disdained?
- That differences are a gift?
- Having a glimpse that our arrogance—which is easy to see in others and very difficult to see in ourselves—is not only irrelevant, it can scare away humility and be very destructive?
- That we need the help of others, especially those we felt better than to help us get out of the way of humility?
- The reality that we need a lot of help from many sources to become who we can be?
- That we often misjudge the sources from which our help will come?

Knowing and Being Known

GRATITUDE

*I have been through some terrible
things in my life, some of which actually happened.*

— MARK TWAIN

Rarely do we stop to remember to be grateful for the connections and intimacy we do have in our lives.

There is no greater satisfaction than knowing and being known. How wonderful it is to connect so fully with ourselves that the process of discovering an otherwise unknown or hidden facet of ourselves is a moment for celebration, even if that information is not so great.

I am 82 now and I remember a few years back when I was confronted with the reality that I do not see or think spatially. The awareness came upon me quite unexpectedly and produced a flood of memories when I had experienced that "handicap" and had not understood it at all. I was so excited to discover that I was "handicapped" in this way. Several of my friends did not want me to use the term *handicapped* and that was exactly what this was, a handicap. As I write this, I still feel the joy and excitement of learning something new about myself at this age. I expect joyfully to be discovering new information about myself and how I relate to others as long as I live.

We need to be reminded to feel grateful for every discovery along the way.

It does not matter how big it is or how small; all new information on the journey can be exciting and eventually makes us more whole.

Everything Is Spiritual/Sacred

GRATITUDE

The peace of men will settle the earth.

— MARY SUMMER RAIN

How wonderful it is to have a time when we are supported to experience the sacredness of gratitude and thanksgiving within ourselves! How good it is to stop to reflect on the sacredness of all the gifts we have been given and to pause to remember deep in our being that everything is spiritual and therefore sacred.

How important it is to pause and take some time to let our gratitude for all we have in our lives seep into our being. We get so busy that gratitude for the presence of the sacredness of our lives seems unimportant at times. We let other things take precedence over our pausing and remembering that we are sacred and everything around us is equally sacred.

We need times to stop and to remember that the sacredness of and spirituality in all creation bathes us continually with little recognition or acceptance.

When we live in and honor that all is spiritual, our lives become so much easier.

Wholeness

GRATITUDE

*. . . our faults cannot hurt God. Nor will our failures interfere
with our own holiness . . . genuine holiness is precisely
a matter of enduring our own imperfections patiently.*

— SISTER THÉRÈSE OF LISIEUX

It is so easy to feel gratitude for the reality that we are all part
of one creation and ultimately are all connected. To live out of
this reality is a challenge in today's world and, ultimately, this
knowing will see us through all the challenges. In trying to live a
new paradigm, the reality of our wholeness gives us the support
we need to risk plunging into the unknown.

It is a great responsibility to be connected to absolutely
everything and it is also a great honor. How lucky we are to have
all these connections! How lucky we are to have all these possibilities for stimulation and growth!

How lucky we are to begin to realize the many planes of
our connectedness and that we are never alone, even when we
actively choose to disconnect.

When we learn to feel gratitude for our constant connection
to the all that is, we are beginning to move into a fuller paradigm
than the one that has been built around us.

Joy

GIVING THANKS

*I am a big man. See all these shells? They are very valuable in our
culture. I could have trunks of them . . . but then I wouldn't be a big
man. A big man gives away what he has and shares with others.*

— NEW GUINEA ELDER

For the native people of this land and most lands, giving
thanks was a comfortable and ongoing process.

Giving thanks was simple because they were aware that
everything they had was given to them and they lived in a land
of abundance. They always had enough—and who needs more
than enough?

In the old times in Ireland, there was a politician who said,
"We Irish do not need to be wealthy. No one needs to be wealthy.
What we need is to have a country where everyone has enough."

Now that is a different paradigm! What would it be like if,
like the Maori *kete* (basket), everyone were to put in what she/
he can and take out only what she/he needs? How much of our
usual stresses come from wanting more than we need?

Do we ever let ourselves feel the joy of having enough?

All Is in Process

THE IMMENSITY OF THE PROCESS

Don't push the river: It flows by itself.

— BARRY STEVENS

Sometimes I think of the process as a flowing river that has everything we need for doing our life.

If, as I now believe, we are here to grow, heal, and learn, the process of our life will always present us with the possibility for all three and more at every turn. Not only can we heal our past (even our ancestors), our present, and our future, we can learn more than we ever could conceive possible. We can grow spiritually, emotionally, and psychologically beyond our wildest beliefs. It is up to us to take advantage of each possibility.

The river of the process of our lives has more opportunities than we could ever imagine. We just do not have all the wisdom, imagination, and knowledge we need to give ourselves or acknowledge the situations we need for our particular healing, growth, and learning.

We have to be willing to plunge into that river which is the process of our lives and *become* the river. There is always the choice to fight the current and drown. There will be times when we smash against the rocks, all the more so if we fight the current. There will be times when the river is rushing and crashing and there will be times when there are quiet eddies with seemingly no movement at all.

And, it is *our* river—*our* process.

When we become the river, life becomes easier, and we do, indeed, flow with the process of our lives. Can you just let yourself believe that there is a process vaster than anything you can imagine and wiser in ways you can never know and you are always already a *part* of it?

Participation

PARTICIPATION AND SPIRITUALITY

I participate, therefore I am and am coming into being.

Participation is the practical presence of our spirituality. It is spirituality in action, not sitting on a shelf in our minds and beings. As we participate, we discover who we are and what is important in who we are.

As we participate, of course we will make mistakes. Mistakes are essential for our growth and wisdom. Yet if mistakes are so essential for our growth, how can we make them and learn from them if we don't participate with every aspect of our lives?

Participation is spirituality in action.

So many of us think that to be spiritual, we need to withdraw, sit, meditate, and be monastic. There is no question but what quiet time is essential for our spiritual health. *And*, in order for us to gather the grist for our spiritual mill to chew on, we need the experiences of our lives on which to reflect. We need to be in our bodies to experience our spirituality and in our activities and interactions for our spiritual selves to grow and learn.

Remember, our spiritual fodder comes from our experiences and our participation in our lives. We all know this truth. We just need to be reminded to remember it. Spirituality is in the living.

Participation is spirituality and spirituality is participation.

Thinking

THE SPIRITUALITY OF OUR THINKING

*Once we start to listen to and trust our
intuition, our lives change . . . for the better.*

There are many levels of reality that are not the usual realm of our thinking. Yet intuition, tapping into the unseen and unknown, and sudden awarenesses are possibilities for us all. Usually these experiences do not come through our thinking minds.

They come while we are busy participating in our lives as a noncontrolled thought, an awareness, a feeling, a hunch, an intuition, a "knowing" of something we have no way of knowing. Our thinking mind tends to want to dismiss this information because most of us have been trained to be suspicious of it. Yet at a very deep level of our being, we *know*, we truly know, that our thinking could probably never have taken us there. When we are open to bypass and not worship our rational mind, we have emptied the teacup and are ready for new tea to offer us new tastes of possibilities.

On a daily basis we need to be reminded that our thinking, rational minds are not our only source of information and the most important information we need at any given moment may come from somewhere else.

What a pity it would be if we miss the whispers of our life.

Beliefs and Assumptions

HEALING, GROWING, AND LEARNING AS PART OF A WHOLE

Do you prefer that you be right or happy?

— A COURSE IN MIRACLES

Our beliefs and assumptions have, in the past, tended to separate us from our true selves and from others. They have acted like barriers and have often been just that to our healing, growing, and learning.

As we seek maturity, we can have some perspective on our youthful exuberance that science—our limited Western science—or religion—our limited perception of religion—was the only way to truth. We believed that all we had to do was slavishly follow the path the culture laid out for us and everything would be all right.

And then, we remember that some of our greatest learnings came when we veered off the path others prescribed for us and had to find our own way. These wanderings may have been painful at the time, and yet, as we look back, they seem to have been just what we needed to move deeper into ourselves and wider beyond ourselves.

Our pain always seemed directly proportionate to our stubbornness and illusion of control supported by our beliefs and assumptions.

Freeing ourselves from beliefs and assumptions that have lost their meaning can be a process in life that gives us new life. One we could never have planned or made happen.

Feelings and Emotions

SPIRITUALITY PERSONIFIED

A closed mind is always fighting to keep everything else at arm's length.

— RICHARD CARLSON

We need to remind ourselves that feelings and emotions and being "emotionally brilliant" are absolutely essential ingredients for experiencing the level of spirituality—personally and culturally—that are essential for living a new paradigm.

A priest once told me that he had studied theology all his life and felt well-versed in his knowledge of the Bible and Catholic teachings and had always prayed for the practice of the experience of God; it was only when he learned to be in touch with his feelings that he *experienced* the practice of the presence of God.

To reiterate, theology is thinking about God. Spirituality is the experience of oneness with God.

In order to make a paradigm shift, we must learn that our feelings and emotions are necessary to lead us to wholeness and our full spiritual selves; in the process we will learn to *live* a new paradigm.

We can never think ourselves into living a new paradigm. This new kind of living requires all that we have and are.

Honesty

THE UNCOMMONNESS OF HONESTY

You want to stand out in a crowd? Try being honest.

Ultimately our unconscious is probably uncomfortable with dishonesty. Lying is a learned trait that can only survive in large numbers if it is culturally reinforced. Children have to learn to lie. They are not born lying. Therefore at some deep level we remember truth-telling. We have only to be reminded to remember.

Some people think that being honest about what others are doing is what honesty is all about. This is the easiest kind of honesty and does require some courage to take on a society's looking at itself honestly. This kind of honesty is embedded in the founding of the United States. Each citizen has the responsibility to keep us honest as a nation. Needless to say, we have failed miserably. And these failures, if we learn from them, will make us stronger in the end.

However, we can never be really honest with the larger issues if we are not honest with ourselves. And being honest with ourselves can be quite a challenge—and is absolutely essential to living a new paradigm.

Changing our unconscious can be an exciting challenge.

Courage

THE SPIRITUALITY OF COURAGE

*I'm the spirit's janitor. All I do is wipe the
windows a little bit so you can see out for yourself.*

— GODFREY CHIPS, LAKOTA MEDICINE MAN

Who knows what courage is? Perhaps it is nothing more than practicing a spirituality that we all know that goes back to a time when we all lived out of the oneness that is the wholeness of the all. That kind of courage is in all of us. It is part of our innate gift of being one with all creation. That kind of courage is buried deep in our own being and is connected to the all that is. It is within us and beyond us. It is the river of the process of being human and part of all creation that connects us with the all. It is a glorious memory of participation that takes us beyond ourselves, within the selves we can be, and is linked to a oneness that we need to be reminded that lives as a memory in every cell of our being. Our judgmentalism removes us from this courage.

When we remember how to practice courage, the opportunities are everywhere in the everyday process of life.

Entitlement

A WORLD WITHOUT ENTITLEMENT

The Great Spirit puts a shadow in your heart when you destroy . . .
— JOE FRIDAY

What would a world look like without the illusion of entitlement? Quite truthfully, we can't know at this point. We can, however, be quite sure that it will look quite different than it does now.

Will everyone be willing to let go of their illusion of entitlement? Probably not! And they will die off and their children will have the opportunity to grow up in a world that is more equal and more filled with gratitude. The most important part of our living is that we are moving toward a different paradigm and we are doing the best we can to make it better than the one in which we are now living.

Will we make these changes perfectly? Of course not! What would be the fun and the learning in that? The best we can do is take the steps that tell us, "Here I stand. I can do no other." And, things will change.

Perhaps we can see the trail of our decisions and our handiwork a hundred lifetimes from now. We did, after all, say that all change is a process, didn't we?

Accepting Our Humanness

OUR FULLNESS OF BEING HUMAN

Zen in its essence is the art of seeing into the nature of one's being, and it points the way from bondage to freedom.

— D. T. SUZUKI

Even though most of us struggle mightily not to accept what we perceive are the "negative" aspects and "limitations" of our being human, we fight accepting the reality and possibility of our greatness even more. And don't even consider asking us to take responsibility for using our potential greatness for the good of all, including ourselves. Ultimately more people stop themselves because of their fear of their greatness than they do for fear of their limitations.

For many, it is terrifying even to imagine what good minds we have, how creative we are, the emotional strength we have, and how much we might achieve if we just deal with our reality and the connection we have with the oneness of the all. We are more fearful of what we *can* be as humans than what we cannot be or who we actually are. We spend so much time focusing on "What if I cannot do it?" which relieves us of taking the responsibility for what might happen if we *do* it, whatever "it" is. We humans are so afraid of the power of the Creator that is naturally within us that we even develop religions to distract us from our reality.

To live out of a new paradigm, we are asked to be fully human and fully spiritual in all aspects and take responsibility for all we have been given and all we are.

Respect

LIVING A NEW PARADIGM

*I was always taught, above all things,
to honor my elders.*

Respect is a bit like pornography, which has been described as "difficult to define, but we know it when we see it." Except with respect, we know it when we *don't* see it. And not seeing it has become the norm. Yet with those few who are mumbling about a new paradigm, we need to "practice respect in all our affairs."

Respect is integral to our reconnecting to our deep spiritual selves. It is a by-product of our moving beyond thinking about a new paradigm, or preaching about a new paradigm, or "changing our consciousness" about a new paradigm. Practicing respect may be when we start to *live* a new paradigm.

To live a new paradigm, we need to get back to an experience of knowing that we are one with the all that is. We need to get back to a spirituality that we accept as our reality. We need to get back to a living of our spirituality before we left the oneness.

Religions came into existence after we left our oneness and were trying to find a way to get back. Perhaps something as simple as respect and the practice of it could at least get our feet on the pathway.

Respecting our elders in all situations might be a good first step.

The Abstractualization of Life

LIVING INTO A NEW PARADIGM

Humor is the WD-40 of healing.

— GEORGE GOODSTRIKER,
KAINAI (BLACKFOOT) ELDER

It is quite possible that in order for us to live a new paradigm we will need to see that our tendency to develop abstract concepts and then try to make them real will actively inhibit our ability to *live* into a new paradigm.

Down deep somewhere we know how to live and be different and all we need is to be reminded that we know about participating in a different way. Then as we participate in a different way, we can trust that something different will happen and that something different does not have to be known or delineated ahead of time or happen all at once. It can even be fun.

If we look back over our lives honestly, we will have to admit that our experiences have added more to our lives than our concepts and abstractions. And if we are really, really honest and open-minded, we will have to admit that life has given us many unplanned opportunities to heal, grow, and contribute that were not brought into being by our concepts and abstractions.

We need daily reminders that abstractions and concepts are not real. They are toys created by humans for humans to play with. Living is real.

Being of Good Spirit

THE LIFE WE ARE GIVEN

*Why should we all use our creative power? Because there is
nothing that makes people so generous, joyful, lively,
bold, and compassionate, so indifferent to fighting
and the accumulation of objects and money.*

— BRENDA UELAND

I have been given life.

Do I *deserve* this life? Maybe, maybe not. Did I do something
to make it happen? Maybe, maybe not. Although I have been
taught that at some deep soul level I "volunteered."

I have opportunities, I have choices, I have options. Is that
not truly amazing? There are so many opportunities for learning. There are so many opportunities for mistakes big and small.
There are so many opportunities to forgive myself and others for
being human and so many other things. How could I not be of
good spirit?

I have been given the human functioning to try to understand this wonderful planet and the way it works. I have been
given the possibility to understand others and how they operate
and even the compassion to perceive why they operate the way
they do.

Most of all, I have been given the opportunity to glimpse
the unknown and the unseen when I get out of my own way and
experience the greatness of all creation.

Why would I not be of good spirit?

Domination Over and the Illusion of Control

OUR SPIRITUALITY

*Our old beliefs and assumptions cannot help us
move into a new consciousness. Beliefs and assumptions
stifle open-mindedness. Letting go can be easier
and more productive than holding on.*

Most of the revealed religions have developed into a focus on Domination Over and the Illusion of Control (Buddhism was a glaring exception and it may be joining the illusion at this point in history). Yet most religions did not start the way they are being practiced in the world of humans.

Inside each of us is a process of being one with all creation and one with our creator. We have come from that place. We can return to that place as we give up the bad habits we have learned in our struggles to find our way as a human race.

We probably never will be completely one with all being, reality, and the process of spirituality—that is one of the limitations of being human. And, we can probably do a lot better than we are doing now.

Realizing the limitations of the paradigm that now dominates the human race and letting go of some of the practices, beliefs, assumptions, and procedures that steer us in a dysfunctional direction will probably add a lot to our journey as individuals and as a species.

Giving up our belief in the necessity to practice domination over others and have the illusion of control over others could be a big step. As we make amends with the way we live our lives, more will be revealed and changes will occur that we could never have imagined.

Humor

HUMOR IS AN ACT OF FAITH

*Imagination was given to us to compensate for what we are not;
a sense of humor was provided to console us for what we are.*

— MACK MCGINNIS

To live a life seasoned with humor and laughter is to live a life of faith. To know humor requires us to believe in something greater than ourselves that is also operative in the universe. To be able to smile, tease, and laugh is an indicator that we have unseen connections that we can trust even when we cannot see them or touch them.

Being able to touch the joyful humor in our lives relieves us of the burden of knowing everything and trying to control everything. Loving ourselves means that we have the humility to see how small we are in the larger scheme of the universe and also lightens the burden of knowing that whatever we do matters.

Humor may well be our doorway to the world of the unknown and the wisdom of the unseen without our ever having to think about it.

Humor is the ultimate paradox of faith.

Beware of the humorless.

Wonder and Awe

THAT THE CREATOR HASN'T GIVEN UP ON US

*As long as I am alive, I can participate in
bringing in healing and the new. That's awesome!*

I have loved writing about wonder and awe. Each page has allowed me to re-experience the feeling, not just the words. For that I am grateful. Yet my wonder and awe move beyond expressing when the phrase "All this, and still the Creator has not given up on us," is presented to me. Now that is awesome!

We still have an opportunity. With all our bumbling, with all our taking long, tedious detours as a human race, with the magnitude of mistakes we have made and continue to make, the very fact that others and I are writing books like this demonstrates that we believe that we still have a chance. We still have a glimmer of hope.

It is a miracle that, as hopeless as we have become as a species, as disrespectful as we have been for all the gifts we have been given, in spite of the destruction we have wrought on this awe-inspiring planet, in spite of the atrocities we have committed and let others commit, in spite of our using our excellent minds to develop more and more destruction to perpetuate on one another, nature, the earth, and all creation . . . in spite of all this, the greatest wonder and awe exists in the place that many of us remember and keep holding in our heads and hearts. This memory brings us to:

"Keep trying!" "Keep trying."

"Remember to look at the big picture."

The Present Can Only Be Our Reality
if We Own Our Past and Our Future

SIMPLIFYING THE COMPLEX

Simplicity is the key.

All too often we find that we cannot understand the simple because we have tried to make everything more complex.

This process of "complexing" the simple is often fueled by our fears, our embellishing of our realities, and our refusal to understand when we accept what we know at any one moment. When we realize how we have "complexed" our universe, we will be open to know much, much more.

Also, we do not need to know more than we are ready to know before we actually need to know it.

How often have we worked ourselves into a dither because we do not know something, or made a decision that is not "ripe" to make, when the reality is we are not ready to know it or cannot do it at that time? For example, why in the world do we believe that we know what a new paradigm will and needs to look like before we have owned our past and present paradigms and healed them? We need to realize that all these processes are happening together. I think my great-grandmother called it putting the cart before the horse—and we have not even owned the cart *or* the horse.

Aren't we dear? We so want to be anywhere except where we are—as individuals and as a species.

Walking in Beauty

GRATITUDE

To us, our house was not unsentient matter—it had a heart, and a soul, and eyes to see us with; and approvals, and solicitudes and deep sympathies; it was of us, and we were in its confidence, and lived in its grace and in the peace of its benediction. We never came home from an absence that its face did not light up and speak out its eloquent welcome—and we could not enter it unmoved.

— MARK TWAIN

An attitude of quiet, simple, humble gratitude is good preparation for remembering the thrill, the healing, the joy, and the simplicity of walking in beauty.

We cannot be taught how to do this. There are no computer courses that will take you there (though some will try). There are no gurus who can guarantee if you just sit in their presence or become a disciple and follow a correct practice you will get there. Something may happen. And that something may feel and be good.

Yet walking in beauty is a state that is already within us. It involves every aspect of our being. It cannot be taught with techniques and we do not need drugs, routines, prescriptions, or supports to get there. The experience of walking in beauty was buried deep inside of us long before we came to consciousness.

We do not need to manufacture walking in beauty.

We just need to get out of the way.

Taking Time

SPIRITUAL TIME

When we think we have no connection, that's tough.
When we realize that the connection has always
been there and, like a switchboard, we just need to
reinsert the plug, that's easy.

For native people, alone time is spiritual time. Basically we know that we are never alone. This fact is core to our lives. The Creator and core of all being is not only always with us, we are one with the all that is.

Also, we are one with nature and all creation, never being alone. When you add to the above that we are all family and always surrounded by family (those in this plane and those on other planes), alone time takes on quite a different meaning.

We do not just need alone time to get away from the buzz of the current culture (which I definitely do at times). We seek alone time in order to reconnect to the essential aspects of our reality, which are always there for us.

Spirituality is a matter of reconnecting with that which is always there and has always been there.

We need to relearn this truth in our lives to build a workable new/old paradigm.

A Belief in Healing

THE WHOLENESS OF HEALING

*Awareness of wholeness is born in the soul
and finds expression in our actions.*

As it is with individuals, so it is with the whole, that the wholeness always wants to move toward a direction of healing.

We get rare glimpses of the wholeness. And we get even rarer glimpses of what needs to happen or how the wholeness could even be healed, by what, or when. Yet as we shed the limited dualistic, mechanistic, materialistic paradigm in which we have been trying to survive, we feel an unnameable something that supports our shift to knowing that everything we are doing as best we can moves the wholeness toward fuller healing. In some strange, unidentified way a belief in the wholeness of healing contributes to the evolution of a new paradigm. We cannot and we do not have to know or explain how, yet our belief in healing supports this evolution's happening on a scale beyond our imagination.

All we have to do is participate in the healing of now. The rest is paradox and inevitable.

Knowing and Living in Several Realities

ARROGANCE WITH "OUR" REALITY

The passion for setting people right is in itself an afflictive disease.
— MARIANNE MOORE

I told a story earlier about two black men who steadfastly stuck with me until I "got it"—that until I faced my own white privilege and the implications of that, I could never really appreciate another's reality. Only in the complete physical, emotional, psychological, and spiritual examination of my own prejudicial assumptions and blind spots (which is a lifetime task) can I free myself to "be" other realities. And this includes the "easy" other realities like sexism, racism, ageism, classism, financial inequality and all the others.

Even if we think we are open-minded and have no prejudice, there are always new levels to explore. How much opportunity we have to face all our assumptions and prejudices about others. Daily we are given circumstances that can teach us how narrow our minds have become. Daily we are given ways to get kicked in the head about our closed-mindedness. Imagine the possibility awaiting us as we open ourselves up to realities other than the physical plane and beyond our mechanistic science. Just because we do not know and understand other realities does not mean that they are not there—even if we have tried to hold on to this illusion of "knowing it all" for centuries.

Moving into a new way of being for humanity and the planet will probably invite us to unknown realities not yet available to us (because of *our* limitations—not because of the limitations of the universe).

Being of Service

DEVELOPING OUR INTUITION

*If we spent as many years knowing about and
studying our intuition as we do math,
where do you think we would be now?*

One of the most exciting and quietly peaceful advantages of being of service is that it provides fertile ground for the development of our intuition.

We certainly do not get much support, help, or encouragement for developing our intuition in the current Western paradigm. In fact, we get more discouragement than encouragement. Yet having a good working intuition may be one of the most important processes of shifting out of the current dominant paradigm.

To be of service, we have to:

1. Be in touch with our bodies, feelings, and awarenesses to know that we are not trying to con ourselves or others.

2. Step outside our usual self-interest world and "normal" way of being in this paradigm so we can trust ourselves.

3. Tune in to the situation and the people there to be able to see 1) if we can be of service in this situation and 2) how we can be of service.

4. Trust our innate knowings of being of service, knowing we will make mistakes and that our thinking and brains will try to take over and fool us. This trusting may take many years to develop.

Good luck, Happy Holidays, and hopefully we all are learning.

Graciousness

ENDING A YEAR WITH GRACIOUSNESS

*Usually it is the simple that leads us
to the complex . . . and back to the simple again.*

Erring in the direction of graciousness could prove to be a very important process in remembering what we already "know." And we need daily reminders of the graciousness that we have tucked away inside each of us.

We have just been lazy and inconsistent in practicing and living out of this graciousness. Just like brushing our teeth and pumicing the calluses off our feet, we need to be reminded that we still know how to both care for our bodies and practice graciousness in the best possible way. If we do not remind ourselves daily and act, both can very quickly get out of hand.

This need to remind ourselves is true on the physical plane and it is also true on the nonphysical plane. We, as humans, need to be reminded of what is important and essential to our very existence. We have a tendency to wander off, get distracted, and forget even the most vital and important. This is just our lot in being human. To err in the direction of graciousness is one of those easily forgotten truths. So here at the end of this year is the reminder to feed our wellspring of true graciousness and err in that direction.

We can, indeed, live a new paradigm.

Moving Out of Our Comfort Zones

REFLECTIONS

Taking stock can be the best way to move forward.

Now that we have spent a year reflecting on our reluctance to move out of our comfort zones and identifying some of the comfort zones that are holding us back as individuals, as a species, and as a planet, perhaps it would be helpful to reflect on some of our possible learnings.

1. Make a list of some of your cherished yet constricting comfort zones you have identified during this year.

2. Note your reactions when you identify some of these comfort zones that are holding you, and in extension the human race, back.

3. List some favorite illusions that you have clung to in spite of their negative effect on you.

4. Look at some of these illusions you have been ready to give up.

5. List what you believe you have worked through and given up or are in the process of giving up.

6. Note where you are in the above processes.

Healing, learning, and growing are our jobs as human beings. What grade would you give yourself this year? Also, ask someone who knows you well and loves you enough to be honest with you what grade they would give you for this year. Is there any change in your level of arrogance?

Letting Go of What We Think We Know

LITTLE CHILDREN

Innocence is not ignorance. It can be very wise.

A very wise teacher once said, "You have to become like little children to enter the gates of heaven." (This is a loose translation.) The same is true for learning to live a new paradigm. To be able to live a new paradigm, we need the freshness, the openness, and the curiosity of little children.

We need to admit that we have no *idea* of where we are going and are not even sure that we would know it if we got there. (We will probably never *get* there.) And, we need to be willing to participate fully in the process of the movement and the going. We need to have the kind of faith that we see in the alcoholic who takes the first tentative steps when she/he has no idea whatsoever what recovery looks like.

We need to learn to trust some people who have lived out of a paradigm that differs from the current dominant one—women and indigenous peoples, in particular—whose knowings and perceptions have been denigrated by the current dominant culture.

This trusting is so difficult for those who are supposed to know and understand everything.

Stepping off the cliff with a good parachute can be so invigorating.

Accepting That Choices and Behaviors Have Consequences

CELEBRATION

You will find that chaos/order are not necessarily a pair of opposites, but that chaos provides a favorable condition to create new order.

— DAVID B. ELLER

During this time of celebration, we can take a moment to reminisce and remember that without consequences for our behavior and choices, we would not have become the people we are today. And those who have tried to avoid consequences legally or otherwise might want to stop to see how much they have squandered by not having to deal with the consequences of their behavior. If we humans are here to heal, learn, and grow, without a doubt having to deal with consequences has resulted in some of our greatest learnings.

The end of the year is a very good time to stop to take a good look and a good laugh at some of the consequences we have set up by our choices and our behaviors. We can learn a lot if we take the opportunity to glean and celebrate our learnings.

And perhaps if we are still too arrogant to admit our avoidance of consequences or our not accepting them gracefully, it probably is not too late to start right now to see what effect our choices and our behavior have had on us.

We need reminders of the effects of the paradigm that we, as a human race, have created to help us thirst for a different way.

Humility

LIVING HUMILITY

Please save me from ever trying to be humble.

Humility is absolutely essential to live into a new paradigm.

It cannot be manufactured, manipulated, or controlled into being.

Humility in its essence is easily mutilated or destroyed. It is very fragile.

Humility, like energy, cannot be created or destroyed; it *can* be scared off.

Humility, should it choose to emerge, is best when its presence is kept unaware. Shedding light on it, or even trying to, results in its fleeting disappearance.

Humility is a thing of the spirit and not part of a mechanistic world.

The minute humility is sighted by the person supposing to have it, it disappears like the breath of the buffalo on a winter's day.

Humility is a by-product, never a direct result. Humility and compassion walk hand in hand.

Knowing and Being Known

THE PROCESS

Being known and knowing another are two of the
most frightening journeys on which we can ever embark.
And, the rewards are infinite.

Knowing oneself is a lifelong process of exploration and surprises. Some of the surprises may not be in keeping with who we thought we were, who we wanted to be, or who we wanted to present to others, and they let us be known to ourselves.

As we are known to ourselves—the good, the bad, the indifferent—we have the opportunity to grow and change. And we also have the opportunity for intimacy with ourselves and others.

When we have no intimacy with ourselves, we can never have intimacy with others. And we need to remember that when we are truly intimate with another, whether it be another person, a dog, or a tree, we change and our relationships change.

As long as we live out of escaping from intimacy, we will not be able to experience these growing changes in ourselves and with others.

Knowing and being known is an ongoing process of grace that continues to unfold throughout our lives. This knowing is living.

Everything Is Spiritual/Sacred

RESPECT

And I knew that when it was time to leave this place it would be sacred land. Sacred land. To carry it in my heart forever was my responsibility, my destiny, and my dream. The land, you see, is a feeling.

— RICHARD WAGAMESE, *KEEPER'N ME*

As we come to recognize the reality that everything—absolutely everything—is sacred and deserves our respect, our lives become easier and more serene. Just the very process of respecting and honoring everything around us opens doors for us to relax and live our lives and not to have to manipulate and control them.

In the current paradigm, respect is in short supply. We do not respect ourselves, we do not respect others, we do not respect nature. We do not respect much of anything.

When we remember what our ancestors knew that all is sacred and everything is imbued with its own kind of spirituality, not only our behaviors, our entire lives start to change and living a new paradigm becomes a possibility.

It does not matter what that paradigm will look like. Why waste our time trying to figure out what the new paradigm will be when we can never know ahead of time? In the process of living respect for all that is around us, a new paradigm will emerge.

Wholeness

THE GROUND OF OUR BEING

Modern ecology can learn a great deal from a people who managed and maintained their world so well for 50,000 years.

— BURNUM BURNUM, ABORIGINAL AUSTRALIAN WRITER

As we realize and live out of our oneness with all creation and the Creator, our beings sigh with relief and open to possibilities. We do not need to know what is ahead or how we will handle whatever, because we are one with it all. When we are connected with the all that is, we find that we are able to act out of that connection and that it will be good for us, even when what we experience hurts or is unpleasant. With our participation, we can handle whatever comes our way.

Often it seems that it is our illusion of our separateness that causes our anxiety. When we really "get" that we are part of a much larger whole and we can participate in and with that whole, it takes the pressure off.

Unfortunately, as human beings we have had poor memories of our reality and our minds have created "realities" that do not exist.

When we are reminded of what we already *know* and in our best moments *experience*, we can move on with our "remembering" leading the way.

Joy

OUR WELLSPRING

We have a tendency to obscure the forest
of simple joys with the trees of problems.

— CHRISTIANE COLLANGE

Joy is that deep wellspring within us that is above, below, and beyond our control. It is a gift we have for being human and is shared with other living creatures.

Joy is the flow of gratitude which springs forth to remind us that we have been given life (and hopefully we will not waste it).

Joy leads us into the deep waters of our being where "out of control" is the norm.

Joy is the wellspring that is shaking our awareness into knowing that we are all connected and connected with the all. We are never alone.

Joy waits patiently for us to rediscover what flowed so freely when we were children and sneaked through even the harshest experiences.

Joy cannot be called on demand like a butler or manufactured, as much as we try. It is only in the letting go and the participating fully in our piece of the wholeness that it peeks out and seeps into us.

Joy is feeling, thought, emotion, and intelligence. It is a deep flowing in our being which can only emerge when we know who we are and have accepted that we will participate as fully as we can in the wholeness of our existence by accepting the all that is one.

We need to be reminded daily to stay out of the way of the flowing joy that is within us.

The End the Beginning

PULLING OUR LIVES BEYOND

Whatever the gains, whatever the loss, they are yours.

— FIVE WOUNDS, NEZ PERCE ELDER

We need endings as humans and we need beginnings.

In all life processes, the old ends so that the new can begin. Yet nothing needs to be lost and we need to hold on to nothing because there will always be more.

The living is not in the thinking. The living is in the participation.

As we realize that we have gone very far off track as a species, the possibility for healing, learning, and growth becomes as every day—every moment. We have made huge mistakes as a species. And it behooves us not to keep making the same ones over and over.

Talking a new paradigm based on concepts and ideas will never move us ahead. We have to participate, make mistakes, learn from them, and move beyond. We and our ancestors have made enough mistakes for us to learn from for centuries.

We can change the foundation out of which we operate, as individuals and as a species. Little nods in a new direction will not be enough at this point.

The old wineskins are beyond repair. Do we have new wine?

ACKNOWLEDGMENTS

I would like to acknowledge all those who have loved me and those who have refused to love me.

I acknowledge all the teachers in my life, who are everyone and everything with whom/which I have interacted. Although I have experienced many great teachers in my life, who is to say which or who is the greatest?

I am so grateful for everyone and everything that has touched me—the loving pleasant and the painful mean.

Only through the living will the importance of the learnings be sifted.

I am grateful to all.

ABOUT THE AUTHOR

Anne Wilson Schaef has a Ph.D. in clinical psychology and an honorary doctorate in Humane Letters from Kenyon College in Kenyon, Ohio. After practicing for many years, she left the field of psychology and psychotherapy in 1984. She has developed her own approach to healing the whole person, coming out of the ancient teachings of her ancestors, which she calls Living in Process. In the past 32 years, she has taught this approach to healing—including healing from the addictive process—throughout the world. She is internationally respected as a speaker, consultant, and seminar leader.

Dr. Schaef is the author of 15 books that have been bestsellers throughout the world and have included a *New York Times* bestseller, a nomination for Best Political Book of the Year, and a two-million-plus bestseller, *Meditations for Women Who Do Too Much*. She has been described as "one of the most important thinkers of our time," "cutting edge," "way ahead of her time," and "having the vision of the eagle." Her favorite and oft-received compliment from readers is that she writes what they have always known but could never articulate. Dr. Schaef loves traveling by ship, gourmet cooking, facilitating the writer within to emerge, being in nature, and gratefully living each day to its fullest. Website: www.annewilsonschaef.com

Hay House Titles of Related Interest

YOU CAN HEAL YOUR LIFE, the movie,
starring Louise Hay & Friends
(available as a 1-DVD program and an expanded 2-DVD set)
Watch the trailer at: www.LouiseHayMovie.com

THE SHIFT, the movie,
starring Dr. Wayne W. Dyer
(available as a 1-DVD program and an expanded 2-DVD set)
Watch the trailer at: www.DyerMovie.com

⌇

THE AFRICAN AMERICANS: Many Rivers to Cross,
by Henry Louis Gates, Jr., and Donald Yacovone

LIGHT THE FLAME: 365 Days of Prayer,
by Andrew Harvey

RETURNING TO THE LAKOTA WAY: Old Values
to Save a Modern World, by Joseph Marshall III

SPONTANEOUS EVOLUTION: Our Positive Future
and a Way to Get There from Here,
by Bruce H. Lipton, Ph.D., and Steve Bhaerman

THE TURNING POINT: Creating Resilience in a
Time of Extremes, by Gregg Braden

All of the above are available at your local bookstore,
or may be ordered by contacting Hay House (see next page).

⌇

We hope you enjoyed this Hay House book. If you'd like to receive our online catalog featuring additional information on Hay House books and products, or if you'd like to find out more about the Hay Foundation, please contact:

Hay House, Inc., P.O. Box 5100, Carlsbad, CA 92018-5100
(760) 431-7695 or (800) 654-5126
(760) 431-6948 (fax) or (800) 650-5115 (fax)
www.hayhouse.com® • www.hayfoundation.org

~~ ~~

Published and distributed in Australia by:
Hay House Australia Pty. Ltd., 18/36 Ralph St., Alexandria NSW 2015
Phone: 612-9669-4299 • *Fax:* 612-9669-4144 • www.hayhouse.com.au

Published and distributed in the United Kingdom by: Hay House UK,
Ltd., Astley House, 33 Notting Hill Gate, London W11 3JQ
Phone: 44-20-3675-2450 • *Fax:* 44-20-3675-2451 • www.hayhouse.co.uk

Published and distributed in the Republic of South Africa by:
Hay House SA (Pty), Ltd., P.O. Box 990, Witkoppen 2068
info@hayhouse.co.za • www.hayhouse.co.za

Published in India by: Hay House Publishers India,
Muskaan Complex, Plot No. 3, B-2, Vasant Kunj, New Delhi 110 070
Phone: 91-11-4176-1620 • *Fax:* 91-11-4176-1630 • www.hayhouse.co.in

Distributed in Canada by: Raincoast Books,
2440 Viking Way, Richmond, B.C. V6V 1N2
Phone: 1-800-663-5714 • *Fax:* 1-800-565-3770 • www.raincoast.com

~~ ~~

Take Your Soul on a Vacation

Visit www.HealYourLife.com® to regroup,
recharge, and reconnect with your own magnificence.
Featuring blogs, mind-body-spirit news,
and life-changing wisdom from Louise Hay and friends.

Visit www.HealYourLife.com today!